MARKETING RESEARCH
WITH **R** AND
PYTHON

MARKETING RESEARCH WITH R AND PYTHON

Howard Pong Yuen Lam

The Chinese University of Hong Kong, Hong Kong

World Scientific

NEW JERSEY · LONDON · SINGAPORE · BEIJING · SHANGHAI · HONG KONG · TAIPEI · CHENNAI · TOKYO

Published by

World Scientific Publishing Co. Pte. Ltd.
5 Toh Tuck Link, Singapore 596224
USA office: 27 Warren Street, Suite 401-402, Hackensack, NJ 07601
UK office: 57 Shelton Street, Covent Garden, London WC2H 9HE

Library of Congress Control Number: 2023935175

British Library Cataloguing-in-Publication Data
A catalogue record for this book is available from the British Library.

ISBN 978-981-127-754-2 (hardcover)
ISBN 978-981-127-869-3 (paperback)
ISBN 978-981-127-755-9 (ebook for institutions)
ISBN 978-981-127-756-6 (ebook for individuals)

For any available supplementary material, please visit
https://www.worldscientific.com/worldscibooks/10.1142/13446#t=suppl

Desk Editors: Sanjay Varadharajan/Julio Hong

Typeset by Stallion Press
Email: enquiries@stallionpress.com

Preface

This book is developed for readers who want to learn about marketing research with R and Python. Readers may have no or little experience in programming in R and Python, and may want to learn what is necessary quickly, and be able to conduct marketing research and run tests easily in R or Python.

A number of marketing research textbooks have used different software packages for years. R and Python are free for anyone to download and install in a personal computer. Instructors and students do not have to go to a computer room in a university to use any software package with license. Instead, students can run R or Python at their own personal computers anytime and anywhere.

This book covers the important frameworks and concepts of marketing and marketing research for developing a new product. For any company, growth comes either from organic growth from sales of existing products, or from launching successful new products. Due to competition in the marketplace, each company's marketer must determine when to develop and launch a new product as an upgrade of an existing product; as another product (line extension) under a current brand with an existing product; or as a new product under a new brand.

So, marketers have to develop a new product concept and test it against a competitive concept. They can analyze data by using R or Python with word cloud, string, Chi-square, correlation, t-test, analysis of variance, regression, sentiment analysis, and web scraping. R and Python programs are available for download and use for other applications. Videos with professional English voice over and sub-titles are posted online at World Scientific for learners to view, pause, try on their own computers, and learn by doing.

Readers can chose to learn R or Python, or both, and know how codes in R can be implemented in Python and vice versa.

The contents of this book are derived from my teaching notes and programs written in R or Python for teaching Marketing Research courses for undergraduate students and Master of Science students at The Chinese University of Hong Kong (CUHK).

About the Author

 **Howard Pong-Yuen Lam** is currently Associate Professor of Practice in Marketing at The Chinese University of Hong Kong (CUHK) Business School. Before joining the academia, he was head of marketing or general manager with rich commercial experience. He has worked at P&G, McDonald's, Coca-Cola, and other multinational companies.

Professor Lam is passionate about solving business problems and developing new theories and frameworks through research. His research interests include branding strategy, new product launch, marketing communications for products with reduced negative attribute. His research studies were published in the *Journal of Marketing*, *Business Horizons*, *Journal of Database Marketing and Customer Strategy Management*, *Journal of the Operational Research Society*, and *Cornell Hotel and Restaurant Administration Quarterly*.

To enhance course relevancy and practicality, he also conducted case research with co-authors and got business cases published by Ivey case centre and listed at Harvard case centre.

He has taught undergraduate courses in marketing research and master courses in marketing research, marketing management, marketing to consumers, management of the corporation.

Professor Lam was born and grew up in Hong Kong. He obtained a Bachelor's degree in computer science, an MBA degree, and a PhD (in marketing), all from CUHK, and an MSc degree in financial management from the University of London. He also completed the General Manager Programme at Harvard Business School Executive Education, and is an affiliate at The Association of Chartered Certified Accountants (ACCA) after completing all the required examinations.

Acknowledgments

I am deeply grateful to the following people who have made this book a reality.

I am indebted to my PhD thesis supervisor and friend for 30 years, Professor Kin Nam LAU. Thank you for your excellent advice for my academic journey.

Thank you to Professor Francisco CISTERNA VERA for agreeing to work with me on the Project of "Videos and eBook of R and Python for Marketing Research and Marketing Analytics Courses."

In 2020–2022, Ms. Shuman LIU was the teaching assistant for my marketing research courses for Master of Science (MSc) in Marketing program at CUHK. She had read all my teaching notes and programs before my students, and gave me valuable suggestions to adjust the difficulty level for students to learn easily.

My former students of the Master of Science (MSc) in Marketing program at CUHK, Ms. Jiahui CHEN, Ms. Siqi GU, Ms. Leilei WU, and Mr. Wenguang ZHANG, in alphabetical order of their family names. They ran R or Python programs with screen recording, prepared a sub-title text file for each video, generated voice over from the sub-title file by using Microsoft OneNote, combined screen recording, sub-title text file, and voice over together to create videos for this book.

I also thank all my former and current students at CUHK for asking me questions so that I can continue improving my teaching to make learning enjoyable and intellectually rewarding.

This book would not have been possible without the support from Mr. Julio Farn Hing HONG, Dr. Yan Hong NG, Mr. Jay POON,

Ms. Siew Lan TAN, and Mr. Mike Ding Yuan TEE (in alphabetical order of their family names) at World Scientific.

I reserve the last word of thanks for my wife, Jane. I hope that our son and daughter will benefit from reading this book for work or study.

Contents

Chapter 1

Marketing

Marketing as Exchange

American Marketing Association (AMA, 2023a) defined Marketing as follows:

> Marketing is the activity, set of institutions, and processes for creating, communicating, delivering, and exchanging offerings that have value for customers, clients, partners, and society at large.

Offerings could broadly refer to the products or services that were of value to customers, and for customers to pay money to buy. Offerings could also refer to ideas such as "if you drink, don't drive". This idea can be of value to a driver and might save his/her life from a car accident. The driver, however, need not have to pay for this idea, and might simply watch an advertisement with this message.

Exchange could be a simple exchange between two parties, a buyer and a seller. Exchange could also occur among three parties, a company, a TV station, and a consumer (see Figure 1.1).

Exchange among four parties could include a buyer, a seller, a celebrity, a TV station. For instance, a seller could invite a celebrity to endorse his product. The celebrity performs a show in a TV station. The buyer likes the celebrity, pays attention to the show on TV, and watches the celebrity's advertisement during the commercial break. The buyer finally buys the product from the seller.

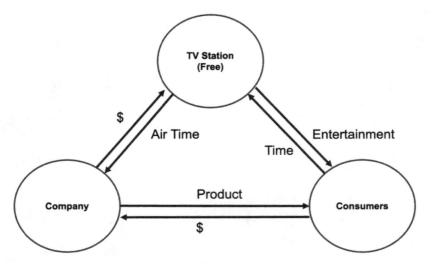

Figure 1.1.   Exchange among company, consumers, TV station.

Consumers, Customers, Company, Competitors, Collaborators, Context

Consumers are important for a marketer of a product/service. Consumers also have choices. They can choose products/services of a company's competitors. Marketing to consumers in different contexts might require the marketer to develop different marketing strategies and programs. The context refers to the culture of a country or other environmental factors. A company also has its suppliers, agencies, or collaborators. Dolan (2019) identified five Cs for marketers to understand and analyze: customers, company, competitor, collaborator, context (see Figure 1.2).

We could add in consumer as another C. Consumers would go to the customer of a company (retailers) to buy a product. For a company, a retailer is one of its customers, while individuals who consume the company's product are the company's consumers.

We could show the relationships among these 6Cs in a diagram and add in the five competitive forces suggested by Porter (2008) for competition for profits: established industry rivals, customers, suppliers, potential entrants, substitute products.

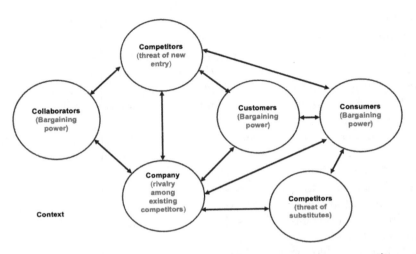

Figure 1.2.   Relationships among consumer, customer, company, competitor, collaborator in a context.

Segmentation, Target, Positioning

If you hit my hand with your hand, you will not hurt me much. If you focused, you could use the sharp point of a pen to go through my hand.

It would be easier if we focused on one individual, and attracted him with the most personalized product/service. With digital marketing, we could have a specific message addressed to one individual, who we consider to be our target.

There are different strategies for segmentation. The life-cycle stage is useful in practice for three reasons. First, marketers can identify for each product/service the key life-cycle stage that consumers need the product/service. Second, marketers can develop actionable marketing programs to recruit new consumers at the life-cycle stage, and retain these existing consumers for repeat purchase. Third, marketers can justify the acquisition cost with the profit that the marketer could receive from the whole life cycle of the consumer.

For example, for a baby diaper brand, the target is a pregnant woman with expected delivery within a few months. If it is the woman's first pregnancy, she would need to decide what diaper brand to buy and use for her baby. After she has made the decision, she would likely stay with using the same diaper brand. So, if a marketer of a diaper brand can convince a young pregnant woman to use the brand, the returns can be high if the woman continues to use the same diaper brand for her baby. When she has her second baby and keeps using the same diaper brand, the benefits would be doubled.

Some life-cycle events with opportunities for different products/services are as follows.

When high school students go to university and live in a dormitory, they can be the target for a number of product/services in personal care (shampoo, shower gels), beauty care, and financial services (banks account, credit cards).

When adults leave their parents and lived on their own, they would need household items like washing machine, refrigerators, microwave ovens.

When a couple has their baby, they would need diaper, milk powder, milk bottle, toys.

After a man and a woman decide to get married, they would need wedding rings, wedding photo, hotel or restaurants for wedding dinner.

For a university graduate, he/she would need a suit or a dress for a job interview, and increase in credit card limit.

When a couple decides to get a divorce, they would need a lawyer, an accountant, a real estate agent service, or a bank mortgage loan for one of them to buy another flat or rent another flat after divorce.

After a man has an accident, he would need medical care, insurance claim, or even funeral services.

After a person retires, he could be the target for volunteering services, medical care, travel.

For positioning, please refer to the chapter on marketing research (Chapter 3).

Branding Strategy

American Marketing Association (AMA, 2023b) defines Brand as follows:

> A brand is a name, term, design, symbol, or any other feature that identifies one seller's goods or service as distinct from those of other sellers. ISO brand standards add that a brand 'is an intangible asset' that is intended to create 'distinctive' images and associations in the minds of stakeholders, thereby generating economic benefit/values.

When marketers develop a new product, they choose (or create) a brand name for it and hope that this name would increase the chances of success of the new product (Lam *et al.*, 2013).

Keller *et al.* (1998, p. 55) proposed that a "suggestive" brand name could convey information regarding a relevant attribute or benefit in a particular product context. They found support on the proposition that compared with a non-suggestive brand name (e.g., Emporium televisions), a brand name that explicitly conveys a product benefit (e.g., Picture Perfect televisions) and produces greater recall of an advertised benefit claim that is consistent with the brand name's connotations is more effective.

Lam and Wong (2022) proposed the hierarchical branding strategy for new products by having three names:

(1) A suggestive given name for the new product that helps consumers recall the key benefits and features of the new **product**.
(2) A suggestive family name for the new product that communicates the benefits of the **product category**.
(3) A corporate name which is suggestive of the key **business** that the corporation is in and the consumer needs it could satisfy.

For example, "fruit pulp orange" was the English back translation for the Chinese given name 果粒橙 for the new product of Minute Maid juice drink with added pulp. Good juice source was the English back translation for the Chinese name 美汁源 to connote the category benefit of the juice category. Minute Maid brand was one of the brands for the Coca-Cola Company. The corporate image of the Coca-Cola Company was that of a company that was trustworthy for producing high quality beverages that were safe for consumption.

When entrepreneurs decide their company names, they should also think about the mission of their companies and the benefits for their customers (if they target business customers) or for their consumers (if they target individuals).

Lam and Lu (2022) reported the example of GoGoVan and LaLaMove. Both companies were founded in 2013 and had "Van" in their company names at that time, "GoGoVan" and "EasyVan" at that time. In 2014, EasyVan decided to rebrand as LaLaMove just in time for its launch in Bangkok because it would offer services from vehicles, such as motorcycles, that were not vans (Horwitz, 2014).

In 2022, the name was GoGoX at the Initial Public Offering, not GoGoVan (*Hong Kong Exchange News*, 2022).

References

AMA (2023a). Definition of marketing. American Marketing Association. https://www.ama.org/the-definition-of-marketing-what-is-marketing/ (accessed on January 15, 2023).

AMA (2023b). Definition of brand. American Marketing Association. https://www.ama.org/the-definition-of-marketing-what-is-marketing/ (accessed on January 15, 2023).

Dolan, R. J. (2019). *Framework for Marketing Strategy Formation*. Harvard Business Publishing, 8153.

Hong Kong Exchange News (2022). https://www1.hkexnews.hk/listedco/listconews/sehk/2022/0614/2022061400009.pdf (accessed on January 20, 2023).

Horwitz, J. (2014). Hong Kong's Easyvan rebrands as Lalamove just in time for launch in Bangkok. *TechinAsia*, November 27. https://www.techinasia.com/hong-kongs-easyvan-rebrands-as-lalamove-just-in-time-for-launch-in-bangkok (accessed on January 20, 2019).

Keller, K. L., Heckler, S. E. and Houston, M. J. (1998). The effects of brand name suggestiveness on advertising recall. *Journal of Marketing*, *62*(1), 48–57.

Lam, Howard Pong-Yuen and Wong, Vincent Chi. (2022). Hierarchical branding strategy for new product launch: Evidence from China. In S. S. Durmusoglu (ed.), *Chinese Innovation and Branding Leaps*. Singapore: World Scientific Publishing, pp. 103–136.

Lam, Howard Pong-Yuen and Lu, Tracy Shiyu. (2022). Corporate branding strategy for new companies in China: Lessons learned from GoGoVan and LaLaMove. In S. S. Durmusoglu (ed.), *Chinese Innovation and Branding Leaps*. Singapore: World Scientific Publishing, pp. 137–150.

Lam, Pong-Yuen, Chan, A., Gopaoco, H., Oh, K. and So, T. H. (2013). Dual branding strategy for a successful new product launch in China. *Business Horizons*, *56*, 583–589.

Porter, M. E. (2008). The five competitive forces that shape strategy. *Harvard Business Review*, *86*(1), 78–137.

Chapter 2

Marketing Research or Not

American Marketing Association (AMA, 2023) defined Marketing Research as follows:

> Marketing research is the function that links the consumer, customer, and public to the marketer through information — information used to identify and define opportunities and problems; generate, refine, and evaluate actions; monitor performance; and improve understanding of it as a process. It specifies the information required to address these issues, designs the method for collecting information, manages and implements the data collection process, analyzes the results, and communicates the findings and their implications.

Continuous improvement is important for a company which offers products. Sales growth either come from existing products or new products. The context is also important for the organization. Which city or country does the company have a presence in and wants to increase sales.

When marketers want to make a decision, they might not need to conduct marketing research. First, they have to know the right problem. They might be able to solve the problem by analytical thinking.

When a marketer wants to develop a new product or upgrade an existing product, they have to know the relative positioning of different products in a product positioning map in the target consumer's mind. The marketer can get consumer feedback and ideas from conducting qualitative research (one-on-one in-depth discussion, or focus group discussion). Afterward, the marketer could develop several product concepts for conducting quantitative research to compare their appeals to consumers.

The Problem

We make personal or business decisions from time to time. Not all decisions would need us to conduct marketing research, which would take time and money.

One example is the need of a machine to count coins collected from buses. If we took this problem as it was, we would create a machine with different sizes of holes to allow coins of different values to be thrown through. Instead of having a machine to count coins, the problem could be seen as that of the mechanism used by a bus company to collect transportation fee from each traveler. What we need is a payment mechanism that could quickly allow each traveler to pay the transportation fee of a journey easily. Different cities have their travel tickets, some have the value stored into the tickets. Some public transportation systems have scanners for travelers to show QR codes from their mobile phones.

Shampoo Promotion Example

After we have a better idea of the real problem, we can try to find a solution without conducting marketing research. For example, instead of conducting marketing research on what would be an appealing gift to offer for a shampoo brand, we could think of the problem as the need of a retailer to benefit from the shampoo brand so as to help the retailer increase its own traffic and sales. For instance, the constraint from retailer was that the value of the gift had to be of HK$5 or more, when the retail price of the shampoo brand of 400 ml was HK$25, that is, 20% for HK$5/HK$25. When the average marketing budget was only 5% for a brand, how could a marketer spend 20% to meet this request from the retailer?

One solution was by having a collaborator, a quick service restaurant, for the promotion (one of the 6Cs mentioned in the chapter about marketing was collaborator). A marketer could convince the quick service restaurant to offer HK$5 cash coupon for each bottle of shampoo brand of 400 ml with the retail price of HK$25. The marketer could negotiate for a discount for each coupon redeemed, so that the marketer only had to pay HK$4. Why would the collaborator agree? Because this promotion would increase traffic through its doors. If a quick service restaurant does not agree, the marketer of the shampoo brand could approach another quick service restaurant.

It is unlikely that a promotion could have 100% redemption rate. If the redemption rate was 25%, one out of four HK$5 coupons would be redeemed. So, the shampoo brand marketer could sell four bottles of shampoo at HK$25 × 4 and pay for one coupon redeemed at HK$4. Hence, the marketing budget for the promotion was HK$4 out of HK$25 × 4 (=HK$100). In effect, the percentage was HK$4/HK$100 = 4%.

One uncertainty for the above calculation is the redemption rate. If the redemption rate was higher than 25% (say at 30%), the final absolute amount of marketing expense would be higher than what the marketer had budgeted for at 25%. For a company with fiscal year from July 1 of one calendar year to June 30 of the following calendar year, the shampoo brand marketer could run the promotion in June–July of a calendar year. He can then charge all coupons collected on or before June 30 to the current fiscal year, and coupons collected on or after July 1 to the next fiscal year.

Chocolate Bar Upsize Example

We also do not have to conduct marketing research if we can use accounting data for financial analysis. If a marketer wanted to decide whether to offer more volume for a chocolate bar with the same price, he could use cost data for breakeven analysis.

If the current price is HK$70 for 200 g chocolate, and the marketer would like to run an upside promotion 15% more at the same price, the new offer would be HK$70 for 230 g chocolate. We did not know the current sales units, and assumed it was S. If our accountant told us that the variable cost of 200 g chocolate was HK$20, we could calculate the new cost of 230 g chocolate as HK$20/200 g × 230 g = HK$23.

We could use the following equation to find the breakeven Sales units, B, for getting the same profit.

$$S \times (\$70 - \$20) = B(\$70 - \$23)$$
$$S\,\$50 = B\,\$47 \tag{2.1}$$
$$\frac{B}{S} = \frac{\$50}{\$47} = 1.06$$

In other words, if the marketer could increase the units sold by 6%, he could achieve the same absolute amount of profit. Would this be

possible? How appealing was it to consumers for the same price and
with 15% more?

There was one more benefit to the marketer. If he was successful
in achieving 6% volume increase for units sold, he could sell more
grams of chocolate too, to increase the volume market share.

If the current market share is 35%, what would the new market
share be?

We could let the market size in gram be M. Then, we could multiply 200 g for each unit by the number of units sold, S, and divide
it by the market size M in gram.

$$35\% = \frac{200\,S}{M} \qquad (2.2)$$

Hence,

$$\frac{S}{M} = \frac{35\%}{200} \qquad (2.3)$$

$$\text{New volume in grams} = 1.06\,S \times 230$$

So, if we assume the market size remained the same at M,

$$\text{New market share} = 1.06\,S \times 230/M$$
$$\text{New market share} = 243.8\frac{S}{M}$$

From Equation (2.3),

$$\text{New market share} = 243.8\frac{35\%}{200} = 42.7\%$$

6% increase in units sold for the upsized chocolate to 230 g could
mean market share increase from 35% to 42.7% if we assume the
market size remained the same at M.

We could also assume that market size might increase slightly by
3%.

$$\text{New market share} = 1.06\,S \times 230/(1.03\,M)$$
$$\text{New market share} = 243.8\frac{S}{(1.03\,M)} \qquad (2.4)$$

From Equation (2.3),

$$\text{New market share} = 243.8\,\frac{35\%}{1.03(200)} = 41.4\%$$

Reference

AMA (2023). Definition of marketing. American Marketing Association. https://www.ama.org/the-definition-of-marketing-what-is-marketing/ (accessed on January 15, 2023).

Chapter 3

Marketing Research Process

This chapter first illustrates one model for consumers to make decisions when the product of a brand has multiple attributes, and consumers can assign relative importance weights to these attributes. Marketers can conduct marketing research using this model by asking respondents to provide importance weights for all attributes and ratings of each attribute for a brand, and then calculate the weighted average scores for two products. As a result of this model, consumers can choose the product of a brand with higher weighted average score.

This chapter then introduces the three key steps in the process of marketing research: positioning map, qualitative research and quantitative research.

Creating a Sustainable Advantage

Kotler *et al.* (2022, p. 150) and Chernev (2019) suggested that there were three core strategies for creating a sustainable advantage for a company: introduce a new attribute, differentiate it from an existing attribute, and build a strong brand.

We could build on their ideas and identified the following three strategies to create sustainable advantages for a brand:

1. When all competitors do not have it, your brand has a "new" attribute.

2. When all competitors have an attribute, your brand has a "better" attribute.
3. When all competitors have better attributes, your **brand is different** and significantly better "overall."

We could also use the following three Chinese phrases (with English translations) to describe these three strategies:

1. **人無我有 (others do not have, I have)**
   The first character 人 means "the other people."
   The second character 無 means "no."
   The third character 我 means "I."
   The fourth character 有 means "have."
2. **人有我優 (others have, I am better)**
   The first character 人 means "the other people."
   The second character 有 means "have."
   The third character 我 means "I."
   The fourth character 優 means "better."
3. **人優我異 (others are better, I am different and better overall)**
   The first character 人 means "the other people."
   The second character 優 means "better."
   The third character 我 means "I."
   The fourth character 異 means "different."

The second Chinese character 優 and the fourth Chinese character 異 together 優異 mean "excellence" in English.

For example, each mobile phone has several key attributes. Samsung introduced a new attribute, a foldable mobile phone, to compete with Apple iPhone, which did not have this feature then.

While both the Samsung mobile phone and Apple mobile phone had cameras with the same resolution, the quality of a Samsung photo was clearer than an Apple photo even after a user zoomed in many times.

Apple, however, had a strong brand that could integrate **B**usiness model, **E**ngineering and **D**esign (BED in short) together to give users an excellent brand experience. Hence, Apple users continued to stay with using iPhone after Samsung had launched a foldable mobile phone with better quality of photos on zooming in.

Multiple Attributes

Using mobile phone as an example again, we illustrate how consumers could evaluate and provide relative importance weights for three attributes: screen size, battery, storage.

Before Samsung introduced the feature of foldability, an individual could compare a model of Samsung with another model of iPhone across three attributes. The sum of different relative important weights was 100%. The value of each attribute rating was between 0 to 10 (Table 3.1).

Mobile phone attributes

$$5\,(\mathbf{20\%}) + 8\,(\mathbf{30\%}) + 9\,(\mathbf{50\%}) = 7.9 \tag{3.1}$$

$$6\,(\mathbf{20\%}) + 7\,(\mathbf{30\%}) + 10\,(\mathbf{50\%}) = 8.3 \tag{3.2}$$

As the weighted average of **8.3** for iPhone was higher than **7.9** for Samsung, an individual was expected to choose iPhone.

The marketers of Samsung had to come up with different strategies to compete. One of them was to increase screen size to make it better than Apple (Table 3.2).

Table 3.1. Comparison of Samsung and iPhone according to attributes.

Relative Importance	Screen Size 20%	Battery 30%	Storage 50%	Weighted Average
Samsung	5	8	9	7.9
iPhone	6	7	10	8.3

Table 3.2. Comparison of iPhone and Samsung with larger screen for Samsung.

Relative Importance	Screen Size 20%	Battery 30%	Storage 50%	Weighted Average
Samsung	10	8	9	8.9
iPhone	6	7	10	8.3

Table 3.3. Comparison of iPhone and Samsung with a new attribute: Foldability.

Relative Importance	Screen Size 10%	Battery 20%	Storage 40%	Foldable 30%	Weighted Average
Samsung	5	8	9	5	7.2
iPhone	6	7	10	0	6

Another strategy followed by Samsung was to add a new feature, foldability (Table 3.3).

The weighted average score of Samsung increased to **7.2**, which was higher than that for iPhone at **6.0**, because the individual had assigned a relative importance weight of 30% to the foldable feature, and a rating of **5** to Samsung with this feature and **0** to iPhone without this feature.

Positioning Map

Most companies have processes to review their business each year. For a portfolio of products that a company has, it can put them into a map with two dimensions, the x-axis and the y-axis, and label these dimensions based on consumer feedback as a simple exercise of putting products of the company and its competitors on a table, to see how they are positioned against each other.

If a consumer thinks two products are similar, she should put them close together. If the consumer thinks two products are dissimilar, she should put them apart. The distance between any two products represents the degree of similarity between the two products. The shorter the distance, the greater the similarity. The longer the distance, the greater the dissimilarity.

For example, a consumer might have consumed carbonated Cola, energy drink, juice drink, water, and tea in the past 7 days. She can position them on the map based on her experience. Similarly, several consumers participated in this exercise of putting products on a table, and discussed among themselves about the same in qualitative research (focus group). They came to a consensus on how to group products based on their similarities. After their discussion,

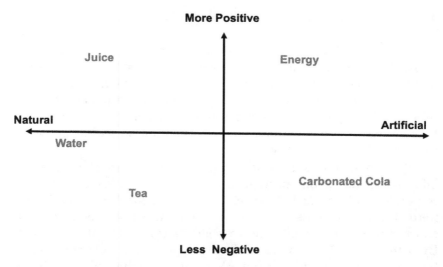

Figure 3.1. Positioning map for various drinks.

they came up with the following map for putting different products together (Figure 3.1).

The x-axis has labels of "artificial" versus "natural". The y-axis has labels of "more positive" and "less negative".

An energy drink that provides vitamins and functional ingredients to energize a consumer was placed in the quadrant of "artificial" and "more positive".

Fruit juices that are nutritious and have positive benefits were placed in the quadrant of "natural" and "more positive".

Carbonated cola drink goes well with hot and spicy food to cool one down, and so it was placed in the quadrant of "artificial" and "less negative".

Tea can also cool one down and has detoxing benefits. It was placed in the quadrant of "natural" and "less negative".

Water is natural and "neutral" between "more positive" or "less negative".

Qualitative Research

Most people would like to be with other people, rather than being alone and not talking to anyone. When you meet and chat with your friend, both you and your friend can freely talk about any topic of interest.

In a one-on-one in-depth discussions or in focus group discussions, the interviewer and the interviewee did not know one another well before the research. So, the interviewer had to introduce herself and also asked the interviewee(s) to introduce himself/herself (themselves). The topic of discussion was not just any topic of interest between you and your friend. Instead, the topic was what marketers wanted to find out from research.

While one-on-one in-depth discussion can give the researcher information about one particular respondent, it takes time and the respondent might not have much to say for some questions. If there were 6–8 respondents in a focus group, the interviewer can ask another respondent while one respondent thinks about the answer. By listening to the answers of the other people, a respondent might be able to build on ideas of the others, and gave his opinions. In this way, focus groups give researchers insights that one-on-one in-depth discussions might not be able to provide. One-on-one in-depth discussions, on the other hand, can allow the respondent to think deeply about a topic without being distracted by the other respondents in the research.

For our study, the interviewer had to prepare a list of questions as a discussion guide for a one-on-one in-depth discussion or a focus group discussion. The interviewer might also be known as the moderator.

The moderator's discussion guide can include some key questions and points of discussion. For example, if the moderator wanted to get some ideas for a new mobile phone model, the moderator might have the following questions:

1. **What brand and model of mobile phone are you using now?**
2. **When did you buy this? Why?**
3. **Had you considered the other brands/models before you bought your current brand/model? Why and why not?**
4. **Have you been using the same brand of mobile phone since you bought your first mobile phone? If no, what is the previous brand of mobile phone that you have used?**

Why have you switched from the previous brand to the current brand?

5. **What are the key features you like in your current mobile phone? Why?**

6. **Is there anything that you dislike about your current mobile phone? Why?**

7. **If you can tell the company that made your mobile phone to create a better mobile phone for you, what will you want the next mobile phone model to have?**

Please pause and think about your answers to these questions before you read the rationale for having these questions, and some possible answers to these questions in the following. While questions mentioned above are for mobile phones, we can also change the product from mobile phone to another product category.

Question 1 is easy to answer for any respondent who has a mobile phone.

Question 2 is also useful for marketers to know about the two "w's", "When" and "Why". If a respondent has bought the current mobile phone 5 years ago, and keeps using it even now, he/she may be quite different from another respondent who has bought the latest model a few months ago. Answers to the question "Why" will also be different for respondents. A respondent may buy it for functional reasons such as because he has lost the previous one and must buy a new one. Another respondent may buy it for emotional reasons such as because the new model comes in a color that he wants.

Question 3 can help marketers know the competitive set of brands and why the respondent will consider these other brands.

Question 4 helps marketers understand the actual brand switching that a respondent has gone through. Marketers do not want to lose users to another brand. Answers to this question can provide useful information for marketers to protect their own brand and keep users.

Questions 5 and 6 are fundamental questions that marketers have to consider for brand satisfaction study: the likes and dislikes of a brand. Answers to these two questions can also help respondents start thinking about what they want for a "better" mobile phone, which is the next question.

Question 7 helps marketers to get ideas from respondents. Each person is unique, and may have suggestions that marketers cannot think of themselves.

Answers from one respondent to these seven questions

1. **What brand and model of mobile phone are you using now?**
   I use Apple iPhone 14 Pro Max.

2. **When did you buy this? Why?**
   I bought it when it was first introduced by Apple a few months ago.

   I know the differences from the previous model are not big. I bought it because of its one difference — the resolution and quality of the photos are better than in iPhone 13, and I want to have the best possible quality of photos.

   When I attend social events for my work, I have to use my iPhone to take photos with guests. Usually, I cannot get back any photo from the professional photographer of the event. Even if I can get photos afterwards, it is usually much later.

3. **Had you considered the other brands/models before you bought your current brand/model? Why and why not?**
   Yes, I know that Samsung's latest model can be folded.
   The screen size can be doubled after the phone is unfolded.

   This feature is unique and appealing to me. However, I am reluctant to switch to Samsung with a different operating system.

   Currently, if I want to view comfortably, I will connect my Apple Mac Pro 16 inches to an external monitor from Apple for me to view at home or in my office.

4. **Have you been using the same brand of mobile phone since you bought your first mobile phone? If no, what is the previous brand of mobile phone that you have used? Why have you switched from the previous brand to the current brand?**
   I bought and used Samsung with big screen for one year when Steve Jobs of Apple insisted on offering only one size. I think we

have to treat people differently. I have big hands. Tim Cook of Apple finally introduced one more size for iPhone. I immediately bought the bigger screen size version of iPhone. I am currently using the latest model of Apple iPhone 14 Pro Max with 6.7-inch (diagonal).

5. **What are the key features you like in your current mobile phone? Why?**
Easy to use it together with the other Apple products so that I don't have to waste time to learn another operating system.

6. **Is there anything that you dislike about your current mobile phone? Why?**
A few years ago, I did not like to carry a power bank with my iPhone when I went out. Although I charged my iphone every night, the power could still run out in about 8 hours. After I have upgraded to the current model, I seldom run out of power now. So, I do not have any major dislike of my iPhone.

7. **If you can tell the company that made your mobile phone to create a better mobile phone for you, what will you want the next mobile phone model to have?**
I hope that one day Apple will launch a new model of iPhone with bigger screen size than iPhone 14 Pro Max at 6.7 inches (diagonal). I understand that not many people will want a bigger size, but I am willing to pay more for a bigger screen.

Based on the answers to each question, the interviewer can ask follow-up questions to clarify or get more information. For Question 7, the moderator may ask follow-up questions based on the answer of the respondent, as follows:

So, what is the ideal screen size of iPhone for you?
Bigger by around 20%.

I see. Why only 20%, why not even bigger?
20% is what I can still hold in my hand and also put in a pocket of my pants.

How about width and height? Do you want Apple to proportionally make it bigger as by keeping the same ratio between width and height, or you want a different ratio?
Keeping the same ratio is fine, but it is frustrating that some Apps cannot be displayed properly now with my iPhone.

The follow-up questions from the interviewer and answers from the interviewee may continue, depending on the extent of the information that the marketer wants to find out.

Quantitative Research

After a marketer has conducted several one-on-one in-depth discussions or focus groups, the marketer can decide whether he wants to have quantitative research to compare different marketing options and choose the best alternative.

For example, a marketer could compare two product concepts, concept A for his new product, and concept B for the competitive product.

He could conduct a quantitative research with 200 respondents in total, for example. He could randomly assign 100 respondents to read product concept A and answer questions about it, and randomly assign another 100 respondents to read the product concept B and answer questions about it. Each of these 200 respondents would either read product concept A or product concept B, but not both. As each respondent is randomly assigned to one of the two product concepts, we can treat the two groups (each with 100 respondents) to be "equal" statistically, and can compare their answers with statistical tests.

A marketer could reduce cost by only having 100 respondents in total, and ask all of them to read both product concepts. The marketer could randomly assign 50 respondents to read product concept A first and then product concept B, and randomly assign another 50 respondents to read product concept B first and then product concept A. A respondent's answers to the first concept might affect his/her answers to the second concept. Hence, one approach is to have the above arrangement (50 respondents for AB, 50 respondents for BA) before answers from all 100 respondents are analyzed by statistical tests to compare A and B.

References

Chernev, A. (2019). *Strategic Marketing Management: Theory and Practice.* Chicago, IL: Cerebellum Press.

Kotler, P., Keller, K. L., and Chernev, A. (2022). *Marketing Management.* 16th edn., Pearson.

Chapter 4

Measurement and Scaling

The four primary scales of measurement are nominal, ordinal, interval, and ratio (Malhotra, 2020, p. 269). Their basic characteristics as summarized by Malhotra (2020, p. 270) are as follows:

Nominal: Numbers identified and classified objects.

Ordinal: Numbers indicated the relative positions of the objects but not the magnitude of differences between them.

Interval: Differences between objects could be compared; zero point was arbitrary.

Ratio: Zero point was fixed; ratios of scale values could be compared.

One example for each scale is as follows.

Nominal Scale

What is your gender?
M — Male
F — Female
The letter M or F simply indicates the gender.

Ordinal Scale

What is your highest level of education completed?

(a) No education
(b) Kindergarten
(c) Primary school

(d) Secondary school
(e) University — Undergraduate
(f) University — Master
(g) University — PhD

We know the order of each level of education.

Secondary school is above primary school.

University — master is above university — undergraduate education.

However, we cannot calculate the difference between secondary school and primary school.

Interval Scale

What is your purchase intention of brand X?
1-definitely will not buy, 7-definitely will buy

1	2	3	4	5	6	7

We usually assume that the difference between 1 and 2, 2 and 3, and so on is the same. We can also use -3 to 3 instead of 1–7.

What is your purchase intention of brand X?
-3-definitely will not buy, 3-definitely will buy

-3	-2	-1	0	1	2	3

We can also assume that the difference between -3 and -2, -2 and -1, and so on is the same. The zero point is arbitrary. If we use the scale of 1–7, we cannot calculate the ratio of the answer of one respondent A with another respondent B. If respondent A gives 6 and respondent B gives 2, we cannot calculate the ratio of 6/2 (3 times), and say that the purchase intention of respondent B is 3 times that of respondent A.

Ratio Scale

What is your weight in kilogram (kg)?_____
What is your height in meter (m)?_____

If respondent A has height of 0.9 m and respondent B has height of 1.8 m, we can calculate the ratio of their heights to be 2 for B versus A ($=1.8\text{m}/0.9\text{m}$).

Number of Points in a Scale

What is your purchase intention of brand X?
1-definitely will not buy, 7-definitely will buy

1	2	3	4	5	6	7

For the above question, we can have 7 points, 5 points, 9 points, or odd number of points if we allow respondents to have a neutral point of view toward a question.

If we have an even number of points (6 points, 4 points, or 10 points), respondents cannot have a neutral point of view toward a question.

The choice may depend on whether a researcher has to compare with past research results of a company or a research agency. If a company has been tracking the purchase intention of a brand for years with a scale with 7 points, it is likely that the researcher has to follow. Similarly, if a research agency has been using a scale of 7 points to measure purchase intention of new product concepts, the new product concept test will likely have the same scale with 7 points. Comparison will be easier as a result.

The number of points in a scale may also depend on the culture of the respondents. Chinese respondents tend to avoid choosing the two extremes. If a researcher has used a scale of 7 points, Chinese respondents can still choose another 5 points if they avoid choosing the 2 extreme points on the scale.

Scale with Multiple Items

Wong *et al.* (2020a) have given a scale with 8 items (questions) to measure an individual's mindset. These 8 questions are as follows:

Please rate your level of agreement with the following statements.
For questions 1–4, 1 = strongly agree and 7 = strongly disagree.

For questions 5–8, 1 = strongly disagree and 7 = strongly agree.

(1) The kind of person someone is, is something very basic about them, and it can't be changed very much.
(2) People can do things differently, but the important parts of who they are can't really be changed.
(3) Everyone is a certain kind of person, and there is not much that can be done to really change that.
(4) As much as I hate to admit it, you can't teach an old dog new tricks. People can't really change their deepest attributes.
(5) Everyone, no matter who they are, can significantly change their basic characteristics.
(6) People can substantially change the kind of person they are.
(7) No matter what kind of person someone is, they can always change very much.
(8) People can change even their most basic qualities.

When the sum of answers to these 8 question is equal to 32 (4×8), the individual is neutral, as he has chosen the mid-point, 4, in a scale with 7 points, in all 8 answers.

If the sum of answers is less than 32, the individual has an entity mindset, and the smaller the value of the sum, the stronger the entity mindset.

If the sum of answers is greater than 32, the individual has an incremental mindset, and the larger the value of the sum, the stronger the incremental mindset.

"People with incremental mindset believe that a person's qualities are contextual and malleable, given sufficient time and effort. In contrast, people with entity mindset believe that attributes are dispositional and unlikely to change" (Wong *et al.*, 2020b).

References

Malhotra, N. K. (2020). *Marketing Research: An Applied Orientation.* 7th edn., United Kingdom.

Wong, Vincent Chi, Su Lei Su and Lam, and Howard Pong-Yuen (2020a). When less is more: How mindset influences consumers' responses to products with reduced negative attributes. *Journal of Marketing,*

OnlineFirst, May 14, 2020. Online supplements. https://journals.sa
gepub.com/doi/10.1177/0022242920920859 (accessed on January 10,
2023).

Wong, Vincent Chi, Su Lei Su and Lam, and Howard Pong-Yuen (2020b).
When less is more: How mindset influences consumers' responses to
products with reduced negative attributes. *Journal of Marketing, 84*(5),
137–153.

Chapter 5

Questionnaire

There are two types of questions, open-ended and close-ended. For a close-ended question, we have to provide options for respondents to choose from. These options have to be mutually exclusive and also completely exhaustive.

Mutually Exclusive

For example, for the question **"Did you drink Coke in the past 7 days?"**, there are only two choices, yes or no, and these two choices are mutually exclusive. That is, the answer has to be either yes or no, and a respondent can only pick one of the two choices.

One may think of questions about gender with choices of male and female as mutually exclusive. In reality, there are more than two choices. If we type "What is your gender?" in the software to help us conduct a survey, www.qualtrics.com, we will get the following few choices automatically from the software:

What is your gender?

(a) Male
(b) Female
(c) Non-binary/third gender
(d) Prefer not to say

Completely Exhaustive

For the question **"What is your annual income from all sources before tax in the last calendar year?"**, if we only give the following two choices for respondents to choose from, these choices are not completely exhaustive to completely capture all income possibilities.

(a) Less than US$5,001
(b) US$5,001–US$10,000

We can increase the number of choices to the following:

(a) Less than US$5,001
(b) US$5,001–US$10,000
(c) US$10,001–US$15,000
(d) US$15,001–US$20,000
(e) More than US$20,000

Choices (a) and (e) cover the situation that a respondent may have income less than US$5,001 or have income more than US$20,000. The other choices, (b), (c), (d), have the same range of US$5,000.

If we have the following four choices, answer c has a range of US$10,000 (US$10,001–US$20,000), two times of the range for choice b of US$5,000 (US$5,001–US$10,000).

(a) Less than US$5,001
(b) US$5,001–US$10,000
(c) US$10,001–US$20,000
(d) More than US$20,000

Ideally, each choice should have the same range. Otherwise, respondents may mistakenly think that the choices have the same range if they have not read the values carefully.

Age

If we ask "How old are you?", different respondents may have different answers, depending on whether they want to round up or not. For a respondent who is born on February 1, 1990, what should be his answer if he has received the questionnaire on January 31, 2023? We will have to know the date that a respondent has answered a questionnaire before we can know his/her age. So, instead of asking all respondents for their ages, we can ask each respondent to let us know the month and year of birth. Afterward, we can calculate ourselves.

What is your month and year of birth?

Month ____

Year ____

Nationality

What is your nationality?

(a) Hong Kong Special Administrative Region (SAR)
(b) Mainland China
(c) British citizen
(d) Canadian citizen

An individual can have more than one nationality or passport. So, we can ask the following question instead.

Do you currently have the following passport(s)?

	Yes	No
Hong Kong Special Administrative Region		
Mainland Chinese citizen		
British citizen		
Canadian citizen		

Frequency

If we want to know the frequency of a respondent in performing a certain activity, how could we ask the question and what options to provide? The following is an example:

How often do you exercise?

(a) Never
(b) Rarely
(c) Occasionally
(d) Regularly

Different respondents may have different interpretations of these words. One respondent may choose "regularly" if he exercises once a month. Another respondent may choose "regularly" if he exercises once a week. So, how could we improve these choices?

How often do you exercise?

(a) About once a day
(b) About once a week
(c) About once a month

These three choices are not precise. If a respondent exercises once every 2 weeks, should he/she choose (b) or (c)? So, we can improve the choices for the question further as follows.

How often did you exercise in the past 4 weeks?

(a) 7 times or less
(b) 8 times to 14 times
(c) 15 times to 21 times
(d) 22 times or more

Finally, different people may define exercise differently. So, we may want to make the question even clearer with a definition for exercise such as "exercise means that you walk, run, play sports on your own or with other people for at least 30 minutes continuously".

Satisfaction

How satisfied were you with the service you received at the restaurant A in your last visit?

(a) Completely satisfied
(b) Mostly satisfied
(c) Somewhat satisfied
(d) Neither satisfied nor dissatisfied
(e) Dissatisfied

These five choices above have three choices that are satisfied, and one choice that is dissatisfied. So, they are not balanced. We can improve by having the same number of positive and negative choices, and asking "how satisfied or dissatisfied ..." instead of "how satisfied ...".

How satisfied or dissatisfied were you with the service you received at restaurant A in your last visit?

(a) Completely satisfied
(b) Somewhat satisfied
(c) Neither satisfied nor dissatisfied
(d) Somewhat dissatisfied
(e) Completely dissatisfied

Two Questions Instead of One Question

Are you satisfied with the service and quality of food in restaurant A?

A respondent may be satisfied with the service in restaurant A, but he may not be satisfied with the quality of food there. So, the above question should be separated into two questions.

Are you satisfied with the service in restaurant A?

Are you satisfied with the quality of food in restaurant A?

Comparison

If your research agency has given you the following research result, will you choose celebrity A or celebrity B for your brand if liking of a celebrity is an important measure?

Liking scale (1-dislike, 7-like)
Celebrity A — mean is 5.5
Celebrity B — mean is 5.2

If we only compare the two means, we may choose celebrity A with a higher value at 5.5.

If the two means come from the following data, what will our choice be then?

Liking	1	2	3	4	5	6	7	Mean
Number of respondents:								
Celebrity A	0	30	0	0	0	0	70	5.5
Celebrity B	0	0	0	0	80	20	0	5.2

Celebrity A has polarizing appeal to all 100 respondents.
30 respondents have given 2 in the scale of 1–7.
Another 70 respondents have given 7.
For celebrity B, 80 respondents have given 5.
Another 20 respondents have given 6.
This example illustrates the importance of examining the data in addition to comparing two means only.

Opening Paragraphs

Different organizations or companies may have their guidelines on what researchers have to inform respondents. The following paragraphs provide key information about a survey, and respect the choice and privacy of respondents.

This asks for your help and consensus to take around 15 minutes to complete the online survey about product concepts. You are free to decline to participate, and have the right to terminate the survey at anytime. The purpose of the investigation is for us to understand your feedback for two different product concepts. Your responses are very important to us, as it helps us receive enough data for quantitative analysis and report preparation and presentation for new products that can better satisfy consumer needs in the future. We look forward to receiving your responses, and hope that you enjoy the experience of completing this survey.

The survey is anonymous. We will take precautions to preserve the confidentiality of the research data and ensure that all reports of the research will be devoid of identifiers. Information obtained will not be publicly disclosed in a fashion that would identify any specific person. The retention period for research data is 3 months after the completion of the survey in January 2023. If there is any question about your rights as a participant in this study, you may contact us at the following email: email-address.

Once again, thanks for your help and contribution.

Questionnaire Structure

The following questionnaire has 10 questions. Researchers can add more questions to suit their needs. Questions 1 and 2 are filler questions to determine whether a respondent is qualified for the survey. Afterward, there are questions for current brand usage, current level of satisfaction of current brand, attribute importance, and demographics.

Filler Questions

1. Are you aged 18 or above?

Yes

No-End the survey

2. Are you using a mobile phone now?

Yes

No-End the survey

Current brand usage

3. What is the brand of your current mobile phone?

a. Apple

b. Samsung

c. Huawei

d. Xiaomi

e. Others, please specify _____

Current level of satisfaction

4. How satisfied are you with your current mobile phone?
Please assign a score from 0 to 100 (0-not satisfied, 100-satisfied).
Score_____

Attributes

5. How important are the following attributes for your choice of mobile phone?

1-not important. 7-important.

(a) Brand
(b) Operating system (i.e. Apple IOS/Google Android, etc.).
(c) Storage
(d) Camera resolution
(e) Foldable

Demographic questions

6. What is your gender?

(a) Male
(b) Female
(c) Non-binary/third gender
(d) Prefer not to say

7. What is your year and month of birth?
Year _____
Month _____

8. What is your highest level of education completed?

(a) No education
(b) Kindergarten
(c) Primary school
(d) Secondary school
(e) University-undergraduate
(f) University-master
(g) University-PhD

9. What is your current marital status?

(a) Single
(b) Living with a partner
(c) Married
(d) Separated
(e) Divorced
(f) Widowed
(g) Prefer not to say

10. What is your personal annual income from all sources before tax in calendar year 2022?

Less than US$50,001
US$50,001–$100,000
US$100,001–$150,000
US$150,001–$200,000
More than US$200,000

Thank you for your time and effort.

Product Concept

Before we actually spend a lot of money to commercially produce a product, we can reduce the risk of product failure by having research findings that prove that the product is appealing to a target group of consumers. We can develop a product concept, and conduct a product concept test among a group of respondents.

The product concept is a description of a product, and it usually includes an opening statement which can resonate with consumers. This will attract consumers and pique their interest to know more about the product, understand what it is, the frame of reference, or the category of the product. Is it a snack, a drink, or what is it? Marketers also want to highlight the key point of difference of a product versus the other competitive products. Marketers also have to provide a reason to believe and summarize the functional and emotional benefits to consumers. If a marketer wants to ask respondents for their purchase intention of a product, the marketer has to give the product's package and price as well.

Lam *et al.* (2013) have given an example as follows:

After a hard day's work, you need some rest and enjoy.

The new potato chip is crispy and delicious, but it does not contain any fat and salt (0% fat, 0% salt).

It is produced by a patented baking process.

Without adding any oil, it nevertheless has a crispy texture. It also has specially added minerals that give it a delicious, slightly salty taste and that are essential for the human body.

Try the new product now.

Product: Potato Chips / Weight: 50g / Price: RMB3

Product concept test is also useful for academic research when we want to compare different scenarios. Wong, Su, and Lam (2020) have given product concept descriptions in their research for two mindsets (entity/incremental) and two attribute framings (neutral/reduced negative attribute). For more details about mindsets, please refer to Chapter 4 in this book, about measurement and scaling. The four product concepts' descriptions are as follows. The key differences among them are highlighted in bold text.

Entity mindset with neutral attribute framing

COPO is a brand of luncheon meat. Now you can eat luncheon meat whenever you feel like it because it is pre-cooked for your convenience.

At COPO, we understand that consumers are committed to consistency over the course of their lives. Just like you, we at COPO remain, we persist, and we keep steady. We always stay the same with you.

Choose COPO for Luncheon Meat!

Entity mindset with reduced negative attribute framing

COPO is a brand of luncheon meat. Now you can eat luncheon meat whenever you feel like it because it is pre-cooked for your convenience.

At COPO, we understand that consumers are committed to consistency over the course of their lives. Just like you, we at COPO remain, we persist, and we keep steady. We always stay the same with you.

Now, COPO Luncheon Meat has had its sodium nitrite reduced by 30% compared to the original recipe.

Choose COPO for Luncheon Meat!

Incremental mindset with neutral attribute framing

COPO is a brand of luncheon meat. Now you can eat luncheon meat whenever you feel like it because it is pre-cooked for your convenience.

At COPO, we understand that consumers change over the course of their lives. Just like you, we COPO people evolve, we develop, and we are flexible. We always change with you.

Choose COPO for Luncheon Meat!

Incremental mindset with reduced negative attribute framing

COPO is a brand of luncheon meat. Now you can eat luncheon meat whenever you feel like it because it is pre-cooked for your convenience.

At COPO, we understand that consumers change over the course of their lives. Just like you, we COPO people evolve, we develop, and we are flexible. We always change with you.

Now, COPO Luncheon Meat has had its sodium nitrite reduced by 30% compared to the original recipe.

Choose COPO for Luncheon Meat!

Questionnaire — Product Concept Test

The following questions are developed, based on the product concept research of Lam *et al.* (2013).

Q1 **After reading the introduction about the product concept, to what degree do you like the product?** (Choose one only) "Please indicate from 1 to 7, where 1 means strongly dislike it, 7 means strongly like it".

Q2 **If this product can be purchased in the place where you regularly shop, which of the following options best describes your likelihood of buying this product?** (Choose one only) "Please indicate from 1 to 7, where 1 means definitely will not buy, 7 means definitely will buy".

[Q3 will only be asked if the answer is 4 to 7 for Q2]

Q3 **If this product can be purchased in the place where you regularly shop, how many times will you buy this product during the next 10 times you buy potato chips?** Enter: _____times

Q4 **How credible is the product description?** (Choose one only) "Please indicate from 1 to 7, where 1 means the least credible, 7 means the most credible".

Q5 **What do you think is the level of uniqueness of this product compared to other potato chips on the market?** (Choose one only) "Please indicate from 1 to 7, where 1 means the least unique, 7 means the most unique".

Q6 **What do you think about this product's relevancy for you?** (Choose one only) "Please indicate from 1 to 7, where 1 means not at all relevant, 7 means very relevant".

Q7 **To what degree do you like the product name [product name option]?** (Choose one only) "Please indicate from 1 to 7, where 1 means strongly dislike it, 7 means strongly like it".

Q8 **Do you think this product name [product name option] is easy to remember?** (Choose one only) "Please indicate from 1 to 7, where 1 means not at all easy to remember, 7 means very easy to remember".

Q9 **What do you think is the influence of this product name [product name option] on the product image?** (Choose one only) "Please indicate from 1 to 7, where 1 means very negative influence, 7 means very positive influence".

Q10 **What is the level of fit of the product name [product name option] and the description of the product?** (Choose one only) "Please indicate from 1 to 7, where 1 means does not fill well, 7 means fits well".

Questions Q1–Q6 are the key measures for marketers to obtain for each product concept. Afterward, we can compare each measure between two product concepts, concept A and concept B. Concept A can be the proposed new product concept. Concept B can be the competitive product concept.

Questions Q7 to Q10 are the key measures for brand names. Marketers can add these four questions to Q1 to Q6 for conducting branded product concept test. The research finding of Lam *et al.* (2013) is that product concepts can receive statistically significant higher purchase intention levels when the brand names have suggestive meanings.

References

Lam, Pong Yuen, Chan, Annie, Gopaoco, Hannie, Oh, Kevin, and So, Tsz Him. (2013). Dual branding strategy for a successful new product launch in China. *Business Horizons, 56,* 583–589.

Wong, Vincent Chi, Su Lei Su and Lam, Howard Pong-Yuen. (2020). When less is more: How mindset influences consumers' responses to products with reduced negative attributes. *Journal of Marketing,* OnlineFirst, May 14, 2020. Online supplements. https://journals.sagepub.com/doi/10.1177/0022242920920859 (accessed in January 10, 2023).

Chapter 6

Analysis of Variance

Variance Test

If we have obtained interval or ratio data from two or more groups
of respondents, we can run analysis of variance to determine whether
there is any statistically significant difference among the groups (Hair
et al., 2021).

Lind *et al.* (2018) have given two examples. First, while two hos-
pitals may have similar average waiting time in the emergency units,
they have different variances. Second, two stocks may have similar
returns, but they have different variances.

The test statistic follows the F Distribution, and F is for Sir
Ronald Fisher (Lind *et al.*, 2018).

If we have the data as follows for the waiting time from placing
an order to getting the first dish of food from two restaurants, we
can ask whether there is a difference in the variation of waiting time
for the two restaurants (see Table 6.1).

The null hypothesis is that there is no statistically significant
difference in the variances.

$$H_0 : \sigma_1^2 = \sigma_2^2$$

The alternative hypothesis is that there is statistically significant
difference in the variances.

$$H_1 : \sigma_1^2 \neq \sigma_2^2.$$

The mean waiting time of Restaurant $A = 17.6$.

The mean waiting time of Restaurant $B = 20.0$

Table 6.1. Calculation of within-group variance of the waiting times at two restaurants.

Restaurant A	Restaurant B	$A - \bar{A}$	$B - \bar{B}$	$(A - \bar{A})^2$	$(B - \bar{B})^2$
20	25	2.4	5	5.76	25
15	22	−2.6	2	6.76	4
16	18	−1.6	−2	2.56	4
19	15	1.4	−5	1.96	25
18	16	0.4	−4	0.16	16
20	19	2.4	−1	5.76	1
17	18	−0.6	−2	0.36	4
16	20	−1.6	0	2.56	0
18	23	0.4	3	0.16	9
17	24	−0.6	4	0.36	16
Mean 17.6	20.0		**Sum**	26.4	104.0

The standard deviation formulation

$$S = \sqrt{\frac{\sum(x - \bar{x})^2}{n - 1}} \tag{6.1}$$

So, we have

$$S \text{ for restaurant } A = \sqrt{\frac{26.4}{10 - 1}} = 1.71 \tag{6.2}$$

$$S \text{ for restaurant } B = \sqrt{\frac{104.0}{10 - 1}} = 3.40 \tag{6.3}$$

While the usual practice is to put the larger of the two sample variances in the numerator, so that the F ratio is larger than 1 (Lind *et al.*, 2018, p. 387), we do not have to know which one of the two sample variances is larger if we use R. R can perform an F test to compare the variance of the two samples from normal populations. We can find more details from typing help ("var.test") in R console.

The F ratio for our example is $1.71^2/3.40^2 = 0.25$ if we compare variances of A versus B.

The F ratio is equal to $3.40^2/1.71^2 = 3.94$ if we compare variances of B versus A.

For both cases, the p-values from R are the same and are equal to 0.05344 which is smaller than 10%. So, if we can accept an error of 10%, we will reject the null hypothesis and accept the alternative hypothesis that there is a statistically significant difference between the two sample variances.

Analysis of Variance

Analysis of variance (ANOVA) allows us to compare means from two or more groups (Iacobucci and Churchill, 2018, pp. 382–385). For example, if store sales of a product in units are as follows for 10 stores when the product is in plastic container or in metal container (Iacobucci and Churchill, 2018, pp. 382–385), we can use ANOVA to compare their means.

Store sales of a product in units

Table 6.2. Sales of plastic containers and metal containers at 10 stores.

Grand mean and group means

We first calculate three means:
The grand mean for 20 values.
The group mean for 10 values of plastic container.

Table 6.2. Sales of plastic containers and metal containers at 10 stores.

Store	Plastic Container	Metal Container
1	432	365
2	360	405
3	397	396
4	408	390
5	417	404
6	380	372
7	422	378
8	406	410
9	400	383
10	408	400

The **group mean** for 10 values of **metal** container.

Grand mean

$$= \frac{[(432 + 360 + \cdots 400 + 408) + (365 + 405 + \cdots 383 + 400)]}{20}$$

$$= \frac{(4030 + 3903)}{20} = 396.7 \tag{6.4}$$

Group mean of plastic container

$$= \frac{(432 + 360 + \cdots 400 + 408)}{10} = 403.0 \tag{6.5}$$

Group mean of metal container

$$= \frac{(365 + 405 + \cdots 383 + 400)}{10} = 390.3 \tag{6.6}$$

Any one of these 20 sales values will deviate from the grand mean of **396.7**.

For example, the sales value of store 1 for plastic container, 432, is different from **396.7** by 35.4 (432 − **396.7**). We can write this difference, 35.4, as follows:

$$35.4 = (432 - 396.7)$$
$$35.4 = (432 - 403 + 403 - 396.7) \tag{6.7}$$
$$35.4 = (432 - 403) + (403 - 396.7)$$

That is, we subtract the mean of plastic container, 403, and then add it back.

So, 35.4 is the sum of two terms.

(432 − 403): The first term is the difference between a particular sales value, 432, and the group mean of plastic container, 403.

(403 − **396.7**): The second term is the difference between the group mean of plastic container, 403, and the grand mean, **396.7**.

We can also calculate the square of the above difference, 35.4 × 35.4 = **1250**.

Furthermore, we can calculate the difference between the sales value of store 1 for plastic container, 432, and the group mean of plastic container, 403. So, we have 432 − 403 = 29.

29 × 29 = **841** (highlighted in gray in Table 6.3).

This is the **within-group variance**.

Table 6.3. Calculation of within-group variance of sales of plastic container.

Store	Treatment	Plastic Container	Variance	Within-group Variance	Between-group Variance
1	1	432	1250	841	40
2	1	360	1343	1849	40
3	1	397	0	36	40
4	1	408	129	25	40
5	1	417	414	196	40
6	1	380	277	529	40
7	1	422	643	361	40
8	1	406	87	9	40
9	1	400	11	9	40
10	1	408	129	25	40
Total			**4030**	**4283**	**3880**	**403**

Finally, we can calculate the difference between the group mean of plastic container, 403, and the grand mean, **396.7**. So, we have 403 − **396.7** = 6.3.

6.3 × 6.3 = **40** (highlighted in gray in Table 6.3).

This is the **between-group variance**.

We can use Excel to perform the above calculation for another 9 sales values of plastic container to generate Table 6.3.

Similarly, we can use Excel to calculate all 10 values of **metal container** to generate Table 6.4.

Each of these 20 sales values may be different from the grand mean, due to natural variation or the fact that it is a plastic or a **metal** container (Iacobucci and Churchill, 2018, pp. 382–385).

Our null hypothesis is that two population means are equal.

H_0 : $\mu_1 = \mu_2$ **two population means are equal.**

Our alternative hypothesis is that there is statistically significant difference between them.

H_1 : $\mu_1 \neq \mu_2$ **two population means are not equal.**

If this is the case, the **between-group variance** will be larger than the **within-group variance** (sampling error).

The **between-group variance** refers to the difference of group mean for plastic container and grand mean, (403.0 may be **different**

Table 6.4.   Calculation of within-group variance of sales of metal container.

Store	Treatment	Metal Container	Variance	Within-group Variance	Between-group Variance
1	2	365	1002	640	40
2	2	405	70	216	40
3	2	396	0	32	40
4	2	390	44	0	40
5	2	404	54	188	40
6	2	372	608	335	40
7	2	378	348	151	40
8	2	410	178	388	40
9	2	383	186	53	40
10	2	400	11	94	40
Total		**3903**	**2501**	**2098**	**403**

from 396.7), and the group mean for metal container and grand mean (**390.3** may be **different from** 396.7).

In summary, we have three variances, the total variance, the between-group variance, and the within-group variance.

Total variance

$$= [(432 - 396.7)^2 + \cdots (408 - 396.7)]^2$$
$$+[(365 - 396.7)^2 + \cdots (400 - 396.7)]^2 = 6785 \qquad (6.8)$$

Within-group variance

$$= [(432 - 403.0)^2 + \cdots (408 - 403.0)^2$$
$$+[(365 - 390.3)^2 + \cdots (400 - 390.3)^2] = 5978 \qquad (6.9)$$

Between-group variation

$$= [10(403.0 - 396.7)^2 + 10(390.3 - 396.7)^2]$$
$$= 806 \qquad (6.10)$$

Total variance

$$= \text{Within-group variance} + \text{Between-group variation.}$$
$$6785 = 5978 + 806 \qquad (6.11)$$

The proof can be found in the end of this chapter.

We can also use formulas to show the above three variances.

Let us use $X_{i,j}$ to indicate the 20 values for 10 stores with two types of containers.

We usually use i to stand for the row of a table, and j to stand for the column of a table.

So, i is the store number and j is the package type (plastic or metal) in the above data set.

If we let SS to stand for "Sum of Squares", we can have the following equations.

$$\text{Total variance} = \text{SS}_{\text{Total}} \tag{6.12}$$

$$\sum_{j=1}^{2} \sum_{i=1}^{10} (X_{i,j} - \bar{X})^2 \tag{6.13}$$

$$\text{Within} - \text{Group variance} = \text{SS}_{\text{Within}} \tag{6.14}$$

$$\sum_{j=1}^{2} \sum_{i=1}^{10} (X_{i,j} - \bar{X}_j)^2 \tag{6.15}$$

$$\text{Between} - \text{Group variance} = \text{SS}_{\text{Between}} \tag{6.16}$$

$$10 \sum_{j=1}^{2} (\bar{X}_j - \bar{X})^2 \tag{6.17}$$

We divide each of these three sums of squares by their appropriate degrees of freedom, to obtain a "mean square" which is an unbiased estimate of the population variance (Iacobucci and Churchill, 2018, pp. 382–385). If there is no difference among population means, these mean squares are all estimates of the same variance, and should not differ more than we would expect by chance (Iacobucci and Churchill, 2018, pp. 382–385).

Let MS_{Total}, $\text{MS}_{\text{Within}}$, $\text{MS}_{\text{Between}}$ be the mean square for **total variance**, **within-group variance**, and **between-group variance**, respectively.

If $\text{MS}_{\text{Between}}$ is significantly greater than $\text{MS}_{\text{Within}}$, we reject the null hypothesis and accept the alternative hypothesis that there is statistically significant difference between the two group means. We view $\text{MS}_{\text{Within}}$ as a measure of the amount of variance in sales of containers that may be expected on the basis of chance, that is, the error variance or chance variance (Iacobucci and Churchill, 2018, pp. 382–385).

The **total** number of **degrees of freedom** is **20 − 1(=19)**, as there is only a single constraint on the grand mean for computing MS_{Total}.

For the **within-group** sum of squares, there are **20 observations** and **2 constraints** (one for each group mean). So, degrees of freedom $= \mathbf{20 - 2 = 18}$.

For **between-group** sum of squares, there are **two values**, one corresponding to each treatment mean, and there is **one constraint** imposed by the **grand mean**. So, degrees of freedom $= \mathbf{2 - 1 = 1}$.

Hence, we have the following equations:

$$MS_{Total} = SS_{Total}/(20 - 1) = 6785/19 = 357.1 \quad (6.18)$$

$$MS_{Within} = SS_{Within}/(20 - 2) = 5978/18 = 332.1 \quad (6.19)$$

$$MS_{Between} = SS_{Between}/(2 - 1) = 806/1 = 806 \quad (6.20)$$

$$F = MS_{Between}/MS_{Within} = 806/332.1 = 2.428 \quad (6.21)$$

If we use R to conduct ANOVA, we will get the following output from R.

	Df	Sum Sq	Mean Sq	F value	Pr($>F$)
Container	1	806	806.5	2.428	0.137
Residuals	18	5978	332.1		

The p-value is 0.137. If the null hypothesis is true (there is no difference between the two group means), there is a 13.7% chance for us to have the data set with the 20 sales values. If we only accept an error of 10%, we cannot reject the null hypothesis to accept the alternative hypothesis that there is a statistically significant difference.

Proof for total variance

= Within-group variance + Between-group variation

Total variance

$$= \sum_{j=1}^{2} \sum_{i=1}^{10} (X_{i,j} - \bar{X})^2$$

$$= [(432 - 396.7)^2 + \cdots (408 - 396.7)^2]$$

$$+[(365 - 396.7)^2 + \cdots (400 - 396.7)^2]$$
$$= [(432 - 396.7)^2 + \cdots (408 - 396.7)^2]$$
$$+[(365 - 396.7)^2 + \cdots (400 - 396.7)^2]$$
$$= [(432 - 403.0 + 103.0 - 396.7)]^2$$
$$+ \cdots (408 - 403.0 + 403.0 - 396.7)^2]$$
$$+[(365 - 390.3 + 390.3 - 396.7)^2$$
$$+ \cdots (400 - 390.3 + 390.3 - 396.7)^2]$$
$$= [(432 - 403.0) + (403.0 - 396.7)]^2$$
$$+ \cdots [(408 - 403.0) + (403.0 - 396.7)]^2$$
$$+[(365 - 390.3) + (390.3 - 396.7)]^2$$
$$+ \cdots [(400 - 390.3) + (390.3 - 396.7)]^2 \tag{6.22}$$

$$\text{Since} (A + B)^2 = A^2 + B^2 + 2AB$$

We can expand terms in the above equation to the following:

$$= (432 - 403.0)^2 + (403.0 - 396.7)^2$$
$$+ 2(432 - 403.0)(403.0 - 396.7) + \cdots$$
$$+ (408 - 403.0)^2 + (403.0 - 396.7)^2$$
$$+ 2(408 - 403.0)(403.0 - 396.7)$$
$$+ (365 - 390.3)^2 + (390.3 - 396.7)^2$$
$$+ 2(365 - 390.3)(390.3 - 396.7) + \cdots$$
$$+ (400 - 390.3)^2 + (390.3 - 396.7)^2$$
$$+ 2(400 - 390.3)(390.3 - 396.7)$$
$$= (432 - 403.0)^2 + \cdots (408 - 403.0)^2 + 10(403 - 396.7)^2$$
$$+ 2(432 - 403.0)(403.0 - 396.7)$$
$$+ \cdots 2(408 - 403.0)(403.0 - 396.7)$$
$$+ (365 - 390.3)^2 + \cdots (400 - 390.3)^2 + 10(390.3 - 396.7)^2$$

$$+\,2(365 - 390.3)(390.3 - 396.7)$$
$$+\cdots 2(400 - 390.3)(390.3 - 396.7)$$
$$= (432 - 403)^2 + \cdots (408 - 403)^2 + 10(403 - 396.7)^2$$
$$+(365 - 390.3)^2 + \cdots (400 - 390.3)^2 + 10(390.3 - 396.7)^2$$
$$= SS_{Within} + SS_{Between}$$

Because the sum of the following series is equal to zero.

$$2(432 - 403.0)(403 - 396.7) + \cdots 2(408 - 403.0)(403.0 - 396.7)$$
$$= 2(432 + \cdots 408 - 403.0 - \cdots 403.0)(403.0 - 396.7)$$
$$= 0(403.0 - 396.7) = 0$$

The sum of 10 numbers minus the sum of 10 means = 0.
Similarly, the sum of the following series is also equal to zero.

$$2(365 - 390.3)(390.3 - 396.7)$$
$$+\cdots 2(400 - 390.3)(390.3 - 396.7)$$
$$= 2(365 + \cdots 400 - 390.3 - \cdots 390.3)(390.3 - 396.7)$$
$$= 0(390.3 - 396.7) = 0$$

The sum of 10 numbers minus the sum of 10 means = 0.

References

Hair, J. F., Ortinau, D. J., and Harrison, D. E. (2021). *Essentials of Marketing Research*. New York, NY.

Iacobucci, D. and Churchill, G. A. (2018). *Marketing Research: Methodological Foundations*. 12th edn., Nashville, TN.

Lind, D. A., Marchal, W. G., and Wathen, S. A. (2018). *Statistical Techniques in Business & Economics*. New York, NY.

Chapter 7

Correlation

If we have collected the following preference data from customers of a restaurant for their first and the second visit, we can plot Preference2 (Pref2) versus Preference1 (Pref1) (see Figure 7.1).

If Pref2 is equal to Pref1 as shown above, they are perfectly and positively correlated.

In general, two variables, X and Y, may correlate positively, negatively, or have no correlation. We can calculate the correlation coefficient with the following formulation:

$$\frac{\sum_{i=1}^{n} (X_i - \bar{X})(Y_i - \bar{Y})}{\sqrt{\sum_{i=1}^{n} (X_i - \bar{X})^2 \sum_{i-1}^{n} (Y_i - \bar{Y})^2}} \tag{7.1}$$

For the numerator, we calculate the difference of each X_i from its mean $\bar{X}$ to get $(X_i - \bar{X})$, and the difference of each Y_i from its mean $\bar{Y}$ to get $(Y_i - \bar{Y})$. We multiply them to get $(X_i - \bar{X})(Y_i - \bar{Y})$.

$(X_i - \bar{X})$ may have positive or negative value.

$(Y_i - \bar{Y})$ may have positive or negative value.

So, their product $(X_i - \bar{X})(Y_i - \bar{Y})$ may also have positive or negative value.

If X and Y are correlated positively, when $(X_i - \bar{X})$ is positive, $(Y_i - \bar{Y})$ is likely to be positive, too, in quadrant 2 of the following chart. When $(X_i - \bar{X})$ is negative, $(Y_i - \bar{Y})$ is likely to be negative, too, in quadrant 4. So, the sum of $(X_i - \bar{X})(Y_i - \bar{Y})$ for all points will likely be positive (see Figure 7.2).

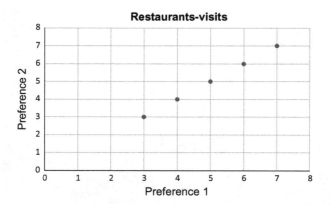

Figure 7.1.   Plot Preference 2 versus Preference 1.

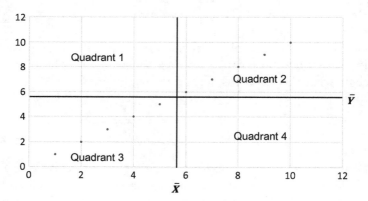

Figure 7.2.   Positive correlation.

If X and Y are correlated negatively, when $(X_i - \bar{X})$ is negative, $(Y_i - \bar{Y})$ is likely to be positive in quadrant 1. When $(X_i - \bar{X})$ is positive, $(Y_i - \bar{Y})$ is likely to be negative in quadrant 4. So, the sum of $(X_i - \bar{X})(Y_i - \bar{Y})$ for all points will be negative (see Figure 7.3).

For the denominator of the correlation coefficient formulation, it can only have positive value because it has two squared terms: $\sum_{i=1}^{n} (X_i - \bar{X})^2 \sum_{i-1}^{n} (Y_i - \bar{Y})^2$.

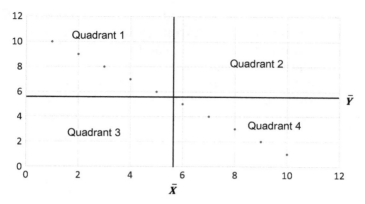

Figure 7.3. Negative correlation.

If each value of X_i is equal to Y_i, the correlation coefficient formulation will be

$$\frac{\sum_{i=1}^{n} (X_i - \bar{X})(X_i - \bar{X})}{\sqrt{\sum_{i=1}^{n} (X_i - \bar{X})^2 \sum_{i-1}^{n} (X_i - \bar{X})^2}} \quad (7.2)$$

The above formulation can be simplified to the following and is equal to 1:

$$\frac{\sum_{i=1}^{n} (X_i - \bar{X})^2}{\sqrt{\sum_{i=1}^{n} (X_i - \bar{X})^2 \sum_{i-1}^{n} (X_i - \bar{X})^2}} \quad (7.3)$$

That is, X and Y are perfectly and positively correlated.

If each value of Y_i is equal to $-X_i$, the correlation coefficient formulation will be

$$\frac{\sum_{i=1}^{n} (X_i - \bar{X})(-(X_i - \bar{X}))}{\sqrt{\sum_{i=1}^{n} (X_i - \bar{X})^2 \sum_{i-1}^{n} (X_i - \bar{X})^2}} \quad (7.4)$$

The above formulation can be simplified to the following and is equal to -1:

$$\frac{\sum_{i=1}^{n} -(X_i - \bar{X})^2}{\sqrt{\sum_{i=1}^{n} (X_i - \bar{X})^2 \sum_{i-1}^{n} (X_i - \bar{X})^2}} \quad (7.5)$$

That is, X and Y are perfectly and negatively correlated.

In general, when we have X and Y, the correlation coefficient formulation will have a value between -1 and $+1$. When the value is zero, X and Y are not correlated. Whether the value of correlation coefficient is statistically significant or not, we can run statistical tests to find out. To run correlation test in R, please refer to the session on correlation in Programming in R of this book. To run correlation test in Python, please refer to the session on correlation in Programming in Python of this book.

Chapter 8

Regression

Bivariate Regression

If we have the following data set with 10 points for X and Y, we can plot them (see Table 8.1).

If we want to find a straight line that can go through as many points as possible and having roughly the same number of points above or below the line, we can manually use a ruler to draw one line, count the number of points above or below the line (see Figure 8.1).

We can keep drawing different lines until we stop and choose one line manually such as $Y = X$.

$Y = X$ is the line that can cross points (0,0), (1,1), (3,3), (5,5), (7,7), (9,9), and have 2 points above it and 2 points below it as shown in the Figure 8.2.

If we are not satisfied with the above method, we may ask whether we have the best line.

To identify the best line, we need a measure.

We can calculate the vertical distance of each of the four points from the line.

Point (2,4) has a distance of $+2$ along the y-axis from the line at (2,2).

Point (6,7) has a distance of $+1$ along the y-axis from the line at (6,6).

Point (4,2) has a distance of -2 along the y-axis from the line at (4,4).

Table 8.1.   *X*-, *Y*-coordinates of data points.

X	0	1	2	3	4	5	6	7	8	9
Y	0	1	4	3	2	5	7	7	6	9

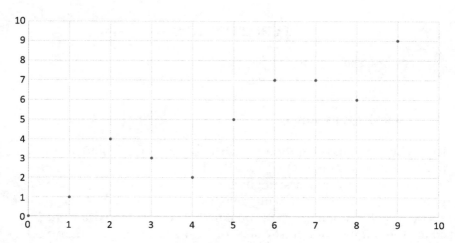

Figure 8.1.   Plot of *Y* versus *X*.

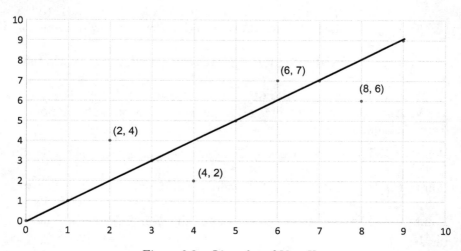

Figure 8.2.   Line plot of *Y* = *X*.

Point (8,6) has a distance of -2 along the y-axis from the line at (8,8).

If we add up the four values, $+2$, $+1$, -2, -2, we get -1.

We know the line cannot go through all points and there is an error.

So, how can we measure the error if the sum of the four values is only -1 because some positive values may offset some negative values?

One measure is to take the absolute value of a value.

If a value is positive, the absolute value of it is its original value.

If a value is negative, the absolute value of it is its positive value.

So, the sum of absolute values is equal to

$$|+2| + |+1| + |-2| + |-2| = 2 + 1 + 2 + 2 = 7 \qquad (8.1)$$

Another measure is the sum of their squares.

$$(+2)^2 + (+1)^2 + (-2)^2 + (-2)^2 = 4 + 1 + 4 + 4 = 13 \qquad (8.2)$$

Which measure should we use? If we choose to use the sum of squared differences, we can derive the values of a and b mathematically for the line $Y = a + bX$.

For the example of $Y = X$, we have $a = 0$ and $b = 1$, where a is the y-intercept and b is the slope of the line.

When we show the lines of $Y = 2 + X$ in Figure 8.3, the y value for each point of $Y = 2 + X$ is above $Y = X$ by a value of 2. While $Y = X$ will cross the point $(0,0)$, $Y = 2 + X$ will cross the point $(0,2)$. So, the y-intercept for $Y = 2 + X$ is at $(0,2)$ and with a value of 2.

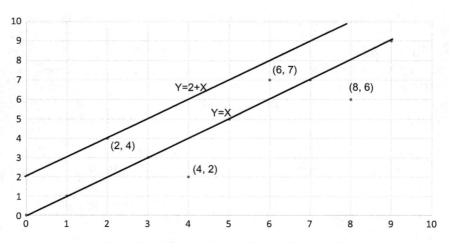

Figure 8.3.   Lines for $Y = X$ and $Y = 2 + X$.

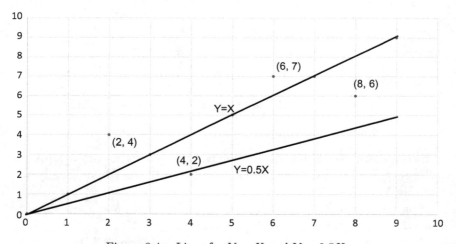

Figure 8.4.   Lines for $Y = X$ and $Y = 0.5X$.

Hence, $a = 2$ is the intercept in the y-axis for $Y = 2 + X$.

When we show the lines of $Y = 0.5X$ in Figure 8.4, the y-value for each point of $Y = 0.5X$ is half of the y-value for $Y = X$.

0.5 is the slope for the line $Y = 0.5X$. 1 is the slope for the line $Y = X$.

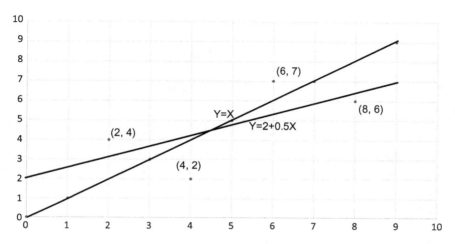

Figure 8.5. Lines for $Y = X$ and $Y = 2 + 0.5X$.

We can also show the lines of $Y = 2 + 0.5X$ in Figure 8.5. The y-value for each point of $Y = 2 + 0.5X$ is 2 plus $0.5X$.

The y-intercept is 2 and the slope is 0.5 for the line $Y = 2 + 0.5X$.

Values of a and b for $Y = a + bX$

To find the value of a and b for the line $Y = a + bX$, to minimize the sum of squared difference of each of the above 10 points for our data set, we can run a program in R or Python, or derive the formula for a and b by partial differentiation.

If we have a regression line $Y = a + bX$, the value of Y from the regression line is equal to $a + bX_i$, for each of our 10 points.

We have i equals to 1–10 to represent the value of 10 points:

$$X_1, X_2, X_3, X_4, X_5, X_6, X_7, X_8, X_9, X_{10}$$

The X values for these 10 points are 0, 1, 2, 3, 4, 5, 6, 7, 8, 9 in our data set.

Let $\tilde{Y}_i$ be the Y value that we can obtain from the regression line $a + bX_i$

That is,

$$\tilde{Y}_i = a + bX_i \tag{8.3}$$

The difference between Y_i and $\tilde{Y}_i$ is equal to

$$Y_i - \tilde{Y}_i = Y_i - a - bX_i \tag{8.4}$$

Mathematically, we can let SS be the sum of squared differences of all these 10 terms. In general, we can put n to be the number of points instead of 10.

$$\text{SS} = \sum_{i=1}^{n}(Y_i - a - bX_i)^2 \tag{8.5}$$

First, we differentiate SS with respect to a by treating the other variables as constant.

$$dSS/da = d\left[\sum_{i=1}^{n}(Y_i - a - bX_i)^2\right]\bigg/ da$$

$$= d\left[\sum_{i=1}^{n}(Y_i - bX_i - a)^2\right]\bigg/ da$$

$$= d\left[\sum_{i=1}^{n}[(Y_i - bX_i) - a]^2\right]\bigg/ da$$

$$= d\left[\sum_{i=1}^{n}[(Y_i - bX_i)^2 - 2a(Y_i - bX_i) + a^2]\right]\bigg/ da$$

$$= \sum_{i=1}^{n}\left\{\frac{d}{da}[(Y_i - bX_i)^2] - \frac{d}{da}[2a(Y_i - bX_i)] + \frac{d}{da}(a^2)\right\}$$

$$= \sum_{i=1}^{n}[0 - 2(Y_i - bX_i) + 2a]$$

$$= \sum_{i=1}^{n} [-2(Y_i - bX_i) + 2a]$$

$$= -2 \sum_{i=1}^{n} [(Y_i - bX_i) - a] \tag{8.6}$$

We set the above equation to zero to find the value of a for the minimum *SS*.

$$-2 \sum_{i=1}^{n} [(Y_i - bX_i) - a] = 0$$

$$\sum_{i=1}^{n} [(Y_i - bX_i) - a] = 0$$

$$\sum_{i=1}^{n} Y_i - b \sum_{i=1}^{n} X_i - na = 0 \tag{8.7}$$

$$\sum_{i=1}^{n} Y_i - b \sum_{i=1}^{n} X_i = na$$

$$\sum_{i=1}^{n} Y_i/n - b \sum_{i=1}^{n} X_i/n = a$$

$$a = \bar{Y} - b\bar{X}$$

Next, we substitute this formulation for a (Equation (8.7)) into SS (Equation (8.5)) and get the following:

$$\text{SS} = \sum_{i=1}^{n} (Y_i - a - bX_i)^2$$

$$\text{SS} = \sum_{i=1}^{n} (Y_i - \bar{Y} + b\bar{X} - bX_i)^2$$

$$\text{SS} = \sum_{i=1}^{n} [(Y_i - \bar{Y}) - b(X_i - \bar{X})]^2 \tag{8.8}$$

$$\text{SS} = \sum_{i=1}^{n} [(Y_i - \bar{Y})^2 - 2b(Y_i - \bar{Y})(X_i - \bar{X}) + b^2(X_i - \bar{X})^2]$$

We differentiate SS with respect to b by treating the other variables as constant.

$$dSS/db = d\left\{\sum_{i=1}^{n}[(Y_i - \bar{Y})^2 - 2b(Y_i - \bar{Y})(X_i - \bar{X})\right.$$

$$\left. + b^2(X_i - \bar{X})^2]\right\}\Big/db$$

$$= \sum_{i=1}^{n}[0 - 2(Y_i - \bar{Y})(X_i - \bar{X}) + 2b(X_i - \bar{X})^2] \quad (8.9)$$

We set the above equation to zero to find the value of b for the minimum *SS*.

$$\sum_{i=1}^{n}[0 - 2(Y_i - \bar{Y})(X_i - \bar{X}) + 2b(X_i - \bar{X})^2] = 0$$

$$\sum_{i=1}^{n}2b(X_i - \bar{X})^2 = \sum_{i=1}^{n}2(Y_i - \bar{Y})(X_i - \bar{X})$$

$$\sum_{i=1}^{n}b(X_i - \bar{X})^2 = \sum_{i=1}^{n}(Y_i - \bar{Y})(X_i - \bar{X})$$

$$b = \sum_{i=1}^{n}(Y_i - \bar{Y})(X_i - \bar{X})\Big/\sum_{i=1}^{n}(X_i - \bar{X})^2$$

$$(8.10)$$

For our data set with 10 points, we can calculate the different terms as shown in Table 8.2.

So, we have

$$b = \sum_{i=1}^{n}(Y_i - \bar{Y})(X_i - \bar{X})\Big/\sum_{i=1}^{n}(X_i - \bar{X})^2$$

$$= \mathbf{73.00}/\mathbf{82.50} = 0.88 \quad (8.11)$$

$$a = \bar{Y} - b\bar{X} = \mathbf{4.40} - 0.88 \times \mathbf{4.50} = 0.42 \quad (8.12)$$

We can also get the above values of a and b from running R or Python.

So, our regression line is

$$Y = a + bX = 0.42 + 0.88\,X \quad (8.13)$$

We can use this to calculate the value of Y from the regression line for value of X between the range of the original values of X, that is,

Table 8.2.   Calculation of SS for X and Y data sets.

X	Y	$X_i - \bar{X}$	$(X_i-X)^2$	$Y_i - \bar{Y}$	$(Y_i - \bar{Y})^2$	$(Y_i - \bar{Y})(X_i - \bar{X})$
0	0	−4.5	20.25	−4.40	19.36	19.80
1	1	−3.5	12.25	−3.40	11.56	11.90
2	4	−2.5	6.25	−0.40	0.16	1.00
3	3	−1.5	2.25	−1.40	1.96	2.10
4	2	−0.5	0.25	−2.40	5.76	1.20
5	5	0.5	0.25	0.60	0.36	0.30
6	7	1.5	2.25	2.60	6.76	3.90
7	7	2.5	6.25	2.60	6.76	6.50
8	6	3.5	12.25	1.60	2.56	5.60
9	9	4.5	20.25	4.60	21.16	20.70
Sum 45	44		**82.50**		76.40	**73.00**
Mean **4.50**	**4.40**					

0–9. However, we should not predict the value of Y for values of X which are outside of this range (Lind *et al.*, 2018, p. 454).

For example, if Y and X are the weight and height of people, and we have estimated a and b in $Y = a + bX$ by using weights and heights of adults with weights greater than 50 kg and heights greater than 1.3 m, we cannot use our regression line of $Y = a + bX$ to predict the weight of a newborn baby with height $= 0.5$ m.

Back to our data set, we can calculate the y-value for each value of X as shown in Table 8.3:

The sum of the squared difference was **11.81**. When we manually found a line of $Y = X$, the sum of the squared difference was 13, larger than 11.81. For the calculation for 13, please refer to the earlier session of this chapter.

We can also calculate the sum of the absolute difference as shown in Table 8.4.

The sum of the 10 absolute values for the differences is **8.50** for the regression line of $Y = 0.42 + 0.88X$. When we manually found a line of $Y = X$, the sum of the absolute value of the difference was 7, smaller than **8.50**. This finding is not surprising, because the regression line minimizes the sum of squared differences, not the sum of the absolute differences.

Table 8.3.   Calculation of the sum of squared difference for $Y = 0.42 + 0.88X$.

X	Y	$Y = 0.42 + 0.88X$	Difference	Difference²
0	0	0.42	0.42	0.17
1	1	1.30	0.30	0.09
2	4	2.19	−1.81	3.28
3	3	3.07	0.07	0.01
4	2	3.96	1.96	3.83
5	5	4.84	−0.16	0.02
6	7	5.73	−1.27	1.62
7	7	6.61	−0.39	0.15
8	6	7.50	1.50	2.24
9	9	8.38	−0.62	0.38
			Sum	**11.81**

Table 8.4.   Calculation of the sum of absolute difference for $Y = 0.42 + 0.88X$.

X	Y	$Y = 0.42 + 0.88X$	Difference	Absolute Value
0	0	0.42	0.42	0.42
1	1	1.30	0.30	0.30
2	4	2.19	−1.81	1.81
3	3	3.07	0.07	0.07
4	2	3.96	1.96	1.96
5	5	4.84	−0.16	0.16
6	7	5.73	−1.27	1.27
7	7	6.61	−0.39	0.39
8	6	7.50	1.50	1.50
9	9	8.38	−0.62	0.62
			Sum	**8.50**

Significance Testing

The strength of association was measured by the coefficient of determination which had value between 0 and 1, and signified the proportion of the total variation in Y that was accounted for by the variation in X with the following equation (Malhotra, 2020, p. 546):

$$\text{For } \tilde{Y}_i = a + bX_i$$

$$H_0 : b = 0 \qquad (8.14)$$

$$H_1 : b \neq 0$$

Null hypothesis H_0: there is no relationship between Y and X.

Alternative hypothesis H_1: there is a statistically significant relationship between Y and X, and b is not equal to zero.

If we do not have a regression line, how can we predict the value of each Y_i from each X_i? One prediction for all X_i is to simply use the mean of all Y_i, that is, $\bar{Y}$.

Of course, not all Y_i will be equal to $\bar{Y}$. There is a difference of $(Y_i - \bar{Y})$ for each point. For example, for the point $(6,7)$, the regression line is below it. The Y-value, 7, is different from the mean of Y at 4.4 by the amount of **2.60** $(= 7.00 - 4.40)$. This difference is indicated by the red line in Figure 8.6.

We then calculate the square of the difference, $(Y_i - \bar{Y})^2$ for each point i, add them up to get the total sum of squares (SS) for Y, SS_{total}, for 10 points in our data set.

$$\sum_{i=1}^{10}(Y_i - \bar{Y})^2 \qquad (8.15)$$

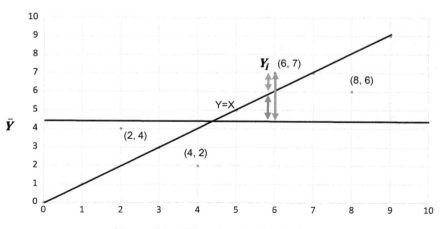

Figure 8.6.   Three types of differences.

After we have got our regression line, we can predict the value of each Y_i as $\tilde{Y}_i = a + bX_i$, that *is* $\tilde{Y}_i = 0.42 + 0.88X_i$.

There is a difference of $(\tilde{Y}_i - \bar{Y})$ for each point i.

For point $(6,7)$, $\tilde{Y}_i = 0.42 + (0.88)(6) = 0.42 + 5.28 = 5.73$.

So, $(\tilde{Y}_i - \bar{Y}) = 5.73 - 4.40 = \mathbf{1.33}$.

This difference is indicated by the blue line in Figure 8.6.

We then calculate the square of this difference, $(\tilde{Y}_i - \bar{Y})^2$, for each point i, add them up to get the total sum of squares (SS) for regression, $\text{SS}_{\text{regression}}$, for 10 points in our data set.

$$\sum_{i=1}^{10}(\tilde{Y}_i - \bar{Y})^2 \tag{8.16}$$

There is still a difference between the actual value of Y_i and the predicated value of $\tilde{Y}_i$ from the regression line, $(Y_i - \tilde{Y}_i)$.

This difference for point $(6,7)$ is equal to $7.00 - 5.73 = 1.27$.

This difference is indicated by the green line in Figure 8.6.

We then calculate the square of this difference, $(Y_i - \tilde{Y}_i)^2$, for each point i, add them up to get the total sum of squares (SS) for residual, $\text{SS}_{\text{Residual}}$, for 10 points in our data set.

$$\sum_{i=1}^{10}(Y_i - \tilde{Y}_i)^2 \tag{8.17}$$

We will see Tables 8.5 and 8.6 to calculate these three differences for all points, and get the total sum of squares for SS_{Total}, $\text{SS}_{\text{Regression}}$, and $\text{SS}_{\text{Residual}}$.

For the example of point $(6,7)$, the differences are highlighted in red, blue, and green.

From Tables 8.5 and 8.6, we can calculate $(\boldsymbol{Y}_i - \bar{\boldsymbol{Y}})^2$, $(\tilde{\boldsymbol{Y}}_i - \bar{\boldsymbol{Y}})^2$, and $(\boldsymbol{Y}_i - \tilde{\boldsymbol{Y}}_i)^2$.

So, we have got the total sum of squares for $(\boldsymbol{Y}_i - \bar{\boldsymbol{Y}})^2$, $(\tilde{\boldsymbol{Y}}_i - \bar{\boldsymbol{Y}})^2$, and $(\boldsymbol{Y}_i - \tilde{\boldsymbol{Y}}_i)^2$.

The three values are **76.40**, **64.59**, and **11.81**, respectively.

$$\text{SS}_{\text{Total}} = \mathbf{76.40}$$

$$\text{SS}_{\text{Regression}} = \mathbf{64.59}$$

$$\text{SS}_{\text{Residual}} = \mathbf{11.81}$$

Table 8.5. Calculation of various differences.

X_i	Y_i	$\bar{Y}$	$\tilde{Y}_i$	$(Y_i - \bar{Y})$	$(\tilde{Y}_i - \bar{Y})$	$(Y_i - \tilde{Y}_i)$
0	0	4.40	0.42	-4.40	-3.98	-0.42
1	1	4.40	1.30	-3.40	-3.10	-0.30
2	4	4.40	2.19	-0.40	-2.21	1.81
3	3	4.40	3.07	-1.40	-1.33	-0.07
4	2	4.40	3.96	-2.40	-0.44	-1.96
5	5	4.40	4.84	0.60	0.44	0.16
6	7	4.40	5.73	2.60	1.33	1.27
7	7	4.40	6.61	2.60	2.21	0.39
8	6	4.40	7.50	1.60	3.10	-1.50
9	9	4.40	8.38	4.60	3.98	0.62
Sum 45	44					
Mean 4.50	4.40					

Table 8.6. Calculation of various sums of squares.

X_i	Y_i	$\bar{Y}$	$\tilde{Y}_i$	$(Y_i - \bar{Y})^2$	$(\tilde{Y}_i - \bar{Y})^2$	$(Y_i - \tilde{Y}_i)^2$
0	0	4.40	0.42	19.36	15.85	0.17
1	1	4.40	1.42	11.56	9.59	0.09
2	4	4.40	2.42	0.16	4.89	3.28
3	3	4.40	3.42	1.96	1.76	0.01
4	2	4.40	4.42	5.76	0.20	3.83
5	5	4.40	5.42	0.36	0.20	0.02
6	7	4.40	6.42	6.76	1.76	1.62
7	7	4.40	7.42	6.76	4.89	0.15
8	6	4.40	8.42	2.56	9.59	2.24
9	9	4.40	9.42	21.16	15.85	0.38
Sum 45	44		Sum	**76.40**	**64.59**	**11.81**
Mean 4.50	4.40					

$$SS_{\text{Total}} = SS_{\text{Regression}} + SS_{\text{Residual}} \qquad (8.18)$$

$$76.40 = 64.59 + 11.81$$

For the proof of $SS_{\text{Total}} = SS_{\text{Regression}} + SS_{\text{Residual}}$, please read Chapter 6 on ANOVA in this book for the proof of total variance = within-group variance + between-group variance.

We can calculate the ratio of

$$SS_{Regression}/SS_{Residual}$$
$$= \frac{64.59}{76.40} = 0.85 \tag{8.19}$$

This ratio is also called the **coefficient of determination** with symbol R^2.

That is, our regression line can explain 85% of SS_{total}, sum of the total variance in the data set.

The overall test can be conducted by using F statistic (Malhotra, 2020, p. 558).

$$F = \frac{SS_{Regression}/k}{SS_{Residual}/(n-k-1)} \tag{8.20}$$

For our data set with $k = 1$ (we only have one X) and $n = 10$, we have

$$= \frac{64.59/1}{76.40/(10-1-1)} = \frac{64.59}{1.48} = 43.77$$

The p-value is 0.0001666.

So, we will reject the null hypothesis and accept the alternative hypothesis that there is a statistically significant relationship between X and Y if we are willing to accept an error of 5%.

We can also show that

$$F = \frac{SS_{Regression}/k}{SS_{Residual}/(n-k-1)} = \frac{R^2/k}{(1-R^2)/(n-k-1)} \tag{8.21}$$

Proof of $F = \dfrac{\text{SS}_{\text{Regression}}}{\text{SS}_{\text{Residual}}} = \dfrac{R^2}{(1-R^2)}$ 　　　　(8.22)

$$R^2 = \frac{\text{SS}_{\text{Regression}}}{\text{SS}_{\text{Total}}} = \frac{\text{SS}_{\text{Regression}}}{\text{SS}_{\text{Regression}} + \text{SS}_{\text{Residual}}}$$ 　(8.23)

$$1 - R^2 = 1 - \frac{\text{SS}_{\text{Regression}}}{\text{SS}_{\text{Regression}} + \text{SS}_{\text{Residual}}}$$

$$= \frac{\text{SS}_{\text{Residual}}}{\text{SS}_{\text{Regression}} + \text{SS}_{\text{Residual}}}$$

Hence, $\dfrac{\text{SS}_{\text{Regression}}}{\text{SS}_{\text{Residual}}} = \dfrac{R^2}{(1-R^2)}$ 　　　　(8.24)

Multiple Regression

For bivariate regression, we only have two variables: the dependent variable, Y, and the independent variable X in $Y = a + bX$.

If we have more than one independent variable, we can still express their relationship with the dependent variable, Y, by a linear equation with multiple variables in multiple regression.

$$Y = b_0 + b_1 X_1 + b_2 X_2 + \cdots b_n X_n$$ 　　　　(8.25)

We can get the values of b_0, b_1, $b_2 \ldots b_n$ from running R or Python.

If we have two independent variables, the above equation becomes

$$Y = b_0 + b_1 X_1 + b_2 X_2$$ 　　　　(8.26)

As an example, if we have the Sales, TV media spending, and Digital media spending in units of US\$'000s for 12 months of the last calendar year in the following data set (see Table 8.7), we can run multiple regression to estimate the coefficients for the regression equation.

By running R or Python, we can get the values of b_0, b_1, b_2 for the regression equation.

$$\text{Sales} = b_0 + b_1 \text{TVSpend} + b_2 \text{DigitalSpend}$$ 　　(8.27)

$$\text{Sales} = -1.6 + 2.0 \, \text{TVSpend} + 3.1 \, \text{DigitalSpend}$$ 　(8.28)

So, the expected change in Sales is 2.0 units when TVSpend is increased by one unit but DigitalSpend does not change.

Table 8.7.   Various expenditures in units of US$'000s.

Month	Sales	TVSpend	DigitalSpend
1	820	183	148
2	805	113	185
3	987	196	189
4	718	166	119
5	772	160	143
6	863	171	173
7	895	194	165
8	923	156	194
9	914	148	199
10	683	117	142
11	645	140	120
12	671	116	146

Similarly, the expected change in Sales is 3.1 units when Digital-Spend is increased by one unit but TVSpend does not change.

When marketing budget is limited, we can prioritize spending and put in DigitalSpend rather than TVSpend, because 3.1 units is larger than 2.0 units.

When TVSpend is increased by one unit and DigitalSpend is also increased by one unit, the expected increase in Sales is $2.0 + 3.1 = 5.1$ units.

If we want to predict Sales for TVSpend = 120 and DigitalSpend = 130, we can substitute these values into the regression equation.

$$\text{Sales} = -1.6 + 2.0(120) + 3.1(130) = -1.6 + 240 + 403 = 641.4$$

For multiple regression, we have to adjust the coefficient of multiple determination, R^2, for the number of independent variables and the sample size by using the following formula (Malhotra 2020, p. 555):

$$\text{Adjusted } R^2 = R^2 - \frac{k(1 - R^2)}{(n - k - 1)} \tag{8.29}$$

For our data set of Sales, TV media spending and Digital media spending for multiple regression, we can use R or Python to conduct F statistic test, and obtain a p-value of 0.0000000004345.

$$R^2 = 0.9917$$

$$\text{Adjusted } R^2 = 0.9917 - \frac{2(1 - 0.9917)}{(12 - 2 - 1)} = 0.9917 - 0.0018444 = 0.9898$$

References

Lind, D. A., Marchal, W. G. and Wathen, S. A. (2018). *Statistical Techniques in Business & Economics*. 17th edn., New York, NY.

Malhotra, N. K. (2020). *Marketing Research: An Applied Orientation*. 7th edn., United Kingdom.

Appendix 1: Hierarchical Branding Strategy for New Product Launch: Evidence from China*

Howard Pong-Yuen Lam and Vincent Chi Wong

1. Introduction

When marketers develop a new product, they choose (or create) a brand name for it and expect that this name can increase the chances of success of the new product. Finding a name when introducing a product to China is more challenging than introducing it to most other countries because Chinese language has thousands of characters, each with many meanings and with pronunciations that vary from region to region (Fetscherin *et al.* 2012). As a result, marketers have to conduct rigorous marketing research on different names proposed by their creative agencies in China.

Thomas *et al.* (2004) suggest that a brand is a promise to consumers and that promise is delivered through source identifiers, the "five second sound bites" of a brand, and a strong identity must be protectable legally. They suggest a protectability continuum from

___

*This article is originally published from Lam, Howard Pong-Yuen and Wong, Vincent Chi (2022), "Hierarchical Branding Strategy for New Product Launch: Evidence from China". In *Chinese Innovation and Branding Leaps*, edited by Serdar S Durmusoglu, Singapore: World Scientific Publishing, 103–136.

77

the strongest to the weakest for a brand name to be: (1) arbitrary (or fanciful), (2) suggestive, (3) descriptive, and (4) generic. "Fanciful identifiers are the strongest and are the most easily protected against copycats. Examples include Clorox bleach, Pepsi Cola, and Kodak. These are invented words that have no other meaning. Arbitrary identifiers like Apple computers are in common linguistic use, but have nothing to do with the product it identifies. On the other hand, a suggestive identifier is one that implies the nature or characteristics of the product. Coppertone suggests that users of that suntan oil will have a coppery-toned tan. Suggestive identifiers are a good compromise between marketing and legal concerns. They communicate information to the customer about the nature of the product and are protectable against use by others. Descriptive identifiers express the function or characteristics of products. Example includes Superglue adhesive. These identifiers describe something about the product. They can't be protected against infringement unless they have become distinctive to the consuming public. A generic is exactly what it sounds like: the category name for a type of good and service. Such terms can never be protected legally" (Thomas *et al.* 2004).

Keller *et al.* (1998, p. 55) proposed that a "suggestive" brand name could convey information regarding a relevant attribute or benefit in a particular product context. They found support on the proposition that compared with a non-suggestive brand name (e.g., Emporium televisions), a brand name that explicitly conveyed a product benefit (e.g., Picture Perfect televisions) and produced greater recall of an advertised benefit claim that was consistent with the brand name's connotations.

For a new product, marketers must also determine a corporate branding strategy. For example, while P&G uses separate brand names without much reference to the corporate brand, Philips uses its corporate brand prominently, and Nestle uses its corporate name as an "endorsement" for its products (Berens *et al.* 2005, p. 35). An important managerial question involves what and how overall corporate branding and product branding strategy can help marketers increase the chance of success of a new product?

This chapter provides insights to marketers when answering the following questions. Should marketers in China follow suggestions of Zhang and Schmitt (2001) or Fetscherin *et al.* (2012) to create corporate name or product brand names from English to Chinese based on phonetic, semantic and phono-semantic methods? Alternatively, should marketers create names with suggestive meanings and if so, what should a name suggest? Should marketers use one name as both corporate name and product brand name or should they create two names with two different meanings for corporate name and product brand name, respectively? Is there a framework for marketers to follow when they develop brand names for launching new products in sequence and deciding on the appropriate corporate branding strategy for the new products? We first start with an overview of brand name translation methods.

2.   Name Translation Methods

Whether a brand name is arbitrary, suggestive, descriptive, or generic in English, marketers and copywriters at creative agencies have to propose different names in the local language. In terms of translation methods, Zhang and Schmitt (2001) and Fetscherin *et al.* (2012) suggest three methods: phonetic, semantic, and phono-semantic. Therefore, certain product brand names may suggest meanings to consumers (semantic and phono-semantic), while others may not (phonetic).

Brand naming using a translation method is more challenging in logographic languages (e.g., Chinese), compared with phonographic languages (e.g., English) because the former languages feature looser correspondence between sound and meaning (Wu *et al.* 2019). Hence, Wu *et al.* (2019) propose to categorize brand name types for logographic languages into alphanumeric, phonetic, phono-semantic, or semantic. They use the Roman transliteration known as the Pinyin system to present the Chinese brand names. Based on whether the Chinese name has similar sound as the English name (Yes, No) and whether the Chinese name has meaning or not, there are four different brand name types as shown in Table 1.

Table 1.   Brand name types in logographic language.

		Meaning	
		No	Yes
Sound	No	Alphanumeric	Semantic
	Yes	Phonetic	Phono-semantic

Alphanumeric and phonetic brand name types are examples of arbitrary brand name mentioned earlier in this chapter. Semantic and phono-semantic brand name types are examples of suggestive or descriptive brand names, depending on the exact meaning of the name.

Wu *et al.* (2019) provide two examples of each brand name type in China, one for a multinational firm and the other for a domestic (Chinese) firm as follows:

Alphanumeric type (sound: no, meaning: no) includes 3M (a multinational from the US) and 360 (a popular internet security software brand in China).

Phonetic type (sound: yes, meaning: no) includes Motorola with Chinese name 摩托罗拉 (Pin-yin: Mou Tuo Luo La), which sounds similar to Motorola in English. Another example is Galanz (the largest microwave oven brand in China) with Chinese name 格兰仕 (Pin-yin: Ge Lan Shi), which sounds like "Galanz" in English.

Semantic type (sound: no, meaning: yes) includes Microsoft with Chinese name 微软 (Pin-yin: Wei Ruan), which means "tiny and soft" in Chinese. Lenovo's Chinese name (Pin-yin: Lian Xiang) means "association" in Chinese.

Phono-semantic (sound: yes, meaning: yes) includes Coca-Cola with Chinese name 可口可乐 (Pin-yin: Ke Kou Ke Le), which sounds like "Coca-Cola" and means "delicious happiness". Another example is E-land (a popular apparel brand in China) has Chinese name 衣恋 (Pin-yin: Yi Lian), which sounds like "E-Land" and means "loving clothes".

We have summarized these brand names from multinational firms and domestic (Chinese) firms in Tables 2 and 3.

Wu *et al.* (2019) summarize the literature on these four brand name types. They gathered studies from primary marketing journals (e.g., *Journal of Marketing Research, Journal of Marketing,* and *Journal of Consumer Research*) and find that most of the studies are set in the US context and use lab experiments, with consumer as the unit of analysis and survey-based dependent measures as opposed to actual consumer choice. In contrast, the study of Wu *et al.* (2019) is set in the Chinese context, where they use observational field data

Table 2. Brand name types in logographic language (multinational firms).

		Meaning	
		No	Yes
Sound	No	3M	Microsoft
	Yes	Motorola	Coca-Cola

Table 3. Brand name types in logographic language (domestic Chinese firms).

		Meaning	
		No	Yes
Sound	No	360	Lenovo
	Yes	Galanz	E-land

with brand (e.g., Honda CR-V) as a unit of analysis and estimate a demand model based on unit sales.

Research on semantic brand names generally examines the relationship between the meaning of a brand name and consumers' brand perceptions and attitudes, mainly in phonographic language contexts. Research has shown that brand names that use familiar words or convey a product benefit (e.g., "Lifelong" brand luggage) enhance brand outcomes such as attitudes, perceptions, and recall (Keller *et al.* 1998; Lee *et al.* 2003; Peterson and Ross 1972).

Using automobile sales data from China and a discrete choice model for differentiated products, Wu *et al.* (2019) relate brand name types to demand, with evidence showing that Chinese consumers preferred vehicle models with semantic brand names (7.64% more sales than alphanumeric), but exhibited the least preference for phono-semantic names (4.92% lower sales than alphanumeric). In China, domestic firms benefited from semantic brand names, whereas foreign firms gained from using foreign-sounding brand names. Entry-level products performed better with semantic brand names, and high-end products excelled when they had foreign-sounding brand names.

Thus, the four-way categorization of brand name types should help multinational firms and domestic (Chinese) firms understand and leverage the association between brand name types and consumer demand.

In another study, Gao *et al.* (2020) summarize prior research on brand name translation in international markets from 2001 to 2020 and develop a theoretical framework that integrates similarity, which focuses on how the translated brand name relates to the original brand name, and informativeness, which focuses on how the translated brand name reveals product content, to study the impact of brand name translations. Gao *et al.* (2020) analyzed Hollywood movies shown in China from 2011 to 2018. The results show that higher similarity leads to higher Chinese box office revenue, and this effect is stronger for movies that perform better in the home market (i.e., the United States). Also, when the translated title is more informative about the movie, the Chinese box office revenue increases. The informativeness effect is stronger for Hollywood movies with greater cultural gap in the Chinese market.

2.1. *Product branding strategy*

In this session, we use two examples to illustrate how marketers can create excellent Chinese brand names for a product with meaning. The first example is the translation of the English brand name of Coca-Cola to Chinese. The Chinese name of Coca-Cola 可口可乐 (Pin-yin: Ke Kou Ke Lei) is an excellent Chinese name with rich meaning, "delicious happiness". " 可口 Ke Kou" means delicious and "可乐 Ke Lei" means happiness. Therefore, Coca-Cola has a suggestive name with meaning related to Coke's functional benefit (delicious) and emotional benefit (happiness).

Another example is from Lam *et al.* (2013). They showed how marketers might increase the chance of success for a new product launch. Since each newborn baby has a given name and a family name, Lam *et al.* (2013) suggest creating a "given name" and "family name" for the "new brand" of the new product. They reported the successful case of using "given brand name" and "family brand name" together — dual product branding strategy — by practitioners in China for the Minute Maid Orange Pulp juice drink launch. A suggestive given brand name helps consumers recall the key benefits and features of the new product. A suggestive family brand name communicates the benefits of the product category. A dual product branding strategy addresses the problem of using only one brand name for a new product launch. After the successful launch of the first new product with two names (given brand name + family brand name), marketers are able to launch other new products under "different" given brand names under the "same" family brand name in the future to meet different consumer needs. An analogue is that the first newborn baby now has younger brothers and sisters, and all of them have the same family name. Marketers may use the same family brand name to introduce different products to build scale for the brand, and are able to clearly differentiate the different product offerings under different given brand names under the same family brand name. When a company acquires a brand from another company, a marketer may position the acquired brand under the same family brand name only if the marketer had defined the business scope of the family brand broadly enough with a suggestive family brand name.

The case and research of Lam *et al.* (2013) provides empirical support for the success of using two names simultaneously in ascending order of abstraction for a new product. For Minute Maid, the Chinese given brand name has three Chinese characters 果粒橙 (Pin-yin: Guo Li Cheng). The meaning of these three Chinese characters is "Fruit Pulp Orange" and is suggestive of its key features and benefits. The Chinese family brand name of the new product is 美汁源 (Pin-yin: Mei Zhi Yuan) which means "Good Juice Source". It is also suggestive and positions Minute Maid as a juice-based wellness parent (family) brand. Lam *et al.* (2013) have described one Minute Maid case for their dual product branding strategy. They have not studied the interaction of corporate branding and product branding. Hence, there is a need to extend their work with empirical support.

2.2. *Corporate branding strategy*

Corporate branding is important for marketers in applying a product branding strategy (e.g., Ajami and Khambata 1991; Buil *et al.*, 2013; Knox 2004). "Consumers' cognitive associations for a company can be both a strategic asset and a source of sustainable competitive advantage. Because influencing these corporate associations is an important strategic task, marketers spend great sums of money each year on corporate advertising and related activities" (Brown and Dacin 1997, p. 68). Corporate brands are more likely than product brands to evoke cognitive associations of common products and their shared attributes or benefits, people and relationships, programs, and values (Keller and Lehmann 2006; Barich and Kotler 1991). A corporate brand provides consumers with expectations of what the corporation will deliver, and a "corporate brand promise" is similar to the "brand promise" of product brands (Argenti and Druckenmiller 2004, p. 368). The key question is what corporate association marketers should create for consumers. Before we provide an answer to this question, we describe the state of knowledge on this topic.

2.2.1. *Monolithic corporate branding strategy/Stand-alone corporate branding strategy*

Marketers can either choose corporate branding strategies in one extreme, that is, to use one corporate name for all products, or another extreme of using one brand name for each product. For example, General Electric mainly uses its corporate name as the brand name for all of its products. The advantage of this strategy is that the marketing investment to build the corporate brand image can benefit all products under the brand image. The disadvantage, however, is that it is difficult to create different brand images for different products. This corporate branding strategy is labeled as "monolithic corporate branding" (Berens *et al.* 2005; Laforet and Saunders 1994; Olins 1989). The other extreme is that marketers create one brand name for each product. The advantage is that marketers can build a clear image for each brand's target audience, whereas the disadvantage is that the brand building investment is high. Berens *et al.* (2005, p. 35) named this corporate branding strategy "stand-alone".

For example, P&G treats corporate name and product brand name as separate, and markets several products of a product category under one, two or more brand names, rather than creating one brand name for each product. For baby care, P&G has Pampers. For beauty and skin care, P&G has two key brands, SK-II and Olay. For hair care, P&G has four key brands, Head & Shoulders, Rejoice, Pantene, and Vidal Sassoon. P&G remains as a corporate brand name only. One major disadvantage of "stand-alone product" branding strategy is that marketers cannot achieve economies of scale in communication. For example, even though P&G is a sponsor of 2022 Winter Olympics in Beijing, P&G has to produce different commercials for different brands (Head and Shoulders, Gillette, etc.) to leverage the Olympics sponsorship and possibly spend significant amount of effort choosing the specific brands they will advertise more than others.

2.2.2. *Corporate brand name and product brand name —*
The same or different?

Some companies such as Coca-Cola and PepsiCo use the same name as company brand name and product brand name. So, the Coca-Cola Company uses the same name, Coca-Cola, as corporate name and as product brand name for cola beverages. The Coca-Cola Company, however, also has a range of products and brands covering many different beverages to meet different needs. The disadvantage of using Coca-Cola as the same name for company and for product of cola beverage is that it is not easy to create the right association for the brand as a company and as a product. Consumers have many different associations for Coca-Cola. As a company, Coca-Cola is friendly to the environment, cares for the community, is sportive and encourages global harmony with Olympics and World Cup sponsorships. As a product brand, Coca-Cola is refreshing, uplifting, and optimistic. These all have positive associations, but evoke different emotions in consumers.

In fact, when many companies grow from small companies into big multinational companies, marketers usually use the brand name for its key product as the corporate brand name. As marketing budget is limited when a company is small, marketers tend to put all the money on different activities into building one name to benefit both the product brand and corporate brand.

The problem arises when a company expands and thus, realizes that the same product brand name cannot be used for other categories. For example, marketers could not use Coca-Cola as the brand name to launch lemon-lime carbonated beverages, and so the Coca-Cola Company had to create the brand Sprite. Similarly, marketers of Coca-Cola China had to create Minute Maid as the family brand name for a juice-based wellness brand. As the associations of Coca-Cola did not fit the consumer healthy nutrition need of Minute Maid, marketers also could not use Coca-Cola Corporate name in a "monolithic" corporate branding strategy. Thus, companies can use "monolithic corporate" branding strategy for one consumer need, and "monolithic corporate" branding strategy for two or more consumer needs.

Marketers can use "monolithic corporate" branding strategy for meeting one consumer need such as "beauty and skin care". The advantage is that the company can focus its resources in building a consistent image for the company and also for all its products. For example, L'Oreal is a leading player in the beauty and skin care market and one of the several globally successful companies in consumer packaged goods industry (See Henderson and Johnson 2012, for a detailed study).

Marketers can also use "monolithic corporate" branding strategy for meeting two or more consumer needs. For example, the product line at Amway at first consisted of just one product, a biodegradable soap (Amway 2014). Subsequently, Amway expanded its business through direct selling business model to distribute its product in more countries, and also expanded its business by acquiring brands or creating brands for meeting different consumer needs. Amway's Nutrilite offers vitamin and dietary supplements for health care. Amway's Artistry offers products for beauty and skin care. However, for consumers and direct sellers who distribute Amway products, Amway has a heritage and image in kitchen cleaning detergent. So, marketers for Amway Artistry may find it difficult to compete with L'Oreal, because Amway has a heritage in detergent, while L'Oreal has a heritage in beauty and skin care. For consumers, it is harder to accept that a company with heritage in detergent can have expertise in producing products for taking care of soft and delicate skin of women. On the contrary, since its founding in 1909, L'Oreal has been pushing the boundaries of science to invent beauty and meet the aspirations of millions of women and men (Henderson and Johnson 2012).

We argue that if marketers are working for a fast moving consumer goods (FMCG) company such as P&G, marketers should evaluate whether or not they should mention the parent brand in product brand's communication. In fact, markets of SK-II do not mention P&G in their communications because P&G company brand may not have strong associations with high-end beauty products.

2.2.3.   *Composite brand — Combination of two existing brand names*

Park *et al.* (1996) investigated the effectiveness of using a composite brand, a combination of two "existing" brand names, as the brand name for a new product. They offered a hypothetical example of the Godiva cake mix by Haagen-Dazs. Their studies reveal that by combining two brands with complementary attribute levels, a composite brand extension appears to have a better attribute profile when it consists of two complementary brands than when it consists of two highly favorable, but not complementary brands (Park *et al.* 1996, p. 453). Although marketers of two companies may negotiate joint promotions, it is not easy for marketers to create a joint venture between two companies for a brand launch (Spyropoulou *et al.* 2011). Furthermore, there are problems with the brand of a joint venture. The profit will be shared between Godiva and Haagen-Dazs. Hence, will there be enough incentive for each company to build (or support) distribution networks for the Godiva cake mix sold by Haagen-Dazs? In other words, for Godiva, the profit from Godiva's products is around two times that of the joint venture products of Godiva and Haazen-Dazs. The same situation applies to Haagen-Dazs' products vs. the joint venture products of Godiva and Haazen-Dazs. Hence, one question for us to ask is: Can marketers create a given name and a family name for a new product without the constraint of using an "existing" brand name of the marketer's own company and negotiate a deal to use another "existing" brand name from another company? If marketers could create names, what names should they create?

2.3.   *Creation of suggestive corporate names*

In this section, we offer insights and recommendations pertinent to the question of what corporate brand names should suggest. Currently, marketers or company founders have at least three approaches to create suggestive corporate names.

2.3.1.   *Suggestive corporate name — Product category*

Burger King, Pizza Hut, Kentucky Fried Chicken (KFC) are suggestive company names for their product offerings and "corporate ability" in different types of food. However, using products sold as company name might limit a company's growth. So, KFC's business suffered much more than McDonald's when there was bird-flu in Asia in 2003. Marketers at KFC also could not reposition KFC easily to offer Chinese food, and had to acquire other companies (Little Sheep in China), or created a new company. In 2005, KFC launched East Dawning 东方既白 (Pin-yin: Dong Fang Ji Bai) to offer Chinese food. East Dawning specializes in serving gourmet Jiangnan[1] cuisine such as Chinese style chicken soup or salty bean. The primary target groups are tourists and visitors in transit because the stores are predominantly located in bustling transportation hubs (Yum China 2020). Some Chinese food like chicken soup or salty bean can be found from the WeChat official account of East Dawning. In summary, these company names suggest to consumers what types of products these companies sell, not what consumer needs these companies will directly satisfy.

Managerial Take Aways

- While the use of suggestive product category names (chicken, pizza or burger) in the corporate name can help consumers know what the products they will have from the company, it limits what the company can offer in the product portfolio in the future.
- This naming approach is based on the product concept, not the marketing concept. Product concept assumes that consumers will buy product with a certain quality, performance or features (Kotler and Keller 2016, p. 43). Marketing concept focuses on what the consumers really need (high quality food delivered with excellent services in a restaurant), rather than the type of product (chicken, pizza or burger) (Kotler and Keller 2016, p. 43).

2.3.2. *Suggestive corporate name — Founders*

Many company founders use their own names to create company names. One key advantage is that the company can benefit from

---

[1]Jiangnan is Pin-yin of the two Chinese characters 江南 which means southern part of the Yangtze river.

awareness and image of the founder. For example, Li Ning, a famous Chinese Olympics gold medalist, performed for several minutes in walking around the ceiling of the Bird Nest stadium before he lighted up the cauldron in the opening ceremony of Beijing 2008 Olympics. Li Ning's performance in Beijing Olympics is an extremely valuable event to build awareness of the corporate brand name of "Li Ning". For Adidas, an Olympics sponsor and competitor of "Li Ning" sports company, the appearance of Li Ning is a major ambush market- ing event. That is, a company, often an event sponsor's competitor, attempts to deflect the audience's attention to itself and away from the sponsor and reduce the effectiveness of the sponsor's message while undermining the quality and value of the sponsorship opportu- nity that the event owner is selling (Meenaghan 1996). However, the major disadvantage of using company founder's name as company name is that the founder may get old, and the sportive image of "Li Ning" may deteriorate. Another disadvantage is that the name may suggest some meaning to consumers which the company may not want. Ning means "inactive" in Chinese, not "active".

Let us now consider how Li Ning could handle taking its brand abroad, especially to Western markets. They can use an approach similar to Lee Kum Kee. Lee Kum Kee was founded as an oys- ter source manufacturer over a century ago. The third generation leader, Mr. Lee Man Tat, set his eyes to make this sauce available to consumers globally. When doing so, the company had to change the brand to LKK so that consumers would not feel alienated with the full name. Following these footsteps, Li Ning can adopt "LN" or "LI-N" when entering into other countries.

We propose that LI-NING be shortened to LI-N instead of LN, because of several reasons. First, the current name is LI-NING, and so LI-N can keep the part about LI, the family name of many Chinese people. Second, LI-N is better than LI in helping consumers relate to the current company name of LI-NING. Third, legally, it is difficult to register a trademark of LI globally and stop all other companies to use LI. It should be easier to get trademark registration for LI-N as a short form for the current one of LI-NING. Lastly, when Chi- nese introduce themselves to foreigners, they first state their family name and then their given name. As it is difficult for foreigners to remember two names, Chinese mainly introduce the family name and give the initial of the given name. So, for "Li Ning", he can introduce himself to foreigners as having family name of LI and initial of N.

In the Western world, Ray Kroc, the key person behind the global success of McDonald's, also decided to use the family name of McDonald's brothers to expand McDonald's business globally. So, McDonald's can offer a range of products, and the name of McDonald's is less limiting than Burger King, Pizza Hut, or Kentucky Fried Chicken and more astute than Kroc Burgers. However, the Chinese company name of McDonald's may require more marketing investment to build than the Chinese company name of "Burger King 汉堡王" which literally means "King of Burger". It is difficult for consumers to remember McDonald's company name, and the name may even create wrong consumer associations. For example, some Chinese consumers think the Chinese phonetic translation of McDonald's is "麦当奴" which means "Mc being slave". The right Chinese company name for McDonald's is "麦当劳" which means "Mc being labour". The confusion arises because the pronunciation of these two Chinese names are the same. These two meanings, right or wrong, however, have little to do with the four pillars for the success of McDonald's: QSCV, which stands for Quality, Service, Cleanliness and Value.

As the full name of McDonald's name is phonetic translation with Pin-yin of "Mai Dang Lao", Chinese has created a short name for it by simply using the first Chinese character of it with the sound of "Mai" and put the second character to be "Ji". About 100 years ago, when Chinese formed a new company, they might simply use their own personal name and added a Chinese character of "Ji" at the end. Ji is the Pin-yin for the Chinese character 记. Its meaning is similar to "entity" in English. So, Chinese may simply say "Mai Ji" 麦记. Hence, we have Lee Kum Kee with Chinese characters of 李锦記 and Pin-yin of "Li Jin Ji" because it was founded by a man, 李锦裳 (Pin-yin: Li Jin Shang). So, the company has the first two Chinese characters of this founder and the third Chinese character is Ji ("Kee" is the romanization of "Ji" in Guangdong accent).

While there are several reasons for the smaller success of Burger King relative to that for McDonald's and KFC in China, the Chinese name of Burger King 汉堡王 (Pin-yin: Han Bao Wang) is also a contributing factor for Burger King's smaller success: Hang Bao Wang has two meanings to Chinese, which may limit its appeal to

Chinese consumers. First, "Hao Bao" means burger. So, it simply communicates to Chinese that Burger King offers burger. While dumplings are popular traditional food among Chinese, burger is not. Compare this to McDonald's in China: To succeed, McDonald's started offering food other than burger. Another problem with the Chinese name of Burger King is its third Chinese character which literally means "King". In Chinese culture, individuals (or other entities) are expected not to stand out too much from a crowd and become too individualistic. Chinese also are educated by their parents and teachers to be humble. So, by claiming itself being the "king" of Burger, Burger King in fact is not humble, and has set up very high expectation for its burger that it may fail to meet. Chinese would expect its burger to be significantly better than the burger from McDonald's. In reality, this is not the case.

English name	McDonald's	KFC	Burger King
Chinese name	麦当劳	肯德鸡	汉堡王
Pin-yin	Mai Dang Lao	Ken De Ji	Han Bao Wang
Meaning	Sounds like McDonald's	"Ken De" sounds like Kentucky. "Ji" is chicken in Chinese	"Han Bao" means burger. "Wang" means king
Translation approach	Phonetic	Phono-semantic	Phono-semantic
Positioning	American burger	Tasty chicken	King of burger
Appeal to Chinese	Average	Strong*	Below average

Note: *The Appeal to Chinese is explained in the paragraph under the table.

As can be seen in the table above, where we compare the three American QSR chains, of the three, KFC's Chinese name has the strongest appeal to Chinese consumers. First, traditionally, Chinese eat a lot of chicken. The time to get one kilogram of chicken meat from a chicken is less than that for getting one kilogram of beef, because it takes longer time for a cow to grow than for a chicken to grow. The cost per kilogram of chicken meat is less than that for beef. So, when budget is limited and Chinese need protein from meat, chicken meat is a lower cost option than beef. Also, the strong flavor of the KFC recipes can create the same taste even though the chicken are sourced locally and from different suppliers. KFC also does not require fresh chicken meat because Chinese cannot taste any difference from fresh chicken or frozen chickens with the strong flavoring of the KFC recipe. On the contrary, McDonald's and Burger King have to maintain its global standard for the beef. Hence, raw material cost is higher for McDonald's than for KFC. So, it is not surprising that KFC can operate profitable stores in many locations while McDonald's and Burger King cannot afford to continue paying even the rent. As a result, McDonald's and Burger King have primarily lost to KFC in China in terms of store opening. In summary, for the four Ps of Marketing (Product, Price, Place, Promotion), both McDonald's and Burger King has lost to KFC in product cost competitiveness (beef vs. chicken) and in terms of places (opening stores).

2.3.3. *Suggestive corporate name — Arbitrary*

The third approach for creating company name is that founders create names with arbitrary suggestive meanings. Some company examples include Alibaba, Amazon, Apple, Baidu, Facebook, Google, and Yahoo. For Baidu, its Chinese name is 百度 with Pin-yin of Baidu.

The name Baidu was inspired by a poem written more than 800 years ago during China's Song Dynasty. "The poem compares the search for a retreating beauty amid chaotic glamour with the search for one's dreams while confronted by life's many obstacles ... Hundreds and thousands of times, for her I searched in chaos/Suddenly, I turned by chance, to where the lights were waning, and there she stood". Baidu, whose literal meaning is "hundreds of times" represents a persistent search for the ideal (Baidu 2020).

2.3.4. *Corporate name — What should it suggest?*

Levitt (2006, p. 1) argues that companies should stop defining themselves by what they produced and instead reorient themselves toward customer needs: "sustained growth depends on how broadly you define your business — and how carefully you gauge your customers' needs. Business will do better in the end if they concentrate on meeting customers' needs rather than on selling products. What business are you really in? Had US railroad executives seen themselves as being in the transportation business rather than the railroad business, they would have continued to grow. Hollywood defined its business in movie, when it was actually in the entertainment business".

In China, we can also find company with name which limits its scope of business. One example is Little Sheep (2020). It used product brand name of 小肥羊 (Pin-yin: Xiao Fei Yang), which literally means little fat sheep. While it can focus on its communication as an expert in offering hot pot with sheep meat, it also limits what it can offer.

Hence, we recommend that the company name should be suggestive of what business the company is in and what the company's mission is. Each successful company must have a purpose expressed in its mission, and the company's mission is relevant to customer, is not changed frequently, and represents "corporate ability". This can also remind executives to continue building business, which will help enhance the "corporate ability" in the chosen business definition and better satisfy customer needs. Focusing on the customer is also consistent with the "jobs to be done" concept: Marketers should develop purposeful brands where products can be "hired" by consumers to perform jobs consumers want to get done (Christensen *et al.* 2005). FedEx, for example, designed its service to perform the job of "I need to send this from here to there with perfect certainty as fast as possible" (Christensen *et al.* 2005, p. 1). "A clear purpose brand acts a two-sided compass: one side guides customers to the right products. The other guides your designers, marketers, and advertisers as they develop and market new and improved products" (Christensen *et al.* 2005, p. 1). We propose that marketers should apply these suggestions of Christensen *et al.* (2005) to "corporate brand name" rather than limiting these suggestions on "product brand name".

We could identify two companies, which have suggestive corporate names on the mission and purpose, namely, Microsoft and Netscape. "Microsoft" represents software for microcomputer. Another example is Netscape. Originally named Mosaic Communications Corporation, the venture was later re-named Netscape Communications Corporation by Andreeseen and Clark (Corts and Freier 2003, p. 2). Navigator, the company's browser, was a spectacular success, capturing more than 60% of the market less than two months after its release in December 1994 (Yoffie and Cusumano 1999, p. 8). Netscape as a company name is suggestive of the future landscape of "Net". Navigator is also a suggestive name for users. It enables them to navigate through the vast network of information on the Internet. When Microsoft launched its product to compete with Netscape's Navigator, Microsoft also used a suggestive name, Internet Explorer (IE), which simply helps users to "explore" the Internet.

In China, the use of Internet is mainly via mobile phones now. So, people communicate and get information through apps on their mobile phones, such as QQ or WeChat, instead of going through browsers on a PC. According to the April 2020 report of China Internet Network Information Center (CNNIC 2020), among people with Internet access, 99% of them go to the Internet via mobile phones, vs. only 35% via laptop computers and 43% via desktop computers. In China, similar to the rest of the world, there are two key operating systems: one for Mac OS (Safari browser) and one for Windows (IE browser). As Microsoft Windows operating system is allowed to be used in China for decades, many websites are designed to be compatible with Internet Explorer.

3. Hypotheses Development: Improving New Product Success by Choosing the Right Branding Strategy

In this chapter, we propose a hierarchical branding strategy with two names for one product, a product *given* name and a product *family* name, and to bind them together on the launch of a new product, and also use a suggestive *corporate* name as an abstract umbrella brand to increase the chance of new product success. The hierarchical branding strategy is based on the classic category-based processing model in social psychology domain.[2] According to Fiske *et al.* (1999), when people form impressions about a new target, they tend to first judge whether the target's attributes fit an established category. If people perceive a fit, a more category-based impression formation process will occur. Specifically, when a new product and the original parent brand are sufficiently similar, consumers view them as belonging to the same category and evaluate the new product

---

[2]Yeo and Park (2006, p. 272) summarized the key conceptual framework for a branding strategy based on the distinction between category-based and piecemeal processing and earlier work such as Fiske *et al.* (1999) and Fiske and Neuberg (1990).

on the basis of the favorableness of this category independently of its specific attributes (Yeo and Park 2006, p. 272). In the case of Minute Maid in China, the use of the same family name (Good Juice Source) for the launch of the first new product (Fruit Pulp Orange) and for the launch of another new product (Fruit Pulp Premium Milk) in effect helped consumers view the two products as belonging to the same category. The particular family name (Good Juice Source) also helped consumers view the two new products as coming from the same source and belonging to the same category. On the contrary, "when consumers perceive a lack of category fit, the extension is given smaller probabilities of success" (Yeo and Park, 2006, p. 272).

The actual challenges for practitioners have inspired us to propose that product *given* brand names, product *family* brand names and *corporate* names play different strategic roles. Marketers can create a suggestive product given brand name for product benefits, a suggestive product family brand name for category benefits and a suggestive corporate name for the business that the company is in that meets consumers' needs.

In China, family name is particularly important. When two Chinese have the same family name, they may feel emotionally connected as they believe that they have the same common ancestors hundreds of years ago. Hence, the suggestion that a corporate name and a family product name be used to convey certain aspects of a new product could resonate much more strongly in the eyes of Chinese consumers. In China, people are strongly devoted to their family names, while for the US or Australia, people may have adopted new names because whoever came to those lands had a new start, giving up their past lives along with their names.

Thus, while we have borrowed the notion of suggestiveness from Keller *et al.* (1998), our proposal is different from previous work conceptually. First, Keller *et al.* (1998, p. 55) propose that a "suggestive" brand name could convey information regarding a relevant attribute or benefit in a particular product context. We propose that we could have two "suggestive" names for a product, a given name and a family name. We also suggest strategic meaning for these two names, the suggestive given name should give meaning for product benefits, the suggestive family name should give meaning for the category benefits. Keller *et al.* (1998) did not study corporate branding and what corporate name should suggest. We extended their work and conducted a study to provide support that corporate name should also be suggestive. We recommend that the suggestive corporate name should give meaning for the business that the company is in that meets consumers' needs.

As it is also important for practitioners to have actionable guidelines on what is "new product success" and "goodness of name", we have developed two constructs. For "new product success", the six items are overall liking, purchase intention, purchase frequency, credibility, uniqueness, and relevancy. We recommend these items for the "new product success" construct because marketers often look at scores of these items to determine whether they can continue product development in a stage-gate process within an organization.[3] Marketers and research agencies have also used these items following the suggestions of Malhotra (2020, p. 341) and Lam *et al.* (2013, p. 587). Although marketers can create different names, they also need to know which one to use. So, we propose another construct, "goodness of name", with four items: overall liking of the product name, influence of the product name on the product image, the level of fit of the product name with the product description, and ease of remembering the product name. Marketers must assess the overall liking of the product name and need a name to enhance the product image that fits the product description. If consumers can easily remember a name, the marketing investment for building awareness of the name will be more efficient. These item measures are also general enough for marketers to use for different product categories.

For details on the research hypotheses, method, analysis and results for Two-Level Hierarchical Branding Strategy and Three-Level Hierarchical Branding Strategy, please see Appendix I of this chapter.

Marketers may increase the chance of success for a new product launch by adopting a hierarchical branding strategy with ascending order of abstraction with three names with different suggestive meanings.

---

[3]For details, please refer to Aaker *et al.* (2019, p. 217) and Hair *et al.* (2021, p. 200).

Below is a summary of our specific suggestions to managers:

Managerial Take Aways

- Use a suggestive given name for the new product that helps consumers recall the key benefits and features of the new product.
- Use a suggestive family name for the new product that communicates the benefits of the product category. By giving the new product a suggestive corporate name, new product success can be further enhanced if the corporate name is suggestive of the key business that the corporation is in and the consumer needs it seeks to satisfy.
- In terms of measures, there are guidelines on what is "new product success" and "goodness of name".

3.1. *Discussion*

There are three key theoretical contributions of our study. One is that the use of a hierarchy of brand names constitutes a new framework of branding for new product launches, providing a consumer-based perspective on new product management strategies. Specifically, the present research suggests that a hierarchy of names provides consumers with additional cognitive cues in tracing the desirable characteristics of an established brand. Second, the new framework is strategic and considers a long-term perspective, as the focus is not on the success of launching one single product, but on the branding strategy for successfully creating an umbrella brand with different products with different given names in sequence. The creation of two names for a new product is similar to what parents will create for their newborn baby, a given name and a family name. The family name reminds consumers of the linkage between the established product/brand equity and the newly launched product (and is also important in Chinese markets), whereas the given name suggests the value/function conveyed by the new product. Third, prior research has suggested that products are akin to humans (Aaker 1997; Aggarwal and McGill 2012; Jordan 2002; Rojas-Méndez *et al.* 2013). Consumers' perceived product personalities play an essential role in determining product evaluation (Aggarwal and McGill 2007), loyalty (Chandler and Schwarz 2010), and risk taking (Kim and McGill 2011). The current research further extends the research of product anthropomorphism to the study of given/family names of brands. With the introduction of given/family names to the product anthropomorphism theory, we are more able to visualize a brand or product with human-like characteristics. In turn, this helps us to advance our knowledge of understanding the emotional bonds between brands and consumers.

4. Conclusion and Future Research

We extend the work of Keller *et al.* (1998) and Lam *et al.* (2013) by pro- posing and empirically demonstrating a three-level hierarchical branding strategy for new product launch, which is characterized by the binding of a suggestive given name and a suggestive family name for a new product. Besides, by putting the new product under a suggestive corporate name, marketers can further enhance new product success if the corporate name is suggestive of the key business that the corporation is in and the consumer needs it seeks to satisfy, especially in China. Because the actual name used is highly important, marketers should treat this factor seriously and ask creative agencies to propose different names with different levels of abstraction. Marketers do not want to use a suggestive name with negative connotations.

A. Appendix I — Research Hypotheses, Method, and Results

A.1. *Two-level hierarchical branding strategy*

The suggestive product *given* brand name helps consumers recall the brand, its benefits or its points of difference. The suggestive product *family* brand name enables marketers to gradually build the parent brand to be an umbrella brand covering the key benefits of the product category; thus, the two names for the product are complementary. By printing *"product given name by product family name"* on the front packaging label, marketers can build awareness of the product family name. Marketers can establish ownership of the "category" via a suggestive family brand name. When the awareness of the first product's given name and family name are at a similar level, marketers can use the same family name to launch a second new product with a second given name, and so on. These steps form the core essence of the two-level hierarchical branding strategy.

H1: A new product with "one suggestive brand name" will receive more positive responses compared to that with "one non-suggestive brand name".

Following H1 and the successful case of Minute Maid in China:

H2: A new product with "one suggestive given brand name plus one suggestive family brand name" will receive more positive responses compared to that with "one non-suggestive brand name".

Furthermore, we hypothesize that:

H3: A new product with "one suggestive given brand name plus one suggestive family brand name" will receive more positive responses compared to that with "one suggestive given brand name plus one non-suggestive family brand name".

A.2.   *Three-level hierarchical branding strategy*

For corporate branding strategies, we empirically tested the use of suggestive or non-suggestive corporate names and their combination with a product given brand name and product family brand name.

H4: A new product with "a suggestive corporate name" will receive more positive responses compared to that with "a non-suggestive corporate name".

H5: A new product with "a suggestive corporate name and another suggestive product family brand name" will receive more positive responses compared to that with a non-suggestive name as both "corporate name and product family brand name".

Furthermore, we propose that using one name as both the corporate name and the product family brand name (e.g., Coca-Cola) is not ideal for communication and therefore may affect consumers' responses. Thus:

H6: A new product with "a suggestive corporate name and another suggestive product family name" will receive more positive responses compared to that with a suggestive name as both "corporate name and product family brand name".

Although the naming strategy of Coca-Cola as both a corporate name and a product family brand name is not ideal for communication, we hypothesize that a suggestive name will nevertheless enable the concept to be associated with more positive responses compared with a "non-suggestive" name as both a corporate name and a product family brand name. Thus:

H7: A new product with a suggestive name as both the "corporate name and the product family brand name" will receive more positive responses compared to that with a non-suggestive name as both the "corporate name and the product family brand name".

Because the suggestiveness of a brand name can produce greater recall of the claimed benefits of the product, which is consistent with the brand name's connotations (Keller *et al.* 1998), we further hypothesize that:

H8: The ease of remembering the product name will be significantly correlated with participants' responses to a new product.

A.3. *Method*

We followed Lam *et al.* (2013) and used a concept test to quantitatively measure consumers' reaction to the same product with different corporate and product brand names using an experimental approach. In terms of product categories, we followed Keller and Aaker (1992) and Lam *et al.* (2013) and chose snacks (i.e., potato chips) because respondents are expected to have purchase and usage experience. For the Chinese family brand names of the stimuli, we followed the approach of Zhang and Schmitt (2001, p. 317) and Lam *et al.* (2013), using fictitious names to minimize any familiarity and prior knowledge factors. The Chinese stimulus names were presented with Chinese characters in the experiment. We used the same procedure as Zhang and Schmitt (2001) and Lam *et al.* (2013), informing all of the respondents that the study involved brand names and that they would be given brand names that might be used for actual products in the future and that might appear on product packaging and promotional materials. We also emphasized the Chinese name in larger, bold typeface in the experimental instrument (Zhang and Schmitt 2001; Lam *et al.* 2013).

We followed Lam *et al.* (2013) and used the same new product concept (Appendix II). While Lam *et al.* (2013) focused on a two-level hierarchical branding strategy, our experiment extended this strategy to a three-level hierarchical structure. There are five product concepts (Table 4) for the different branding strategies. We develop family names with a higher level of abstraction than given names. We have two suggestive corporate brand names (i.e., A and C) for the branding strategy of using a suggestive given product brand name and a suggestive parent product brand name so as to rule out the possible interpretation that the findings were due to the uniqueness of a name.

To test our hypotheses, we conducted two experiments with nested within-designs. Study 1 tested our hypotheses concerning

Table 4. Five product concepts in study 1.

Concept	A	B	C	D	E
Number of names	Two names	Two names	Two names	One name	One name
Parent brand name	Suggestive	Non-suggestive	Suggestive	Suggestive	Non-suggestive
Sub-brand name	Suggestive	Suggestive	Suggestive		
Parent brand name — English	Xiang Su	Ke Li	Xiang Su	Potato "zero" chip	Ke Li
Parent brand name — Chinese	香酥	克立	香酥	马"零"薯	克立
Sub-brand name — English	Potato "Zero" Chip	Potato "Zero" Chip	"Zero" Potato Chip		
Sub-brand name — Chinese	马"零"薯	马"零"薯	"零"薯片		

a two-level hierarchical branding strategy (family, given brand names) for new products (H1–H3), while study 2 tested our hypotheses for a three-level hierarchical branding strategy (family, given brand names, and corporate name; H4–H8). A global research agency conducted the research fieldwork in Shanghai, China and provided statistical significance tests at the 95% confidence level. The agency conducted online interviews with a total of 1,000 respondents (50% male and 50% female, average age of 29) across two studies.

A.3.1. *Study 1*

Study 1 had a 2 (number of product names: one vs. two) × 2 (name suggestiveness: suggestive vs. non-suggestive) nested-within design. The design generated five branding concepts as shown in Table 4: concept A (suggestive family/suggestive given brand names), B (non-suggestive family/suggestive given names), C (suggestive family/suggestive given names), D (one suggestive name), and E (one non-suggestive name). We counterbalanced the order of presenting the five concepts to rule out any recency/primacy effect(s).

A.3.1.1. Study 1 — Procedure and measures

A global research agency conducted 500 online interviews (50% female and 50% male, average age of 29) in China. All respondents must have consumed potato chips in the previous three months. We presented five new product concepts to each participant and measured their responses with regard to their overall liking and purchase intention on each product concept. Consistent with the previous literature (e.g., Fock *et al.* 2011), we asked participants to rate their purchase intentions using two items: *very likely/very unlikely* (7-point) and *purchase frequency*. We asked participants to note the number of purchases of the presented product out of ten potato chip purchases and transformed the purchase frequency (10-point) linearly into a 7-point scale. We then combined the two items to generate a purchase intention index ($a = 0.71$). We used a single item to capture overall liking: *like a lot/dislike a lot* (7-point) (Hoek *et al.* 2013). Based on Bergkvist and Rossiter's (2007) recent research, for constructs in marketing that consist of a concrete singular object (i.e., attitude/liking of ads or brands), a single-item measure should be used to maximize the predictive validity.

A.3.1.2.   Study 1 — Results of the responses to a new product

The results of a repeated-measure ANOVA revealed a significant difference between participants' purchase intentions regarding the new product for the five different concepts, $F(4, 1996) = 39.79$, $p < 0.001$. To reveal the nature of the difference, we conducted a follow-up contrast. Consistent with the literature and the prediction in H1, participants showed significantly higher intentions to purchase the product for concept D ($M = 4.77$, $SD = 1.21$) than for concept E ($M = 4.24$, $SD = 1.36$, $F(1, 1996) = 118.60$, $p < 0.001$). Participants' purchase intention for concept A ($M = 4.67$, $SD = 1.24$) was significantly higher than that for both concepts E ($M = 4.24$, $SD = 1.36$, $F(1, 1996) = 82.95$, $p < 0.001$) and B ($M = 4.42$, $SD = 1.30$, $F(1, 1996) = 25.68$, $p < 0.001$), empirically supporting H2 and H3. The same pattern of significant results was obtained by replacing concept A with concept C. The statistical result concerning overall liking replicated that concerning purchase intention.

A.3.2.   *Study 2*

While Study 1 focused on a two-level hierarchical branding strategy, Study 2 extended this strategy to a three-level hierarchical structure. That is, Study 2 aimed to test the use of suggestive or non-suggestive corporate brand names, family brand names and given brand names. Study 2 differed from Study 1 in the following aspects. First, Study 2 took corporate brand names into consideration and tested the proposed multiple-name branding strategy in a broader context. Second, based on the results of Study 1, Study 2 kept given brand names constant as suggestive and focused on the additional value of corporate brand names. Third, Study 2 used the measurement approach of a global marketing research agency to enhance the linkage between theory and practice.

    Study 2 employed a 2 (number of product names: two vs. three names) × 2 (name suggestiveness: suggestive vs. non-suggestive) nested within-design. The design generated five branding concepts, as shown in Table 5: concept P (suggestive corporate name/suggestive

Table 5. Five corporate name and product brand name concepts in study 2.

Concept	P	Q	R	S	T
Corporate brand name	Suggestive	Suggestive	Non-suggestive	Suggestive	Non-suggestive
Corporate brand name — English	Quality health source	Health happy source	Yi Er Na	Quality health source	Yi Er Na
Corporate brand name — Chinese	优健源	健乐源	伊尔纳	优健源	伊尔纳
Product family brand name	Suggestive	Suggestive	Suggestive	Suggestive	Non-suggestive
Product family brand name — English	Xiang Su	Xiang Su	Xiang Su	Quality health source	Yi Er Na
Product family brand name — Meaning	Scented crispy	Scented crispy	Scented crispy	Quality health source	No meaning
Product family brand name — Chinese	香酥	香酥	香酥	优健源	伊尔纳
Product given name	Suggestive	Suggestive	Suggestive	Suggestive	Suggestive
Product given name — English	Potato "Zero" Chip	Potato "Zero" Chip	Potato "Zero" Chip	Potato "Zero" Chip	Potato "Zero" Chip
Product given name — Chinese	马"零"薯	马"零"薯	马"零"薯	马"零"薯	马"零"薯

product family brand name/suggestive product given brand name), Q (the same structure as P, but a different corporate name), R (non-suggestive corporate name/suggestive family name/suggestive given name), S (a suggestive name as both corporate and family names/suggestive given name), and T (a non-suggestive name as both corporate and family names/suggestive given name). We developed corporate names with a higher level of abstraction than family names and given names.

A.3.2.1. Study 2 — Procedure and measures

The same global research agency conducted another 500 online interviews (50% female and 50% male, mean age of 29) in China. We presented five new product concepts to each participant with their order counterbalanced. Following the modern practical marketing research, we selected six items that are commonly used by marketing managers (overall liking, purchase intention, purchase frequency, credibility, uniqueness, and relevancy) to capture participants' responses towards the new product. An overall "new product success" index was generated by averaging these six items (Zhang and Schmitt 2001; $a = 0.92$). Finally, following Hong and Sternthal's (2010) research on processing fluency, we used a single item, *very easy/very difficult* (7-point), to measure the ease with which participants could remember the product name.

A.3.2.2. Study 2 — Results

The results of a repeated-measure ANOVA revealed a significant differ- ence for the five concepts in terms of "new product success", $F(4, 1996) = 2.91$, $p < 0.05$. Consistent with the predictions in H4, H5, and H6, the results of *a priori* contrasts showed that concept P ($M = 5.53$, $SD = 1.14$) received a significantly higher score in terms of "new product success" than that of concepts R ($M = 5.48$, $SD = 1.13$, $F(1, 1996) = 4.93$, $p < 0.05$), T ($M = 5.43$, $SD = 1.16$, $F(1, 1996) = 17.88$, $p < 0.001$) and S ($M = 5.49$, $SD = 1.06$, $F(1, 1996) = 4.13$, $p < 0.05$). The same pattern of significant results was found when replacing concept P with concept Q in the analysis. Furthermore, concept S scored higher than T ($F(1, 1996) = 6.00$,

$p < 0.05$), providing empirical support for H7. Finally, a regression analysis showed that the new product success index can be well predicted by the ease with which participants could remember the product concept on a significant level ($t = 19.60$, $p < 0.001$), with a large explanation power ($R^2 = 0.44$; Cohen 1992). These results lend support to our prediction in H8.

Our research has several limitations. We have only focused on the product concept test before a product is launched on the market. Although this is an important early stage in product qualification within a stage-gate process, we have not conducted research on the product and usage stages or other later stages. In terms of product categories, we have only focused on potato chips within the snack food category out of many fast-moving consumer goods. We hope that this chapter encourages more researchers to test suggestive names in product concept tests and report their findings. Our research findings may not be applicable to industrial products when buyers place more importance on functional attributes than on the suggestiveness of a brand name.

A.   Appendix II — New Product Concept in English

After working for a long time, you need some rest.

The new potato chip is crispy and delicious, but it does not contain any fat and salt (0% fat, 0% salt).

It is produced by a patented baking process. Without adding any oil, it nevertheless has a crispy texture. It also has specially added minerals that are essential for the human body and give it a delicious, slightly salty taste.

Try the new [Branding option] now.
Corporate Brand Name: [Branding option]
Family Product Brand Name: [Branding option]
Given Product Brand Name: [Branding option]
Product: Potato Chips
Weight: 50 g
Price: RMB3

References

Aaker, J. L. (1997). Dimensions of brand personality, *Journal of Marketing Research*, 34(3), 347–356.

Aaker, D. A., Kumar, V., Leone, R. P., and Day, G. S. (2019). *Marketing Research, Adaption of Marketing Research*, 11th ed., New Delhi: Wiley.

Aggarwal, P. and McGill, A. L. (2007). Is that car smiling at me? Schema congruity as a basis for evaluating anthropomorphized products, *Journal of Consumer Research*, 34(4), 468–479.

Aggarwal, P. and McGill, A. L. (2012). When brands seem human, do humans act like brands? Automatic behavioral priming effects of brand anthropomorphism, *Journal of Consumer Research*, 39(2), 307–323.

Ajami, R. A. and Khambata, D. (1991). Global strategic alliances: The new transnationals, *Journal of Global Marketing*, 5(1–2), 55–69.

Argenti, P. A. and Druckenmiller, B. (2004). Reputation and the corporate brand, *Corporate Reputation Review*, 6(4), 368–374.

Amway (2014). http://www.amway.com/about-amway/our-company/heritage/history-timeline (accessed on July 5, 2014).

Barich, H. and Kotler, P. (1991), A framework for image management, *MIT Sloan Management Review*, 32(4), 94–104.

Berens, G., van Riel, C. B. M., and van Bruggen, H. G. (2005). Corporate associations and consumer product responses: The moderating role of corporate brand dominance, *Journal of Marketing*, 69(3), 35–48.

Bergkvist, L. and Rossiter, J. R. (2007). The predictive validity of multiple-item versus single-item measures of the same constructs, *Journal of Marketing Research*, 44(2), 175–184.

Baidu (2020). http://ir.baidu.com/company-overview (accessed on November 10, 2020).

Brown, T. J. and Dacin, P. A. (1997). The company and the product: Corporate association and consumer product responses, *Journal of Marketing*, 61(1), 68–84.

Buil, I., Martínez, E., and de Chernatony, L. (2013), The influence of brand equity on consumer responses, *Journal of Consumer Marketing*, 30(1), 62–74.

Chandler, J. and Schwarz, N. (2010). Use does not wear ragged the fabric of friendship: Thinking of objects as alive makes people less willing to replace them, *Journal of Consumer Psychology*, 20(2), 138–145.

Christensen, C. M., Cook, S., and Hall, T. (2005), Marketing malpractice, the cause and the cure, *Harvard Business Review*, 83(12), 74–83.

CNNIC (2020). https://www.cnnic.net.cn/hlwfzyj/hlwxzbg/hlwtjbg/2020 04/P020200428596599037028.pdf (accessed on November 10, 2020).

Cohen, J. (1992). A power primer, *Psychological Bulletin*, 112(1), 155–159.

Corts, K. and Freier, D. (2003). Brief History of the Browser Wars, Harvard Business School Case, 9-703-571, June 9, 2003.

Fetscherin, M., Alon, I., Littrell, R., and Chan, A. (2012). In China? Pick your brand name carefully, *Harvard Business Review*, 90(9), 26.

Fiske, S. T. and Neuberg, S. L. (1990). A continuum of impression formation, from category-based to individuating processes: Influences of information and motivation on attention and interpretation. In *Advances in Experimental Social Psychology*, ed. M. Zanna, Vol. 23, pp. 1–74. San Diego, CA: Academic Press.

Fiske, S. T., Lin M., and Neuberg, S. L. (1999). The continuum model: Ten years later. In *Dual-Process Theories in Social Psychology*, eds. S. Chaiken and Y. Trope, pp. 231–254. New York: Guildford.

Fock, H., Chan, A. K., and Yan, D. (2011), Member-organization connection impacts in affinity marketing, *Journal of Business Research*, 64(7), 672–679.

Gao, W., Ji, L., Liu, Y., and Sun, Q. (2020). Branding cultural products in international markets: A study of Hollywood movies in China, *Journal of Marketing*, 84(3), 86–105.

Hair, J. F., Ortinau, D. J., and Harrison, D. E. (2021). *Essentials of Marketing Research*, New York: McGraw Hill.

Henderson, R. M. and Johnson, R. (2012). L'Oreal: Global brand, local knowledge, *Harvard Business School*, 9, 311–118.

Hoek, A. C., Elzerman, J. E., Hageman, R., Kok, F. J., Luning, P. A., and Graaf, C. D. (2013). Are meat substitutes liked better over time? A repeated in-home use test with meat substitutes or meat in meals, *Food Quality and Preference*, 28(1), 253–263.

Hong, J. and Sternthal, B. (2010). The effects of consumer prior knowledge and processing strategies on judgments, *Journal of Marketing Research*, 47(2), 301–11.

Jordan, P. W. (2002). *The Personalities of Products. Pleasure with Products: Beyond Usability*, London: CRC Press, pp. 19–47.

Keller, K. L. and Aaker, D. A. (1992). The effects of sequential introduction of brand extensions, *Journal of Marketing Research*, 24(1), 35–50.

Keller, K. L. and Lehmann, D. R. (2006). Brands and branding: Research findings and future priorities, *Marketing Science*, 25(6), 740–759.

Keller, K. L., Heckler, S. E., and Houston, M. J. (1998). The effects of brand name suggestiveness on advertising recall, *Journal of Marketing*, 62(1), 48–57.

Kotler, P. and Keller, K. L. (2016). *Marketing Management*, 15th ed., New York: Pearson.

Kim, S. and McGill, A. L. (2011). Gaming with Mr. Slot or gaming the slot machine? Power, anthropomorphism, and risk perception, *Journal of Consumer Research*, 38(1), 94–107.

Knox S. (2004). Positioning and branding your organisation, *Journal of Product and Brand Management*, 13(2), 105–111.

Levitt, T. (2006). What business are you in? Classic advice from Theodore Levitt, *Harvard Business Review*, 84(10), 126.

Laforet, S. and Saunders, J. (1994). Managing brand portfolios: How the leaders do it, *Journal of Advertising Research*, 34(5), 64–76.

Lam, P. Y., Chan, A., Gopaoco, H., Oh, K., and So, T. H. (2013). Dual branding strategy for a successful new product launch in China, *Business Horizons*, 56(5), 583–589.

Lee, Y. H. and Ang, S. H. (2003). Interference of picture and brand name in a multiple linkage ad context, *Marketing Letters*, 14(4), 273–288.

Little Sheep (2020). www.littlesheep.com (accessed on November 7, 2020).

Malhotra, N. K. (2020). *Marketing Research: An Applied Orientation*: Global edition (7th ed.), New Jersey: Prentice Hall.

Meenaghan, T. (1996). Ambush marketing — A threat to corporate sponsorship, *Sloan Management Review*, Fall, 38(1), 103–113.

Olins, W. (1989). Corporate identity: Making business strategy visible through design. London: Thames and Hudson.

Park, C. W., Jun, S. Y., and Shocker, A. D. (1996). Composite branding alliances: An investigation of extension and feedback effects, *Journal of Marketing Research*, 33(4), 453–466.

Peterson, Robert A. and Ross, I. (1972). How to name new brands, *Journal of Advertising Research*, 12(6), 29–34.

Rojas-Méndez, J. I., Papadopoulos, N., and Murphy, S. A. (2013). Measuring and positioning nation brands: A comparative brand personality approach, *Corporate Reputation Review*, 16(1), 48–65.

Spyropoulou, S., Skarmeas, D., and Katsikeas, C. S. (2011). An examination of branding advantage in export ventures, *European Journal of Marketing*, 45(6), 910–935.

Thomas, L. M. and Murry, N. M. (2004). Avoiding identity crisis, *Marketing Management*, 13(3), 44–45. We have added citation and a few paragraphs into the article.

Wu, F., Sun, Q., Grewal, R., and Li, S. (2019). Brand name types and consumer demand: Evidence from China's automobile market, *Journal of Marketing Research*, 56(I), 158–175.

Yeo, J. and Park, J. (2006). Effects of parent-extension similarity and self-regulatory focus on evaluations of brand extensions, *Journal of Consumer Psychology*, 16(3), 272–282.

Yoffie, D. B. and Cusumano, M. A. (1999). Building a company on Internet time: Lessons from Netscape, *California Management Review*, 41(3), Spring 1999.

Yum China (2020). http://www.yumchina.com/brand (accessed on November 7, 2020).

Zhang, S. and Schmitt, B. H. (2001). Creating local brands in multilingual international markets, *Journal of Marketing Research*, 38(3), 313–325.

Appendix 2: Corporate Branding Strategy for New Companies in China: Lessons Learned from GoGoVan and LaLaMove[*]

Howard Pong-Yuen Lam and Shiyu (Tracy) Lu

1. Introduction

When entrepreneurs have a new business idea for an innovative good or service, they usually found a new company and create a company name to pursue the opportunity. They want their companies and offerings of products to be appealing to customers. Therefore, they make several key decisions on company and product names that have long-term implications. First, should the company name and the product/service brand name be the same? Second, should the company name suggest a meaning? If so, what meaning should the name suggest? In this chapter, we review literature and then summarize the key lessons learned from the company names of two startup companies, GoGoVan and LaLaMove. Subsequently, we provide insights,

---

[*]This article is originally published from Lam, Howard Pong-Yuen and Lu, Tracy Shiyu (2022), "Corporate Branding Strategy for New Companies in China: Lessons Learned from GoGoVan and LaLaMove". In *Chinese Innovation and Branding Leaps*, edited by Serdar S Durmusoglu, Singapore: World Scientific Publishing, 137–150.

offer recommendations for managers and recommend future research directions.

Entrepreneurs could choose different corporate branding strategies from one extreme of "using one corporate name for all products" to another extreme of "using one brand name for each product". If entrepreneurs use one brand name for each product, they can build a clear image for each brand's target audience. However, the disadvantage is that the brand building investment is high, because consumers have resistance to brand switching when a new brand is introduced (Lam *et al.* 2010). The importance of the decision to pick a brand name for the company and for its products become more elevated since many new firms, if successful in their domestic markets, will consider entering the Chinese market. Chinese law requires every company to register a Chinese name before they start operating in China. Choosing a name for the China market is a big challenge because the Chinese language has thousands of characters, each with many meanings and with pronunciations that can vary from region to region (Fetscherin *et al.* 2012). See the P&G example in the box below.

P&G vs. Coca-Cola in China

P&G treats its corporate name and product brand names as separate and markets several products of a product category under one or more brand names. For P&G, the company name comes from the family names of its two founders (Procter and Gamble). P&G in English had no "suggestive" meaning for what is offered. When P&G had to register a company with a Chinese name in 1988 for its entry into the mainland China market, the leadership team in P&G Hong Kong asked a creative agency to propose a Chinese name for P&G. Eventually, 宝洁 (Chinese Pin-yin: Bao Jie) was chosen because the number one brand in terms of sales and profit for P&G Hong Kong in 1988 was Pampers, which has a Chinese name of 帮宝适 (Chinese Pin-yin: Bang Bao Shi, meaning: Help Baby Comfort). 宝洁 translates to 'baby clean' as 宝 (Bao) means "baby" and 洁 (Jie) means "clean". Later on, in the 1990s, P&G started offering many other brands/products in multiple categories. Unfortunately, the Chinese name was limiting because 'Baby Clean' was not congruent with P&G's wide variety of product categories.

(*Continued*)

(*Continued*)

When the Chinese name of P&G was decided by the Hong Kong team, they primarily thought about having the name with phonetic translation sounds similar to "Procter and Gamble", and did not consider creating a company name from a strategic point of view based on the future scope of business. For about two years in 1993–1994, P&G China top management forced all brand managers to limit their 30 seconds TV commercial duration to 28 seconds so that they could add a 2 second P&G corporate end-tag. The message was "P&G quality products make your life better". However, most creative agencies and brand managers resisted this change because managers of big P&G brands such as Rejoice, they did not want to spend a lot of media investment to build the corporate brand awareness of P&G. The awareness of the product brand, Rejoice, was much more important than the corporate brand of P&G to remind consumers to buy Rejoice. The managers of small brands or new brands in 1993–1994 also want to spend their limited marketing budget to build awareness of their brands, not building awareness of P&G's corporate brand P&G. In the end, the two-second end-tag requirement lasted only about two years. Although, we did not find any P&G spokesperson to publicly admit that the Chinese name of P&G was wrong, what we noticed was that P&G staff and other marketers simply referred P&G in English instead of Chinese. All Chinese with basic school education would have learned the 26 English letters of A–Z. So, P&G was easy for all Chinese to refer to anyway. The fact that Chinese referred to the English of P&G instead of its Chinese name indicated that the Chinese name for P&G was not as good as its Chinese name. Compare P&G's experience to Coca-Cola's. Coca-Cola, the first multinational firm allowed back in China in 1978, chose a very good Chinese name: 可口可乐 (Pin-yin: Ke Kou Ke Le), meaning "delicious happiness".

2. Brief Literature Review: Corporate Branding Strategies

The branding strategies of small- and medium-sized enterprises (SMEs) are somewhat different from large enterprises, So, we now discuss literature on SME branding strategies. SMEs had resource constraints in terms of time and money in hiring marketers for advertising and conducting marketing activities. As such, SMEs' approaches to the brand management style, operations, and functions are different from large enterprises. Prior studies found that trademarks registration and marketing expenses could create benefits in subsequent years and were likely to show a cumulative effect over time (Agostini *et al.* 2015). In addition, studies found that SMEs that focused on brands could achieve a distinct performance advantage over rivals by understanding customers' needs and brand perceptions, creating relevant and valued brands, supporting the brand consistently over time, effectively communicating the brand's identity to internal and external stakeholders and creating a coherent brand architecture (Berthon *et al.* 2008).

Some researchers studied drivers of brand credibility, defined as ability of the brand to deliver its promise, in consumer evaluation of global brands and domestic brands in an emerging market context (Srivastava *et al.* 2020). For global brands, perceived brand globalness and brand authenticity had a positive impact on brand credibility, but perceived local iconness had no significant influence because consumers may feel challenged to ascribe iconic associations as being a credible signal for global brands (Srivastava *et al.* 2020). For domestic brands, perceived brand globalness had a negative and significant effect on brand credibility. A possible reason for the negative effects of perceived brand globalness is that as domestic brands move into global markets to build brand value, emerging market consumers may feel that the domestic brand manifests a loss of commitment to its home market (Srivastava *et al.* 2020, p. 857).

More recently, prior studies noted the impact of the usage of the first- or second-person pronoun in the brand names, which was common in many products and companies such as iPhone or YouTube. Prior studies found that the usage of the first-person pronoun "I" and of the second-person pronoun "you" in a brand name could have positive impact on brand attitudes when they fit with the overall brand positioning (Kachersky and Carnevale 2015). The use of "you" had positive impact when the offering was positioned for its social benefits, while the use of "I", had greater positive impact when the offering was positioned for its personal benefits (Kachersky and Carnevale 2015).

The marketing investment of building two different names (a company name and a product brand name) is higher than that of building only one name. However, there are major long-term implications for marketing and for the business development of a company. The cost saving of using one name for two purposes, corporate brand image and product brand image, could limit the long-term growth of a company.

When companies grow from small companies into big multinational companies, these companies might have the same name as the product brand name and the company name. As marketing budgets were limited when the company was small, marketers tended to put all the money for different activities into building one name that benefited both the product brand and company brand.

3.   Lessons Learned from GoGoVan and LaLaMove

Should company use the name "van" or "move"? The case of GoGoVan and LaLaMove can be an excellent example. Both GoGoVan and LaLaMove provided a platform to connect drivers with people who had to deliver goods. Both companies were founded in 2013 in Hong Kong and branched out of Hong Kong into Southeast Asia and China. Both companies attracted prominent investors from Mainland China and other countries after these expansions (Leung 2017). GoGoVan was Hong Kong's first unicorn with a valuation of over $1 billion in September 2017 following a merger deal with the China-based 58 Suyun (Russell 2017). 58 Suyun was the freight division of 58 Home, a subsidiary of the New York-listed 58.com. 58 Home owned the majority of the merged entity after the merger and brought together backers such as Tencent and Alibaba. The merger would also create Asia's largest online platform in the intracity logistics and freight business (Perez 2017). The first step for the combined entity was to run GoGoVan services in the 40 cities where 58 Suyun operated and expand the combined coverage to 100 cities in the following 12 months (Barreto and Zhu 2017). In October 2017, LaLaMove received a valuation that was just below $1 billion mark (Russell 2017) after announcing its Series C funding of $100 million led by mainland's VC firm, Shun-Wei Capital, which was cofounded by Xiaomi's chief executive Lei Jun (Leung 2017).

Both GoGoVan and LaLaMove offered transportation and logistics services on-demand, very much in the same style that Uber works for passengers (Russell 2017). They were the Uber models of urban transportation for moving things, not people (Horwitz 2014). LaLaMove founder and CEO Shing Chow (Chow) estimated the logistics market in China alone was worth $1.7 trillion a year, and Uber was among those to take a look at the possibilities (Russell 2017). Uber had tried a logistic model in Hong Kong, but its "Uber Cargo" service was eliminated less than two years after its launch (Russell 2017). Although Uber could not do it on its own with enough income to sustain, it did not give up. Uber identified partner for synergy and income. On July 19, 2018, Uber had a press release to announce its exclusive global partnership with Cargo, the startup that provided in-car commerce to the rideshare economy. The partnership aimed to delight riders with snacks, beverages, electronics, and beauty products while on a trip (Uber and Cargo 2018). As of November 2020, Uber and Cargo had teamed up to increase rideshare earnings with Uber's cartop display program.[1]

In fact, Both GoGoVan and LaLaMove were similar in company names when they were founded in 2013. Both had "Van" in their company names, "GoGoVan" and "EasyVan". In 2014, EasyVan decided to rebrand as LaLaMove just in time for its launch in Bangkok because it would offer services from vehicles, such as motorcycles, that were not vans (Horwitz 2014). In an interview by Apple Daily, a Chinese newspaper in Hong Kong, Chow, Lalamove's founder, said that when EasyVan was founded, its main competitor was GoGoVan (*Apple Daily News* 2017). However, as GoGoVan exploited its first mover advantage, EasyVan decided to enter the South East Asia Market in 2014 and realized that motorcycles were more popular than vans in Bangkok. Bangkok was not the only country for such

---

[1]The cartop display program allows driver to install a display on top of his vehicle to show ads while he drives to make extra cash (Drivecargo.com 2020).

change in company name from EasyVan to LaLaMove. The other countries also had different transportation vehicles which were not vans. Therefore, Chow changed the company name to LaLaMove and added services from motorcycles.

The Chinese name for GoGoVan was 高高客货车 (Kim 2014) with Pin-yin of "Gao Gao Ke Huo Che". Gao meant "high" in English and has a sound similar to "Go" in English. The three Chinese characters of "Ke Huo Che" is the Chinese phrase for van, while "Ke" means "customer", "Huo" means "goods" and "Che" means "car". About one year ago, GoGoVan changed its company name to GoGoX. So, the founders also realized the limitation of using Van only for its platform.

The Chinese name for LaLaMove is 货拉拉 and has a Pin-yin of "Huo La La". "Huo" means "goods" and "La" means "move". Therefore, the decision of Chow to change the name of EasyVan to LaLaMove was consistent with the proposal to use benefit/job to be done for consumers in the company name, "move goods". If Lalamove is a corporate name, it can have product name such as EasyVan under it (Lalamove EasyVan) for matching the two sides of the platform: those who need Van and those who drive Van. Similarly, it can have Lalamove EasyBike for matching the two sides of the platform: those who need bicycles and those who ride bicycles.

4. Insights, Recommendations and Research Results

In this section, we identify and offer insights, recommendations and research results pertinent to the question of what company names are currently being suggested and what they should suggest. Entrepreneurs have several approaches to create suggestive company names. First, they use names such as Burger King, Pizza Hut, Kentucky Fried Chicken (KFC) to suggest "corporate ability in a product category" for different types of food categories. Second, simply use names of founders to create company names. Examples include Li Ning from China and McDonald's from the US. Third, create special suggestive company name. Examples include Alibaba and Baidu from China, Amazon and Google from the US. Baidu is the Chinese pin-yin for 百度. Bai means hundred. Du means angle. So, the two Chinese characters together mean hundred angles or directions.

These two Chinese characters are also included in a Chinese poem. It describes how a man searches a lady from hundred directions. Fourth, the mission and purpose of the company expressed as the benefit that company can bring to consumers. Example is LaLaMove as mentioned earlier.

For Google, for example, the term "google" itself is a creative spelling of googol, a number equal to 10 to the 100th power (Dictionary.com 2020). The Chinese name for Google has two Chinese characters 谷歌 (Pin-yin: Gu Ge) which is a phonetic translation for Google. The English back translation for the first Chinese character 谷 is "valley" and for the second Chinese character 歌 is "song". So, Chinese will not get the original meaning of Google from the Chinese name.

The case of GoGoVan and LaLaMove showed the importance of getting the name right when a company was formed. It was also important to know whether using a suggestive company name of "van" was better or worse than the other naming alternative of using "move". Therefore, we followed Zhang and Schmitt (2001) and Lam *et al.* (2013) and used a concept test to quantitatively measure consumers' reaction to four different overall concepts created from two company concepts with two company names (GoGoVan or LaLaMove) using an experimental approach as follows.

We emphasized the Chinese company name in larger and bold type-face in the experimental instrument, that is, the concept board shown to respondents. For the two company concepts, we created a "van" concept using the App description for the GoGoVan App and created a "move" concept using the App description for the LaLaMove App. These descriptions would be shown to any individual before he/she decided to download the App. People who had installed these apps were excluded from the study. As a result, we had a total of four concepts. First, the "van" company concept with the "GoGoVan" company name. Second, the "van" company concept with the "LaLaMove" company name. Third, the "move" company concept with the "LaLaMove" company name. Fourth, the "move" company concept with the "GoGoVan" company name.

A research agency conducted the research fieldwork in a central location in Beijing in January 2019. The researchers conducted 400 interviews among adults (age over 18), and randomly assigned them to one of the four concepts (50% male and 50% female, with an average age of 34). For the company name, we used the four measures, liking, memorability, impact of image, and name's fit with concept, to capture participants' responses toward the company name. We used a 7-point scale for all metrics. We conducted statistical significance tests at the 95% confidence level, and we showed the research results in Table 1. The five key findings were summarized as follows for the results of on company concepts and company names.

First, we compare row "b" with row "a" in Table 1. For the company concept of "van", the use of LaLaMove as a company name could generate significantly higher overall liking, purchase intention, credibility, uniqueness, relevancy scores on the company concept than the use of GoGoVan as a company name. Furthermore, "LaLaMove" as a company name could also generate significantly higher overall liking, memorability, impact on image and name's fit with concept.

Second, we compare row "c" with row "d" in Table 1. For the company concept of "move", the use of LaLaMove as a company name also generated significantly higher overall liking, purchase intention, credibility, uniqueness, and relevancy scores than the use of GoGo-Van as a company name. "LaLaMove" as a company name could also generate significantly higher overall liking, memorability, impact on image and name's fit with concept.

Third, if we use the same company name, "GoGoVan", then using "move" as a company concept was better than using "van" as a company concept for generating significantly higher overall liking, purchase intention and credibility (by comparing row "d" with row "a" in Table 1). If we use the same company name, "LaLaMove", then using "move" as a company concept also was better than using "van" as a company concept for generating significantly higher overall liking, purchase intention, credibility, uniqueness and relevancy (by comparing column "c" with column "b" in Table 1).

Fourth, we could compare row "c" with row "a" in Table 1. The use of the "move" company concept with the "LaLaMove" company name generated significantly higher overall liking, purchase intention, credibility, uniqueness, and relevancy scores than the use of the "van" company concept with the "GoGoVan" company name. The "LaLaMove" name was also significantly better than "GoGo-Van" in this comparison because of the significantly higher scores on overall liking, memorability, impact on image and name's fit with concept.

Table 1. Research results.

Company Concept

Combination			Overall Liking		Purchase Intention		Credibility		Uniqueness		Relevancy	
Company concept + Company name		#	Mean	(95% CI)	Mean	(95% CI)	Mean	(95% CI)	Mean	(95% CI)	Mean	(95% CI)
GoGoVan	GoGoVan	a	4.7	(4.5–4.9)	4.53	(4.35–4.71)	4.37	(4.18–4.56)	4.08	(3.87–4.29)	4.18	(4–4.36)
GoGoVan	LaLaMove	b	5.25	(5.07–5.43)	5.51	(5.36–5.66)	4.98	(4.82–5.14)	4.59	(4.38–4.8)	5.16	(4.94–5.38)
LaLaMove	LaLaMove	c	5.71	(5.57–5.85)	5.88	(5.73–6.03)	5.49	(5.31–5.67)	4.95	(4.77–5.13)	5.43	(5.21–5.65)
LaLaMove	GoGoVan	d	5.11	(4.92–5.30)	4.87	(4.69–5.05)	4.89	(4.68–5.10)	4.55	(4.34–4.76)	4.66	(4.43–4.89)
Multiple Comparisons			c > b, d, a; b and d > a;		c > b > d > a		c > a, b, d; b and d > a		c > a, d; b and d > a		c and b > d > a	

Company Name

Combination		#	Overall Liking		Memorability		Impact on Image		Name's Fit with Concept	
Company concept + Company name			Mean	(95% CI)	Mean	(95% CI)	Mean	(95% CI)	Mean	(95% CI)
GoGoVan	GoGoVan	a	4.01	(3.76–4.26)	3.61	(3.33–3.89)	4.33	(4.16–4.5)	4.28	(4.09–4.47)
GoGoVan	LaLaMove	b	5.53	(5.37–5.69)	5.77	(5.58–5.96)	5.39	(5.25–5.53)	5.39	(5.24–5.54)
LaLaMove	LaLaMove	c	5.68	(5.5–5.86)	5.97	(5.79–6.15)	5.64	(5.49–5.79)	5.71	(5.54–5.88)
LaLaMove	GoGoVan	d	4.32	(4.07–4.57)	3.73	(3.45–4.01)	4.51	(4.31–4.71)	4.69	(4.48–4.90)
Multiple Comparisons			c and b > d > a		c and b > d > a		c and b > d > a		c and b > d > a	

Note: We used the Post Hoc Tests for Multiple Comparisons and only the statistically significant mean difference ($p < 0.05$) among a, b, c, d were shown.

5. Conclusions, Limitations and Future Research Directions

We proposed and empirically demonstrated that if a company name was suggestive of the key business of the corporation and the consumer needs it satisfies, it generates significantly higher scores when measuring a company's concept and when measuring a company's name. Because the actual name used is so important, marketers should take the naming task seriously and ask creative agencies to propose names using the proposals and research findings in this chapter.

Chapter Takeaways

- Use a suggestive name and to use the same name for both the new product and for the new company; the selected name should suggest the job that the product and company could perform for the company's customer.
- Naming is strategic and should be considered from a long-term perspective, as the focus is not solely on the success of launching one single product but also on creating a successful company.
- If entrepreneurs want to incorporate a new company to do business in China, they are required by the government to have a Chinese company name. Although an English company name is not required, it is better to have both Chinese and English company names when the company is formed. Then, there won't be a need to go through company name registration/name addition process to add an English company name.

Our research has a few limitations. We had only studied startup companies in transportation, namely, GoGoVan and LaLaMove. We hope this chapter will encourage more researchers to test suggestive company names in other industries and report their findings. We expect that results will be similar in other fast moving consumer goods (FMCG) industries. For more expensive products (e.g., refrigerators, washing machines) with longer purchase cycle, buyers will likely choose a company/product after going through rational comparison of the key attributes of different products. The effect of the name of a company or product may be less significant than the case for FMCG industries.

In terms of cultures and countries, we conducted the fieldwork for this study in Beijing and the questionnaire was in Chinese. Because different languages require a different number of characters to express the same meaning, the total number of characters and pronunciations required to express a name may be longer in English than in Chinese. The total number of characters and pronunciations might affect a respondents' comprehension of different names as a whole. In the Chinese education system, students study Chinese language before they get admission into university. They have to learn many Chinese phases with four Chinese characters, and also use these phases in their daily conversations and in major festivals too. For example, in the Chinese New Year, they will wish their friends 身体健康 (Pin-yin: Shen Ti Jian Kang) which means "healthy body". As a result, marketer could use different combinations of four Chinese characters to create memorable and likeable taglines for their brands when entering the Chinese market. A watch brand, Titus, had used a total of 14 Chinese characters in its selling line as follows:

不在乎天长地久 (Pin-yin: Bu Zai Hu Tian Zhang De Jiu)
只在乎曾经拥有 (Pin-yin: Zhi Zai Hu Ceng Jing Yong You)

For Chinese, the first three Chinese characters in the first line (Bu Zai Hu) and the first three Chinese characters in the second line (Zhi Zai Hu) have contrast. The second and the third characters are the same (Zai Hu) which means "care" in English. The first character in the first line, "Bu", means "no". The first character in the second line, "Zhi", means "only". So, together, the sentence structure for the first line and the second line means "I don't care" and "I only care". The remaining four Chinese characters in the first line "Tian Zhang De Jiu" and in the second line "Ceng Jing Yong You" are popular Chinese phases with four Chinese characters and so Chinese can easily understand their meaning. "Tian Zhang De Jiu" means "as long as heaven and earth". "Ceng Jing Yong You" means "as short as a moment of us together".

So, the meaning in English for these 14 Chinese characters is:

I don't care how long heaven and earth will last.
I only care about the short moment of us together.

References

Agostini, L., Nosella, A., and Filippini, R. (2015). Brand — Building efforts and their association with SME sales performance, *Journal of Small Business Management*, 53, 161–173. 10.1111/jsbm.12185.

Apple Daily News (2017). EasyVan 改名 Lalamove, Call 車貨運平台攻電單車突圍 (English back translation from author — EasyVan changed name to LaLaMove. Platform for calling vehicles for delivery offered motorcycles as well to achieve breakthrough). https://hk.finance.appledaily.com/finance/daily/article/20170620/20061974 (accessed on January 20, 2019).

Barreto, E. and Zhu, J. (2017). HK's GOGOVAN, China's 58 Suyun follow merger with $200 mln fundraising, Market News, *Reuters*, August 31, 2017. https://www.reuters.com/article/hongkong-gogovan-fundraising/hks-gogovan-chinas-58-suyun-follow-merger-with-200-mln-fundraising-idUSL4N1LH3N5 (accessed on January 20, 2019).

Berthon, P., Ewing, M. T., and Napoli, J. (2008). Brand management in small to medium-sized enterprises, *Journal of Small Business Management*, 46(1), 27–45.

Dictionary.com (2020). November 5, 2020. https://www.dictionary.com/browse/google.

Drivecargo.com (2020). November 7, 2020. https://drivecargo.com.

Fetscherin, M., Alon, I., Littrell, R., and Chan, A. (2012). In China? Pick your brand name carefully, *Harvard Business Review*, 90(9), 26.

Horwitz, J. (2014). Hong Kong's Easyvan rebrands as Lalamove just in time for launch in Bangkok, *TechinAsia*, November 27, 2014. https://www.techinasia.com/hong-kongs-easyvan-rebrands-as-lalamove-just-in-time-for-launch-in-bangkok (accessed on January 20, 2019).

Kachersky, L. and Carnevale, M. (2015). Effects of pronoun brand name perspective and positioning on brand attitude, *Journal of Product and Brand Management*, 24(2), 157–164.

Kim, Y.-H. (2014). 人人投资的高高客货车要解决大城市物流难题 (English back translation from author: RenRen invested in GoGoVan to solve the logistic difficulty in big cities), *The Wall Street Journal (simplified Chinese edition)*. https://cn.wsj.com/articles/CN-TEC-20141118173807 (accessed on January 20, 2019).

Lam, P. Y., Chan, A., Gopaoco, H., Oh, K., and So, T. H. (2013). Dual branding strategy for a successful new product launch in China, *Business Horizons*, 56(5), 583–589.

Lam, S. K., Ahearne, M., Hu, Ye., and Schillewaert, N. Resistance to brand switching when a radically new brand is introduced: A social identity theory perspective, *Journal of Marketing*, 74(6), pp. 128–146.

Leung, H. (2017). Lalamove scores $100M investment from China: Is this Hong Kong's next unicorn? *Forbes*, October 10, 2017. https://www.forbes.com/sites/hannahleung/2017/10/10/lalamove-scores-100m-investment-from-china-is-this-hong-kongs-next-unicorn/#242c164136a3 (accessed on April 1, 2021).

Perez, B. (2017). GoGoVan to become Hong Kong's first US$1 billion start-up after merger with 58 Suyun, *South China Morning Post*. August 28, 2017. https://www.scmp.com/tech/china-tech/article/2108658/gogovan-become-hong-kongs-first-us1-billion-start-after-merger-58.

Russell, J. (2017). Logistics on-demand startup Lalamove raises $100M as it approaches a $1B valuation. *Techcrunch*, October 10, 2017. https://tech-crunch.com/2017/10/10/lalamove-raises-100m/ (accessed on January 20, 2019).

Srivastava, A., Dey, D. K., and Balaji, M. S. (2020). Drivers of brand credibility in consumer evaluation of global brands and domestic brands in an emerging market context, *Journal of Product and Brand Management*, 29(7), pp. 849–861. https://doi.org/10.1108/JPBM-03-2018-1782.

Uber and Cargo (2018). November 7, 2020. https://drivecargo.com/en-us/uber.

Zhang, S. and Schmitt, B. H. (2001). Creating local brands in multilingual international markets, *Journal of Marketing Research*, 38(3), 313–325.

Appendix 3: Dual Branding Strategy for a Successful New Product Launch in China*

**Pong Yuen LAM, Annie CHAN, Hannie GOPAOCO,
Kevin OH, and Tsz Him SO**

Abstract

Marketers may increase the chance of success for a new product launch by using a sub-brand name and a parent brand name simultaneously. In this paper, we report the successful case of using two brand names — dual branding strategy — by practitioners in China for the Minute Maid Orange Pulp juice drink launch. A suggestive sub-brand name helps consumers recall the key benefits and features of the new product. A suggestive parent brand name communicates the benefits of the product category. A dual branding strategy addresses the problem of using only one brand name for a new product launch. After the successful launch of the first new product by a parent brand, marketers are able to launch other new products under other sub-brand names in the future to meet different consumer needs. Marketers may use the same parent brand to introduce different products to build scale for the brand and are able to clearly differentiate the different product offerings under different sub-brand names. If a company acquires a brand from another company, a marketer may position the acquired brand as a sub-brand under the

---

*This article is originally published from Lam, Pong Yuen, Chan, A., Gopaoco, H., Oh, K. and So, T.H. (2013), "Dual branding strategy for a successful new product launch in China," *Business Horizons*.

parent brand if the marketer has defined the business scope of the parent brand broadly enough and with a suggestive parent brand name.

Keywords: Branding strategy, line extension, new product launch, product name, Minute Maid, China market

1. Branding Strategies for New Products

1.1. *Introduction*

Marketers often conduct research to qualify the product concepts of new products before they launch the new products in the market. Marketers want to create and select product concepts with higher purchase intention scores and overall liking scores to increase the chances of success in the marketplace. Given a product concept, should the brand name be suggestive or non-suggestive to enhance the product concept scores? How many names should the marketer create for a new product?

1.2. *Suggestive or non-suggestive brand names*

Keller, Heckler and Houston (1998) have examined the effects of a brand name's meaning. Their findings indicate that compared with a non-suggestive brand name (e.g., Emporium televisions), a brand name that explicitly conveys a product benefit (e.g., PicturePerfect televisions) produces the greater recall of an advertised benefit claim that is consistent with the brand name's connotations. Keller *et al.* (1998, p. 56) state the following implication of their research findings: "marketers may be better off adopting more flexible branding strategies when introducing new products by using non-suggestive brand names if they anticipate the possibility of a later need to advertise additional benefit claims. Alternatively, if marketer chooses suggestive brand names to introduce new products, they must be willing to commit enough time and resources to reposition the brand if it later becomes necessary or must be willing to introduce new brands or sub-brands to capture product positions that would be difficult to attain with existing meaning-laden brand names. Nevertheless, such marketing maneuvers could be a long and expensive process." For instance, Procter & Gamble (P&G) marketers created the suggestive Chinese brand name of "Soft Smooth 飘柔" to introduce

Rejoice, its innovative 2-in-1 shampoo and conditioner product, to Hong Kong and mainland China. The ability to conveniently obtain soft and smooth hair was a key benefit for consumers that used this 2-in-1 product, and Rejoice achieved market share leadership within one year of its launch. However, in subsequent years, P&G could not easily add other new hair care products under the Rejoice brand name. In particular, a large group of consumers wanted "healthy and shiny" hair, and these consumers preferred to use shampoo and conditioner in a stepwise fashion. On the other hand, the key benefit of Rejoice was the convenience of achieving soft and smooth hair through the use of one bottle of a 2-in-1 shampoo and conditioner product. Furthermore, the Chinese brand name for Rejoice suggested its "Soft Smooth" effects. As a result, P&G could not effectively reposition Rejoice to offer other hair care benefits or use the Rejoice brand to introduce profitable hair styling products to "fix" hair. Instead, P&G had to create another new brand, Pantene, and heavily invest in building Pantene's brand image and its ability to produce "healthy and shiny" hair. The Chinese name for Pantene, 潘婷, was non-suggestive, and was the Mandarin phonetic translation of Pantene.

1.3. *One name or two names?*

Could we launch a new product with two names at the same time, a suggestive sub-brand name and a suggestive parent brand name? Is this approach a better branding strategy for practitioners than committing time and resources to reposition a brand later? A suggestive sub-brand name communicates the new product's features and benefits, whereas a suggestive parent brand name allows marketers to add other new products with other sub-brand names in the future. If a dual branding strategy with two names works for a new product launch, the marketer is then able to build the business in three strategic steps: first, launch and build the sub-brand to a critical mass by focusing on the key attributes and benefits of the sub-brand; second, communicate the overall umbrella benefit of the parent brand; and third, introduce other line extensions with other sub-brand names and continue to build scale for the parent brand.

In fact, marketers in the Coca-Cola Company innovatively used two brand names simultaneously for the successful launch of the Minute Maid Orange Pulp juice drink in China in 2004. This new product launch created by marketers in China was the winner of the Coca-Cola Company's best new product launch in the second year of its launch. The extraordinary success of Minute Maid Orange Pulp also drove strong performance generally for the Coca-Cola Company in China (2007 company annual report, page 33). Minute Maid Orange Pulp also grew into the Coca-Cola Company's 14th brand to achieve annual retail sales of more than US $1 billion (2010 company annual report, p. 2). This brand was also the Coca-Cola Company's first billion brand launched from an emerging nation — China (2010 company annual report, p. 3).

The organization of this paper is as follows. First, we identify the key lessons that were learned from the successful Minute Maid launch case. We subsequently provide insights, offer recommendations, and report research results. We conclude the paper by highlighting the study's limitations and recommending future research directions.

2. Dual Branding for a Successful New Product Launch — The Case of Minute Maid in China

Marketers at Coca-Cola Company applied innovative thinking to the launch of the Minute Maid brand in China. In 2003, the non-alcoholic ready-to-drink beverage market in China was large and growing. Among non-carbonated ready-to-drink beverages, tea, juice, dairy and water had higher than average growth rates. In 2003, the Coca-Cola Company already had market share leadership in the carbonated beverage category with four brands — Coke, Sprite, Fanta and Smart. Therefore, a pragmatic concern for marketers at the Coca-Cola Company in China was the question of how many brands to launch for the company to achieve a leadership position in the non-carbonated beverage category.

Instead of creating several brands for the juice category, the marketers of Minute Maid chose to use two names, a sub-brand name and a parent brand name, to introduce the first new product. The key marketing challenge was to ensure the success of the first new product. Thus, what was the first new product and what was the best Chinese name for it and for Minute Maid? What was the roadmap in building Minute Maid with a sub-brand name and a parent brand name without creating confusion in consumer communications?

The first new product was a juice drink with a juice content of 10%. The price of the beverage was less than 100% juice brands. Although there was a market for pure 100% juice in the metro markets of Beijing, Shanghai and Guangzhou, 10% juice drinks were the biggest segment in the category for the entire country. A 100% juice would be too expensive for marketers to be able to reach the mass market. When the juice content is 10%, the Chinese government allowed it to be classified as a "juice drink." The cost of 10% juice also enabled marketers to set the sales price at a level similar to that of other juice drink brands, teas and other non-carbonated beverages. However, a special, yet quite simple ingredient — orange pulp — was required for the brand to stand out in the juice drink crowd and to achieve profits in this low-margin market (Patton 2007).

Researchers at the Coca-Cola Company's innovation center in Shanghai conceived of a juice drink with added pieces of orange pulp, a unique proposition that gave the brand a real point of differentiation in the crowded Chinese juice market (Patton 2007). Replicating the Minute Maid Orange Pulp texture was not easy. It would take competitors a long time to create the right texture. The mixing speed in the production tank could not be too fast, or the pulp would be destroyed, nor could it be too slow (Patton 2007). Because the orange pulp was such an important ingredient and proposition for the new product, the marketers of Minute Maid also challenged the traditional approach of launching the product under one brand name. Instead, there were two names — the sub-brand name, "Guo Li Cheng 果粒橙", and the parent brand name, "Mei Zhi Yuan 美汁源." "Guo Li Cheng 果粒橙" was a sub-brand name in Mandarin and meant "Fruit Pulp Orange." This name was suggestive of the key features and benefits of the new product, the presence of pulp in orange juice. "Mei Zhi Yuan 美汁源" was the brand name in Mandarin for Minute Maid and meant "Good Juice Source." This name was also suggestive and positioned Minute Maid as a juice-based wellness parent brand.

Although the Coca-Cola Company had an excellent distribution system with its bottling network, the marketing expenditures for any new product required business justification. Practitioners at the Coca-Cola Company had to convince bottlers to launch the new product in their bottling territories with product concept research findings, new product financials and, preferably, successful lead market results. The launch of a juice drink with 10% pulp with two names in China was innovative, and there was no precedent from other countries for practitioners to present to bottlers in China. In fact, not all of the bottlers launched the new product in the first year of the launch, 2004. Only four out of 30 bottlers launched Minute Maid Orange Pulp in April 2004. The bottlers only allocated the media weight that was recommended by professional media agency for a new product launch. Minute Maid Orange Pulp was only one of the many new products/brands for bottlers in China. In a franchising system, the bottlers (franchisees) did not have to agree with the Coca-Cola Company (franchisor) about which products to launch or how much to spend on advertising. In practice, the Coca-Cola Company could not force bottlers to spend enormous amounts for advertising over and above what a professional media agency would recommend. Given all of these challenges, the practitioners must ensure the success of the first new product, "Fruit Pulp Orange" by "Good Juice Source."

Therefore, the marketers of Minute Maid prioritized their marketing efforts in communicating the "Fruit Pulp Orange" by "Good Juice Source" in the first year of the product launch in 2004. The marketers wanted consumers to remember and recall the unique benefits and features of the new product, the fruit pulp. Hence, they put "Fruit Pulp Orange" in a bigger font size than "Good Juice Source" on the packaging label. They created a proprietary bottle design with a pulp orange shape in the upper part of the bottle. In television advertising, they communicated only "Fruit Pulp Orange" and did not mention "Good Juice Source." Although the advertising law in China did not allow advertisers to mention competitive brands, the marketers of Minute Maid ingeniously created a competitive message with the sub-brand name of "Fruit Pulp Orange" as follows: Not all juice drinks were the same; "Fruit Pulp Orange" uniquely contained real fruit pulp that felt great in your mouth. This message clearly communicated the similarity (juice drink) and the difference (the fruit pulp).

After 12 months in the first four leading markets in China — Shanghai, Hangzhou, Nanjing and Xian — Minute Maid achieved the number one or two position in ACNielsen market share in each of these four markets (Patton 2007). As a result, all of the other bottlers wanted to launch Minute Maid in 2005. However, in the same year, a competitive Taiwanese brand, Kang Shi Fu, finally figured out how to produce a juice drink with pulp. In the first few months of Kang Shi Fu's launch of its juice drink with pulp, Minute Maid started new advertising and integrated marketing communications at retail stores with a new message : Not all juice drinks with pulp were the same, "Fruit Pulp Orange" from "Good Juice Source" had softly extracted sunny pulp. In other words, the marketers at Minute Maid started to communicate the source and goodness of the pulp from "Good Juice Source", Minute Maid. The point of reference was juice drink with pulp, and the point of difference was the "Good Juice Source's pulp."

In 2007, Minute Maid Orange Pulp's unit case volume grew more than 60% in China and was the number one juice drink brand in the key metropolitan markets (Company 2007 annual report, page 20). In 2008, the Coca-Cola Company introduced Minute Maid Orange Pulp to five new markets outside of China, and the unit case volume for the brand increased more than 40 percent in China (Company 2008 annual report, page 24). Globally, the Coca-Cola Company was the market leader in juices and juice drinks (Company 2008 annual report, p. 5).

In 2010, after successfully building scale and achieving a leadership share in the juice category, the Coca-Cola Company used Minute Maid, "Good Juice Source", as the parent brand and launched another sub-brand, "Guo Li Nai You 果粒奶优", to enter the smoothie (juice plus dairy) category in China. "Guo Li Nai You 果粒奶优" was a sub-brand name in Mandarin and meant "Fruit Pulp Premium Milk." Because the marketers had already established a strong parent brand in Minute Maid, the marketing spending required to launch "Guo Li Nai You" by Minute Maid was less than it would have been to launch the product with a completely new brand name. Displaying all Minute Maid products on the shelf in a supermarket was also more eye-catching than displaying multiple juice drink brands. A new sub-brand product from an established parent brand could also increase trade confidence and consumer interest in trying the new product. Thus, dual branding strategy could be one strategy to the point raised by Tauber (1981), "launching a new product/brand is time consuming and needs a big budget to create awareness to promote a product's benefits."

3. Insights, Recommendations, Research Results

In this section, we offer insights, recommendation and research results pertinent to the question of Keller and Lehmann (2006, p. 749),

"For new-to-the-world products, what should be the relative empha-sis on building the brand versus establishing and growing the cat-egory?" Our answer is to use a sub-brand name for the product's benefit and a parent brand name for the category's benefit.

A suggestive sub-brand name conveys relevant attribute or benefit information and may offer two important benefits (Keller *et al.* 1998). First, even in the absence of any marketing activities, the semantic meaning of a suggestive sub-brand name should enable consumers to infer certain attributes or benefits. Second, the suggestiveness of a sub-brand name should facilitate marketing communication efforts designed to link corresponding product attributes or benefits to the sub-brand.

For a new product launch to be successful, marketers must ensure that consumers are aware of the product's benefits that are different from anything that is currently available to consumers from other competing brands. Marketers also want to highlight the benefits, the attributes and the reasons why consumers should try the new product of a sub-brand and switch from their existing brands. Furthermore, such differences should be meaningful to consumers and appeal to a large enough consumer segment so that the new product has a large enough scale, rather than being too much of a niche product. If mar-keters are able to successfully build the business of the first sub-brand by the parent brand to be of a large enough scale, the marketers may then launch other sub-brands under the same parent brand in the future. Hence, the parent brand name should ideally have a broad enough meaning to allow marketers to add new sub-brands in the future in the same category or related categories. The sub-brand name should be memorable to consumers so that the marketers are able to build sub-brand awareness and also remind consumers about the benefits and attributes of the new sub-brand to entice them to try the product.

Hence, marketers will need a sub-brand name that is suggestive of the key benefits and attributes of the new product and a parent brand name that is suggestive of the category's benefits. Dual branding strategy may be one answer to the question of Keller and Lehmann (2006, p. 749): "What should be built into a pioneer brand to retard future competition?" By investing in the sub-brand name of "Fruit Pulp Orange" during the first two years of the product's launch, the marketers of Minute Maid successfully owned "pulp" and retarded future competitive entry. By pairing the sub-brand name with the parent brand name on the packaging label and in store communications, marketers were able to gradually increase the brand awareness of the parent brand among the consumers of all of the products in the category and thereby own the category benefit of juice-based wellness.

In 2009, China's Ministry of Commerce rejected Coca-Cola's acquisition of Hui Yuan, a market leader in the 100% juice market segment of China. If this acquisition had been successful and if the Coca-Cola Company had continued to use a dual branding strategy for Minute Maid, Coca-Cola marketers could have used Hui Yuan as a sub-brand of the Minute Maid parent brand. In this scenario, the Chinese name for Minute Maid, "Mei Zhi Yuan" (which literally translates as "good juice source") would have provided positive connotations for "Hui Yuan." Furthermore, the second Chinese character for "Hui Yuan" and the third Chinese character for "Mei Zhi Yuan" are the same; this character means "source" in English. Thus, marketers could join the Minute Maid and Hui Yuan brand names if Coca-Cola's acquisition of Hui Yuan eventually succeeds.

A dual branding strategy is an important strategic choice for Chief Marketing Officers to consider. It is much more difficult to merge two companies and two brands than to add a sub-brand under a successful parent brand. If marketers consistently introduce new products as sub-brands and build the parent brand into a large mega-brand, then these marketers may be able to successfully introduce brands that are acquired from different companies as sub-brands of the acquiring company's mega-brand.

Although the Minute Maid case provides useful insights, practitioners may nevertheless want to consider more actionable advice on whether using two suggestive names is better than other naming alternatives in a dual branding strategy. Therefore, we conducted research by following the suggestion of Dolan (1992). We used a concept test to quantitatively measure consumers' reactions to different product/brand concepts and screened multiple concepts to identify the best one. In terms of product categories, we followed Keller and Aaker (1992) and chose foods that could be eaten as snacks because respondents are expected to have purchase and usage experience. For the Chinese parent brand names of the experiment, we followed the approach of Zhang and Schmitt (2001, p. 317), using fictitious names to minimize any familiarity and prior knowledge factors. The Chinese stimulus names are presented with Chinese characters in the experiments. We used the same procedure as Zhang and Schmitt (2001, p. 318), informing all of the respondents that the study involved brand names and that they would be given brand names that might be used for actual products in the future and that might appear on product packaging and promotional materials. We also emphasized the Chinese name in larger, bold typeface (Zhang and Schmitt 2001, p. 318).

For the new product concept in English, please refer to Appendix I. There are five product concepts (Table 1) for the different branding strategies. We have developed two suggestive sub-brand names for the branding strategy of using a suggestive sub-brand name and a suggestive parent brand name. For the fourth product concept, we tested the sub-brand name of "potato zero chip" (马"零"薯). For the fifth product concept, we tested the sub-brand name of "zero potato chip" ("零"薯片). By testing two suggestive sub-brand names, instead of only one, we were able to obtain more empirical support that the research finding is not due to the uniqueness of one particular suggestive sub-brand name.

Table 1. Five product concepts

Concept	One	Two	Three	Four	Five
Number of names	Two names	Two names	Two names	One name	One name
Parent brand name	Suggestive	Non-suggestive	Suggestive	Suggestive	Non-suggestive
Sub-brand name	Suggestive	Suggestive	Suggestive		
Parent brand name — English	Xiang Su	Ke Li	Xiang Su	Potato "zero" chip	Ke Li
Parent brand name — Chinese	香酥	克立	香酥	马"零"薯	克立
Sub-brand name — English	Potato "zero" chip	Potato "zero" chip	"Zero" potato chip		
Sub-brand name — Chinese	马"零"薯	马"零"薯	"零"薯片		

A leading global research agency conducted the research field-work in Shanghai, China and provided statistical significance tests at the 95% confidence level. The researchers conducted 500 online interviews and randomly assigned respondents to one of the five concepts. The key research results are summarized as follows. First, using one suggestive brand name will lead to significantly higher purchase intent and overall liking scores in product concept tests than using one non-suggestive brand name. Second, using two suggestive names will lead to significantly higher purchase intent and overall liking scores in product concept tests than using one non-suggestive brand name. Third, using two suggestive names will lead to significantly higher purchase intent and overall liking scores in product concept tests than using a suggestive sub-brand name and a non-suggestive parent brand name.

4. Conclusions, Limitations and Future Research Directions

When marketers decide to use only one brand name to launch a new product, choosing a suggestive brand name will lead to higher purchase intent and overall liking scores in product concept tests than using a non-suggestive brand name. If marketers use a dual branding strategy, they should use two suggestive names. A dual branding strategy allows marketers to use the parent brand name to launch other products in the future without having to reposition the brand. If P&G marketers in the 1980s had considered dual brand strategy, they might not have launched four shampoo brands in China, namely, Rejoice, Head & Shoulders, Pantene and Vidal Sassoon. Because "Rejoice" in Chinese meant "soft and smooth", Rejoice could not offer hair styling products to "fix" hair. P&G had to invest a huge marketing budget to build a new brand, Pantene, (with non-suggestive brand name) to offer shampoo, conditioner and hair styling products.

However, we do not recommend that marketers simply choose a dual branding strategy for all of their new products. There exist situations in which marketers must create different brands and brand images to appeal to distinct groups of target consumers. A sports drink brand for an individual achiever may not be appropriate for consumers who like to socialize with their friends through leisure sports. In China, for example, PepsiCo positioned Gatorade as a sports drink for athletes and other consumers who played sports seriously and sought greater athletic performance. By contrast, Danone positioned Mizone as a flavored water drink that contained added vitamins and minerals and was designed for most consumers to quench their thirst after engaging in leisurely exercise activities with their friends. The market share of Mizone flavored water was much higher than the market share of Gatorade sports drink because Mizone flavored water had a larger target demographic segment and projected a brand image that was more relevant to the majority of consumers. Mizone flavored water and Gatorade sports drink are different products with different brand images and appeal to different consumers groups. Although Danone had used Mizone as the brand to introduce another new product, Mizone sports drink, to compete with Gatorade, the Mizone sports drink had very low market share and was not successful.

There are also other limitations of this study. The Minute Maid success may only be applicable to fast-moving consumer goods. The research conducted for potato chips is also within a fast-moving consumer goods category. Will the findings of this research be applicable to slow-moving industrial goods when buyers place greater importance on a product's functional attributes? Practitioners for slow-moving industrial goods should consider using dual branding strategy and report their findings.

Another limitation of this research is the use of the Chinese language. Will there be similar results when the brand names are in English, Japanese, or other languages? One key difference for naming in Chinese and in English is the sequencing of the group and the individual. The Chinese put their names in the order of family name and then the given name. Therefore, the Chinese call their prime minister WEN Jiao Bao, rather than Jiao Bao WEN. WEN is the family name. Jiao Bao is the given name. Conversely, Americans put their given names or first names before the family name. Thus, for Minute Maid, the Chinese call it "Good Juice Source, Fruit Pulp Orange" rather than "Fruit Pulp Orange by Good Juice Source." Researchers may want to investigate whether the differences between the Chinese and Americans in naming conventions or preference will affect their reactions to the sequencing of "sub-brand" and "parent brand."

In practice, it is difficult for marketers to create a suggestive name and legally register the name because names that may be registered are unique and cannot be too generic. Thus, marketers have to explain to the company lawyer that as long as the parent brand name can be registered legally, there is enough protection for a brand. Why must sub-brand names be registered? In the case of Minute Maid, although the competitor, Kang Shi Fu, may also launch and name the product "Fruit Pulp Orange", consumers may nevertheless choose the "Fruit Pulp Orange" by "Good Juice Source", that is, Minute Maid. Marketers may also create a unique font type for "Fruit Pulp Orange" and register the font type to help differentiation. A good suggestive name for a product feature is difficult to create, and marketers should not simply give up the name because it cannot be legally registered.

Marketers may also learn from Apple, which has launched products with the names of iPod, iPhone and iPad. While these three products are different, all of them have "i" at the beginning of their names. All of these products also have similar looks and feels in terms of design, user friendly interface, and the unique iTunes software from Apple. One sees each name as having two parts, "i" and "Pod" for iPod, "i" and "Phone" for iPhone, and "i" and "Pad" for iPad. Both parts are quite suggestive. The key advantage of this naming approach by Apple is that it enables practitioners to create one "suggestive" name with two suggestive parts to allow for registration if the name has not been previously conceived of and registered by another company. Thus, Apple may register iPod, iPhone and iPad. Although Apple must pay a huge sum of money, US $60 million, to another company in mainland China in 2012 to buy the iPad trademark for use in mainland China, iPad is a trademark that may be legally registered.

The effect of the company name probably also affects the success of a new product with a suggestive sub-brand brand name and a suggestive parent brand name. Using the example of Minute Maid again, what would happen to the product concept test scores with and without mention of the Coca-Cola Company's name in the product concept? Although the advertising of Minute Maid in China did not mention that it was a product of the Coca-Cola Company, on the back label of the Minute Maid Orange Pulp juice drink, there was a small line that indicated that it was manufactured and produced by the Coca-Cola Company.

If mentioning the company name was not useful for enhancing the image of a new product, marketers should skip it. For example, after P&G acquired a high-end cosmetic company, SK-II, in the early 1990s, P&G did not market SK-II as a brand under P&G's company name. Finally, if the founder of a company launches a new product for a new company, should the company name be suggestive or non-suggestive? Should the name of the company be broad enough, based on "in which business the company wants to be?" Alternatively, should the founder focus on ensuring the success of the first new product by the company, and change the company name later when there is a business requirement to do so? For example, Apple could change its company name from "Apple computer" to "Apple Inc." to expand its business definition.

We hope that this paper inspires practitioners to rethink the branding process when they launch new products. We close this paper with the Chinese saying for parents who are naming their newborn babies: "Do not worry about the inborn heritage of your baby, worry about the consequence of giving your baby a bad name." Parents may give their baby a Chinese name that means "work hard", and the child may try to meet the expectations of the parents by "working hard" rather than "working smart." Every newborn baby has a given name and a family name. Should a new product have a sub-brand name and a parent brand name?

References

Coca-Cola Company Annual Reports (2007, 2008, 2010). Retrieved July 29, 2012, from http://www.thecoca-colacompany.com/investors/annu al_other_reports.html

Dolan, R. J. (1992). Concept Testing. *Harvard Business School*, 9-590-063, Rev. 3/23/92.

Keller, K. L. and Aaker, D. A. (1992). The effects of sequential introduction of brand extensions. *Journal of Marketing Research*, 24(1), 35–50.

Keller, K. L. and Lehmann, D. R. (2006). Brands and branding: research findings and future priorities. *Marketing Science*, 25(6), 740–759.

Keller, K. L., Heckler, S. E. and Houston, M. J. (1998). The effects of brand name suggestiveness on advertising recall. *Journal of Marketing*, 62 (1), 48–57.

Patton, D. (2007). The Just-Drinks Interview — Howard Lam, Coca-Cola China, Retrieved May 13, 2012, from http://www.just-drinks.com/ interview/the-just-drinks-interview-howard-lam-coca-cola-china_id905 88.aspx.
Tauber, E. M. (1981). Brand franchise extensions: new products benefit from existing brand names. *Business Horizons*, 24(2), 36–41.
Zhang, S. and Schmitt, B. H. (2001). Creating local brands in multilingual international markets. *Journal of Marketing Research*, 38(3), 313–325.

Appendix I — New product concept in English

After working for a long time, you need some rest.

The new potato chip is crispy and delicious, but it does not contain any fat and salt (0% fat, 0% salt).

It is produced by a patented baking process. Without adding any oil, it nevertheless has a crispy texture. It also specially added minerals that are essential for the human body and give it a delicious, slightly salty taste.

Try the new [branding option] now.
Company: an international company.
Brand: [Branding option]
Sub-brand: [Branding option]
Product: Potato Chips
Weight: 50 g
Price: RMB3

Appendix 4: Programming in R

1. Installation

R is a free software for different computer operating systems.

To download it, please visit the following website. https://www.r-project.org.

Then, choose the latest link under Getting Started on the home page to "Download R", and follow the steps to install it into your computer.

After you have installed R, you can start the R console, and see the following screens.

You can start using it to do simple operations.

You can also install the R Studio so that you can more easily write, modify, and execute R programs in an environment.

To download R Studio, please visit the following websites: http://RStudio.com or https://posit.co/.

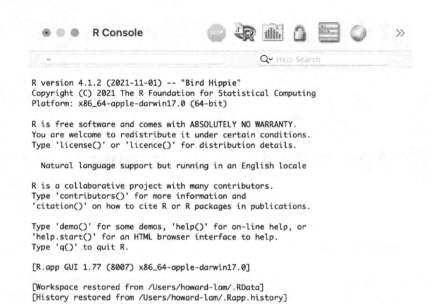

Figure A4.1.   R-console-screen.

2.   R Console

After you have downloaded R from the website, https://www.
r-project.org, installed and run it from your computer, you will see
the R Console.

While you are at the R Console, you will see the following sign
which is an R prompt.

>

That is, R is ready to take your command.

You can say hello to the world by typing:

```
print("Hello World")
[1]  "Hello World"
```

If you want to get help on a topic such as **mean**, you can type:

```
help(mean)
```

This will open up a menu for you to read more information about `mean`.

We can treat R-console as a calculator, too. To calculate the sum of two numbers, you can type

```
8+2
[1] 10
```

You can also use print to tell R that you want it to print the result for you to see. When we use RStudio, we have to use **print** to specifically tell R to print out the result. Without **print** in RStudio, you will not get any output.

```
print(8+2)
[1] 10
```

```
print((8+2)*3)
[1] 30
```

The [1] from R tells you that you are going to read the "first" term [1] in this line. If there is another line, R will give another number for the number of terms. For example, if you type the following, you will get the second line with [11] and the third line with [21], because the first "hello" is the eleventh term in line 2, and the 21st term in line 3.

```
c(rep("hello",30))
```

```
 [1] "hello" "hello" "hello" "hello" "hello" "hello" "hello" "hello" "hello" "hello"
[11] "hello" "hello" "hello" "hello" "hello" "hello" "hello" "hello" "hello" "hello"
[21] "hello" "hello" "hello" "hello" "hello" "hello" "hello" "hello" "hello" "hello"
```

Figure A4.2. Output of `c(rep("hello",30))`.

rep stands for replicates. **c** is a function which combines its arguments.

When you see the R prompt >, you can press the up arrow on your keyboard to get what you have typed previously.

At the R Console, if you want to know what directory (or folder) you are in now, you can type **getwd()** which means get working directory.

```
getwd()
[1] "/Users/pongyuenlam"
```

You can set working directory to the one that you like as follows if you have created such working directories before.

You can create such a directory by using your computer system's method (no need to use R).

```
setwd("/Users/pongyuenlam/Documents/R-folder")
```

If you want to list files in the current directory, type

```
list.files()
```

3. RStudio (Hello World, Comment, **readline**)

Although we can continue working on the R console, it is better to use RStudio because it allows us to easily create, read, modify, execute, and save our R program files.

After you have downloaded R Studio from http://RStudio.com or https://posit.co/, installed and run it from your computer, you will see the R Studio Interface. Please install R Console before you install R Studio. It is convenient in R Studio to save the R-script file (that is, the R program) and other data files together into a folder, the working directory.

We can say hello to the world by typing:

```
print("Hello World")
[1] "Hello World"
```

You can also write a program to perform calculations.

```
x<-1
y<-2
print(x+y)
[1] 3
```

This program assigns a value of 1 to x, a value of 2 to y, adds them up and prints the sum.

To let RStudio know the folder for the different programs and data files for your project, choose "file" at the top menu bar, then "Open Project." You can then choose the folder in your computer.

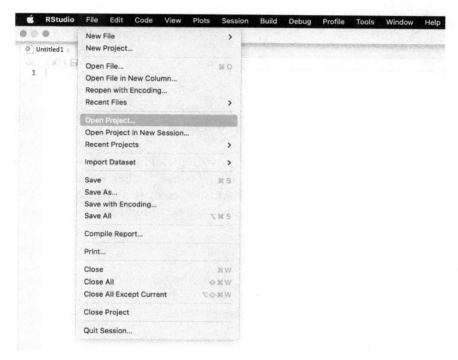

Figure A4.3. R-Studio-screen.

If you want to remind yourself or let other programmers know the meaning of a line, you can add a comment by putting a special symbol of # in a line. R will ignore what you put after # because R knows that it is for humans to read, not for computers to execute.

```
L<-7 # Assigns the value of 7 to variable L
W<-2 # Assigns the value of 2 to variable W
print(L*W) # Print the result of L multiplied by W
 (area of a rectangle)
[1] 14
```

We can make a program more general by allowing users to enter the value for L and W.

Please execute **Area1.R**

```
L<-readline()
W<-readline()
Area<-as.numeric(L)*as.numeric(W)
print(Area)
10
20
[1] 200
```

Listing 3-1-Area1.R

readline() allows us to enter anything (including characters) and so we have to tell R that we want to convert what we have entered (**10**) as numeric value. Then, R will not treat it as the string **"10"**.

We can also have a prompt message to remind users as shown in the following program.

Please execute **Area2.R**

```
L<-readline("Please enter the length ")
W<-readline("Please enter the width ")
Area<-as.numeric(L)*as.numeric(W)
print(Area)
Please enter the length 10
Please enter the width 20
[1] 200
```

Listing 3-2-Area2.py

4.   Arithmetic Operations

We can use operators $(+ - * /)$ for adding, subtracting, multiplying, and dividing two numbers. We can use $\wedge$ for raising to a power.

```
8+2
[1] 10
```

```
8-2
[1] 6
```

```
8*2
[1] 16
```

```
8/2
[1] 4
```

```
8^2
[1] 64
```

```
16^0.5
[1] 4
```

```
8+2*3
[1] 14
```

Because R will calculate 2*3 to be 6 first, and then perform the calculation of 8+6.

```
(8+2)*3
[1] 30
```

Because R will know that it has to calculate (8+2) to get 10 before 10 is multiplied by 3 to get 30.

5. Assignment Operations

We can assign value to a variable by typing <- with two keys in our keyboard.

These two keys are the < (less than sign) and the - (hyphen).

What you type are four keys X, <, - and 1 for the first line below.

```
X<-1
Y<-2
Z<-X+Y
print(Z)
[1] 3
```

<- is what R programming language has chosen to use as "an assign-
ment operator" to tell the computer that we want it to calculate the
value from the "right-hand side" and then assign to the variable in
the "left-hand side."

Please note that we are not dealing with algebra here. In algebra,
it is impossible that **X=X+1**. If we have initialized the value of **X** to
be 1, **X+1** is then equal to 2. So, 2 will be assigned to the variable in
the left-hand side, **X**.

```
X<-1
X<-X+1
print(X)
[1] 2
```

R treats capital letters and small letters differently. So, if you type
print(x), you will get an error, because R does not have anything
for **x**. R only knows that there is a variable **X** (not **x**).

Similarly, you can type the following:

```
X<-1
x<-2
print(x)
[1] 2
```

X has a value of 1.
x has a value of 2.
X and **x** are two different variables.

If we want to manipulate multiple values, we can set up a vector
and name it as **x**.

```
x<-c(1,3,5,7,9)
```

x is simply a series of numbers.
c means that we want to combine its arguments.

To view the content of **x**:

```
print(x)
[1] 1 3 5 7 9
```

To view the structure of x, and find out that it is numeric with five values.

```
str(x)
num [1:5] 1 3 5 7 9
```

To view the content of a particular element in x,

```
print(x[3])
[1] 5
```

We can have operations on vector:

```
y<-c(x+1)
print(y)
[1] 2 4 6 8 10

y<-c(x+10)
print(y)
[1] 11 13 15 17 19

y<-c(x,10,11,12,x)
print(y)
[1]  1  3  5  7  9 10 11 12  1  3  5  7  9
```

6. Functions

First, let's take a simple data set for us to use and perform simple calculations by hand.

Suppose we have 12 people with heights (in cm) as follows, from low to high.

120, 130, 140, 150, 160, 170, 180, 190, 200, 210, 220, 230.

The median is the average of the 6th and 7th numbers when we have 12 numbers. So, it is equal to $(170 + 180)/2 = 175$.

The first quantile separates 25% of the data from the remaining 75% of data. So, it is in the $0.25 (n + 1) = 0.25 \times 13 = 3.25$ ordered position. Its value is then $= 140 + 0.25 (150 - 140) = 142.5$.

The third quantile separates 75% of the data from the remaining 25% of data. So, it is in the 0.75 (n + 1) = 0.75 × 13 = 9.75 ordered position. Its value is then = 200 + 0.75 (210 − 200) = 207.5.

Please execute **Functions.R**

```
data<-c(120,130,140,150,160,170,180,190,200,210,220,230)
print(quantile(data,type=6))
0%        25%      50%     75%       100%
120.0     142.5    175.0   207.5     230.0
```

Listing 6-1-Functions.py

```
data<-c(120,130,140,150,160,170,180,190,200,210,220,230)
print(summary(data,quantitle.type=6))
  Min.    1st Qu.   Median    Mean    3rd Qu.    Max.
  120.0   147.5     175.0     175.0   202.5      230.0
```

As there are different methods to calculate quantile, we have to specify that **type=6** for us to use the above method.

```
x<-c(1,3,5,7,9)
print(range(x))
[1] 1 9

print(length(x))
[1] 5
```

Because **x** has five values, 1, 3, 5, 7, 9.

```
min(x)
[1] 1
```

The minimum value of the five values of **x** is 1.

```
max(x)
[1] 9
```

The maximum value of the five values of **x** is 9.

```
sum(x)
[1] 25
```

Because $1 + 3 + 5 + 7 + 9 = 25$

```
mean(x)
[1] 5
```

Because $25/5 = 5$

```
y<-((x-mean(x))^2)
print(x)
print(y)
[1] 1 3 5 7 9
[1] 16 4 0 4 16
```

Each value in **y** is the square of (x-mean(s)). For example, 16 is equal to $(1 - 5)^{\wedge}2$.

```
print(sum(y))
[1] 40
```

```
print(sum(y)/(length(x)-1))
[1] 10
```

```
print(var(x))
[1] 10
```

var stands for variance

```
print(sd(x))
[1] 3.162278
```

sd stands for standard deviation = square root of variance. Because $10^{\wedge}0.5 = 3.162278$

```
print(prod(x))
[1] 945
```

Because $1 \times 3 \times 5 \times 7 \times 9 = 945$

```
print(sort(x, decreasing=TRUE))
[1] 9 7 5 3 1
```

```
print(sort(x, decreasing=FALSE))
[1] 1 3 5 7 9
```

7. Library

"All R functions and data sets are stores in packages. Only when a package is loaded is its content available",

Source: *An Introduction to R*, https://cran.r-project.org/doc/manuals/r-release/R-intro.html#Packages.
For example, if we want to load **wordcloud**, we can type

```
library(wordcloud)
```

When we execute it, RStudio will ask us whether we want to install the package if it has not been installed before.
To see which packages are currently loaded, type

```
search()
```

8. Conditions

There are six relational operators for us to compare two variables.

< less than
> greater than
<= less than or equal to
>= greater than or equal to
== equal
! = Not equal

We can test the following program.

Relational-operator1.R

```
inx<-readline("Please enter a number ")
iny<-readline("Please enter a second number for comparison")
x<-as.numeric(inx) y<-as.numeric(iny)
if (x==y) print ("=")
if (x<=y) print("<=")
if (x>=y) print(">=")
if (x<y) print("<")
if (x>y) print(">")
if (x!=y) print("not equal")
```

Listing 8-1-Relational-operator1.R

We can also combine two conditions with the symbol | or &.

| means or.
& means and.

condition 1 or condition2
condition1 | condition2 is TRUE when we have:
condition1 is TRUE, condition1 is TRUE.
condition1 is TRUE, condition2 is FALSE.
condition1 is FALSE, condition2 is TRUE.

condition1 | condition2 is FALSE when we have:
condition1 is FALSE, condition2 is FALSE.

condition 1 and condition2
condition1 & condition2 is TRUE when we have:
condition1 is TRUE, condition1 is TRUE.

condition1 & condition2 is FALSE when we have:
condition1 is TRUE, condition2 is FALSE.
condition1 is FALSE, condition2 is TRUE.
condition1 is FALSE, condition2 is FALSE.

We can test the following program.

Relational-operator2.R

```
inx<-readline("Please enter x ")
iny<-readline("Please enter y ")
x<-as.numeric(inx)
y<-as.numeric(iny)
if ((x==1) | (x==2)) print ("x is equal to 1 or 2")
if ((x==1) & (y==1)) print ("x=1 and y=1")
```

Listing 8-2-Relational-operator2.R

For the following program, **Multiple-choices.R**, we can execute different blocks of statements within { }, depending on the choice of the user.

Multiple-choices.R

```
x<-readline("Please enter a choice A B C D ")
if (x=="A")
{
  print("You have chosen A")
} else
{
  print("You have not chosen A")
}

x<-readline("Please enter a choice A B C D ")
if (x=="A")
{
  print("You have chosen A")
} else if (x=="B")
{
  print("You have chosen B")
} else
{
  print("You have not chosen A or B")
}
```

Listing 8-3-Multiple-Choices.R

```
x<-readline("Please enter a choice A B C D ")
if (x=="A")
{
  print("You have chosen A")
} else if (x=="B")
{
  print("You have chosen B")
} else if (x=="C")
{
  print("You have chosen C")
} else
{
  print("You have not chosen A, B, C")
}
```

We usually will indent (i.e., put some spaces at the start of the line) under a condition to make it easier for us to read lines under different conditions.

9. Loop

If we want to print numbers 1–5, we can type **print** 5 times.

```
print(1)
print(2)
print(3)
print(4)
print(5)
[1] 1
[1] 2
[1] 3
[1] 4
[1] 5
```

We can also perform the above step 5 times if we use a do-loop.

Loop-do.R

```
for (i in 1:5)
  print(i)
[1] 1
[1] 2
[1] 3
[1] 4
[1] 5
```

Listing 9-1-Loop-do.R

If we execute the program, we will generate the above output.

i can also be of values 2–6.

```
for (i in 2:6)
  print(i)
[1] 2
[1] 3
[1] 4
[1] 5
[1] 6
```

i can also count down from 6–1.

```
for (i in 6:1)
  print(i)
[1] 6
[1] 5
[1] 4
[1] 3
[1] 2
[1] 1
```

We can use for-loop to calculate the sum of 1–3.

```
sum<-0
for (i in 1:3)
{
  sum<-sum+i
  print(sum)
}
[1] 1
[1] 3
[1] 6
```

We set **sum** equal to 0 before the for-loop.

When **i** is equal to 1, we calculate **sum** plus **i** as 0 plus 1 which is equal to 1. Then, we assign 1 to sum.

When **i** is equal to 2, we calculate **sum** plus **i** as 1 plus 2 which is equal to 3. Then, we assign 3 to sum.

When **i** is equal to 3, we calculate **sum** plus **i** as 3 plus 3 which is equal to 6. Then, we assign 6 to sum.

In this way, we can calculate the cumulative sum of 1+2+3.

Usually we will execute more than one line in a loop. So, we will use the open bracket symbol { and the close bracket symbol } to indicate the lines that we want to execute together.

In a for-loop, we need to specify a variable such as **i**.

If we use a while-loop, we can simply set a condition for the loop to be executed.

For example, we can set a variable such as **done** to be "N" (that is not done yet).

We can set variable **i** equal to 1 before we start running the while-loop.

While **done** is equal to "N", we will do the lines within the open bracket { and close bracket }.

Loop-while.R

```
done<-"N"
i<-1
while (done=="N")
{
  print(i)
  i<-i+1
  if (i>5) done="Y"
}
[1] 1
[1] 2
[1] 3
[1] 4
[1] 5
```

Listing 9-2-Loop-while.R

So, we will print the value of **i**.

Increase the value of **i** by 1 and assign it back to **i**.

In this case, we want to end the while-loop when **i** is greater than 5, because we only want to print 1 to 5.

To end the while-loop, we use if statement in the last line to check and change the value of variable **done** to another value which is not **N**. In the program, we have set **done** to **"Y"** which means Yes.

When **done** is equal to **"Y"**, the condition of **done** equal to **"N"** is **FALSE**. As a result, the while-loop will stop.

We can enhance the program to calculate the sum of 1 to 5

```
done<-"N"
i<-1
sum<-0
while (done=="N")
{
  sum<-sum+i
  print(sum)
  i<-i+1
  if (i>5) done="Y"
}
```

```
[1] 1
[1] 3
[1] 6
[1] 10
[1] 15
```

If we execute the program, we will get the sum of $1+2+3+4+5$ which is 15.

10. Read and Write File

We can use Excel to create a file, and then save it as a comma-separated values (CSV) file.

Suppose the content of Students.csv is as follows:

```
StudentID,Gender,Height,Weight
1,M,180,72
2,M,170,70
3,M,160,60
4,F,150,72
5,F,140,70
6,M,165,60
7,F,155,50
8,M,167,90
9,F,175,66
10,M,190,80
```

To read the above file into **s**, type

```
s <- read.csv("Students.csv")
```

To display the structure of **s**, type

```
str(s)
'data.frame':10 obs. of  4 variables:
$ StudentID: int  1 2 3 4 5 6 7 8 9 10
$ Gender   : chr  "M" "M" "M" "F" ...
$ Height   : int  180 170 160 150 140 165 155 167 175 190
$ Weight   : int  72 70 60 72 70 60 50 90 66 80
```

s is a data frame with each row for one observation and each column for one variable.

To display the dimension (the number of rows and the number of columns), type

```
dim(s)
[1] 10 4
```

To display the number of rows, type

```
nrow(s)
[1] 10
```

To display the number of columns, type

```
ncol(s)
[1] 4
```

To print the entire content, type

```
print(s)
      StudentID Gender Height Weight
1          1       M     180     72
2          2       M     170     70
3          3       M     160     60
4          4       F     150     72
5          5       F     140     70
6          6       M     165     60
7          7       F     155     50
8          8       M     167     90
9          9       F     175     66
10        10       M     190     80
```

To print the first 3 rows, type

```
print(s[1:3,])
     StudentID Gender Height Weight
1         1       M     180     72
2         2       M     170     70
3         3       M     160     60
```

To print the first six rows, type

```
print(head(s))
      StudentID Gender Height Weight
1             1      M    180     72
2             2      M    170     70
3             3      M    160     60
4             4      F    150     72
5             5      F    140     70
6             6      M    165     60
```

To print the last six rows, type

```
print(tail(s))
      StudentID Gender Height Weight
5             5      F    140     70
6             6      M    165     60
7             7      F    155     50
8             8      M    167     90
9             9      F    175     66
10           10      M    190     80
```

To know the variable names, type

```
names(s)
[1] "StudentID" "Gender"     "Height"      "Weight"
```

To know the name of the third column, type

```
names(s)[3]
[1] "Height"
```

To print the value at row 3 and column 2, type

```
s[3,2]
[1] "M"
```

To print row 3, type

```
s[3,]
      StudentID Gender Height Weight
3             3      M    160     60
```

To print column 2, type

```
s[,2]
[1] "M" "M" "M" "F" "F" "M" "F" "M" "F" "M"
```

To print column Height, type

```
s[,"Height"]
[1] 180 170 160 150 140 165 155 167 175 190
```

To print column Height, we can also type

```
s$Height
[1] 180 170 160 150 140 165 155 167 175 190
```

To print columns 2 to 4, type

```
s[,2:4]
   Gender Height Weight
1       M    180     72
2       M    170     70
3       M    160     60
4       F    150     72
5       F    140     70
6       M    165     60
7       F    155     50
8       M    167     90
9       F    175     66
10      M    190     80
```

To print columns 1, 3, and 4, type

```
s[,c(1,3,4)]
   StudentID Height Weight
1          1    180     72
2          2    170     70
3          3    160     60
4          4    150     72
5          5    140     70
6          6    165     60
7          7    155     50
8          8    167     90
```

```
9           9    175    66
10         10    190    80
```

c is a function which combines its arguments.
To print rows 1, 3, and 5, type

```
s[c(1,3,5),]
      StudentID Gender Height Weight
1          1       M    180     72
3          3       M    160     60
5          5       F    140     70
```

To print the summary of **s**, type

```
print(summary(s))
  StudentID        Gender            Height          Weight
 Min.   : 1.00  Length:10         Min.   :140.0  Min.   :50.0
 1st Qu.: 3.25  Class :character  1st Qu.:156.2  1st Qu.:61.5
 Median : 5.50  Mode  :character  Median :166.0  Median :70.0
 Mean   : 5.50                    Mean   :165.2  Mean   :69.0
 3rd Qu.: 7.75                    3rd Qu.:173.8  3rd Qu.:72.0
 Max.   :10.00                    Max.   :190.0  Max.   :90.0
```

To get the subset from **s** with male students, type

```
ms <- subset(s, Gender=="M")
print(ms)
   StudentID Gender Height Weight
1       1      M     180     72
2       2      M     170     70
3       3      M     160     60
6       6      M     165     60
8       8      M     167     90
10     10      M     190     80
```

To get the subset from **s** with female students.

```
fs <- subset(s, Gender=="F")
print(fs)
      StudentID Gender Height Weight
4          4       F    150     72
5          5       F    140     70
```

7	7	F	155	50
9	9	F	175	66

To get the subset from **s** with gender not equal to **"M"**.

```
fs2 <- subset(s, Gender!="M")
print(fs2)
     StudentID Gender Height Weight
4         4      F     150     72
5         5      F     140     70
7         7      F     155     50
9         9      F     175     66
```

To get the subset from **s** with height > 160.

```
hs <- subset(s, Height>160)
print(hs)
      StudentID Gender Height Weight
1          1      M      180     72
2          2      M      170     70
6          6      M      165     60
8          8      M      167     90
9          9      F      175     66
10        10      M      190     80
```

To create and write to a CSV file with row names, type

```
write.csv(hs,"height.csv")
```

The content of height.csv is as follows:

```
"","StudentID","Gender","Height","Weight"
"1",1,"M",180,72
"2",2,"M",170,70
"6",6,"M",165,60
"8",8,"M",167,90
"9",9,"F",175,66
"10",10,"M",190,80
```

To create and write to a CSV file without row names, type

```
write.csv(hs,"height2. csv", row.names = FALSE)
```

The content of height2.csv is as follows:

```
"StudentID","Gender","Height","Weight"
1,"M",180,72
2,"M",170,70
6,"M",165,60
8,"M",167,90
9,"F",175,66
10,"M",190,80
```

11.   Graphics-Bar Chart

Please execute program Bar-chart.R

For the following example, there are students from Marketing, Accounting, Finance, Management. We use **rep** (replicates) to generate a data frame, Students, with 4 students in Marketing, 6 in Accounting, 3 in Finance, 7 in Management.

```
Students<-c(rep('Marketing',4), rep('Accounting',6),
 rep('Finance',3), rep('Management',7))
print(Students)
[1] "Marketing"  "Marketing"  "Marketing"  "Marketing"
 "Accounting" "Accounting"
[7] "Accounting" "Accounting" "Accounting" "Accounting"
 "Finance"    "Finance"
[13] "Finance"    "Management" "Management" "Management"
 "Management" "Management"
[19] "Management" "Management"
```

Listing 11-1-Bar-chart.R

```
print(table(Students))
Accounting    Finance    Management    Marketing
     6            3            7            4
```

If we want to know the sum of these numbers, we can use **sum**.

```
print(sum(table(Students)))
[1] 20
```

To generate a Bar Chart, we can use the following line.

col means color.
xlab means x label.
ylab means y label.
ylim means y limit, the minimum value and maximum value of y.
main means the main title for the chart.

```
barplot(table(Students), col=c("purple", "red", "blue",
"yellow"), xlab="Major", ylab="Count", ylim=c(0,10),
main="Students by Major")
```

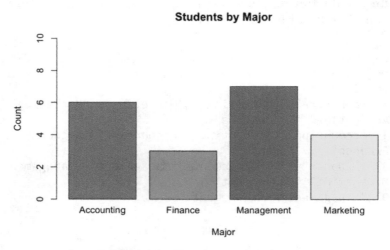

Figure A4.4. Bar chart, vertical.

To save the graph into your computer, you can click "Export," "Save as image," choose the path where you want it to be saved and click "Save."

You can do a Screen Capture from your computer.

For Apple, you can press three keys together: Shift-Command-4.

For Windows, you can press two keys together: Control+PrtScn.
PrtScn stands for Print Screen.

We can also add the function **sort** to the above statement.

```
barplot(sort(table(Students)), col=c("purple", 'red', "blue",
"yellow"), xlab="Major", ylab="Count", ylim=c(0,10),
main="Students by Major")
```

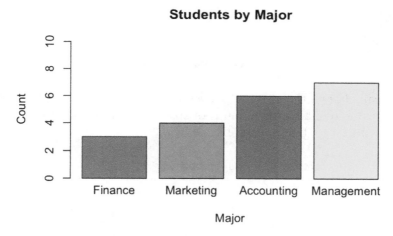

Figure A4.5. Bar chart, vertical sorted.

To create a bar chart horizontally, we can add **horiz=TRUE** as one of the arguments, and specify **legend.text=rownames(table (Students))**.

```
barplot(sort(table(Students)), horiz=TRUE, col = c('purple',
'red', 'blue', 'yellow', 'green'), xlab = 'Major', ylab='Count',
ylim=c(0,10), main='Students by
Major',legend.text=rownames(table(Students)),axisnames=FALSE)
```

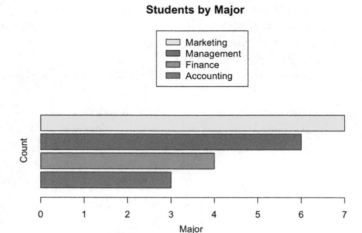

Figure A4.6.   Bar chart, horizontal.

We can change the spacing between the bars by adding **SPACE=0.5**. The value refers to the amount of space (as a fraction of the average bar width) left before each bar.

```
barplot(sort(table(Students)), space=0.5, horiz=TRUE, col =
c('purple', 'red', 'blue', 'yellow', 'green'), xlab = 'Major',
ylab='Count', ylim=c(0,10), main='Students by
Major',legend.text=rownames(table(Students)),axisnames=FALSE)
```

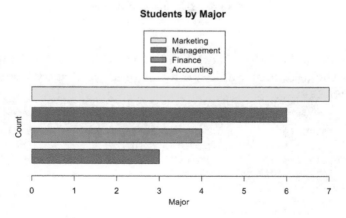

Figure A4.7.   Bar chart, horizontal spacing.

12.   Graphics-Pie Chart

Please execute program Pie-chart.R

For the following example, there are students from Marketing, Accounting, Finance, Management. We use **rep** (replicates) to generate a data frame, Students, with 4 students in Marketing, 6 in Accounting, 3 in Finance, 7 in Management.

```
Students<-c(rep("Marketing",4), rep("Accounting",6),
rep("Finance",3), rep("Management",7))
print(pie(table(Students)))
```

Listing 12-1-Pie-chart.R

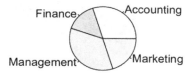

Figure A4.8.   Pie chart 1.

In general, we can have the following values and labels for a pie chart.

```
values<-c(3,5,6,9)
pielabels<-c("A","B","C","D")
pie(values,labels=pielabels, main="Pie Chart")
```

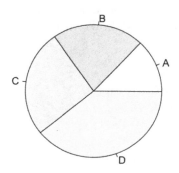

Figure A4.9.   Pie chart 2.

If we want to specify our own colors, we can add

```
col=c("purple","red",  "blue","yellow").
```

```
values<-c(3,5,6,9)
pielabels<-c("A","B","C","D")
pielabels<-paste(pielabels,values)
pie(values,labels=pielabels, col=c("purple","red",
"blue","yellow"), main="Pie Charts")
```

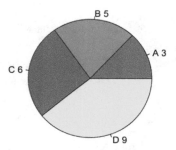

Figure A4.10.   Pie chart 3.

If we want to have % into the pie chart, we can calculate the sum of values, divide each value by the sum, round it up or down. Afterward, we can create the **pielabel** by combining the percentage calculated with the symbol **%** and then a separator (**sep**) which is empty. That is, two double quotes **""** as shown in the following.

```
values<-c(3,5,6,9)
pielabels<-c("A","B","C","D")
percentages<-round(values/sum(values)*100)
pielabels<-paste(pielabels,percentages)
pielabels<-paste(pielabels,"%",sep="")
pie(values,labels=pielabels,  col=c('purple', 'red',
'blue','yellow'),main="Pie Charts")
```

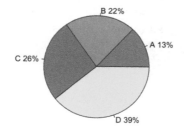

Figure A4.11.   Pie chart 4.

If we have a space between the two double quotes for **sep=" "**, we will get a space between the percentage calculated and the symbol %.

Instead of specifying the four colors or more colors if we have more values, we can use the function of rainbow to create colors automatically. We can also set **clockwise=TRUE** to get the following result of A being at the top of the chart, followed by B, C, and D in clockwise direction.

```
pie(values,labels=pielabels,
col=rainbow(length(pielabels)),clockwise=TRUE,
main="Pie Charts")
```

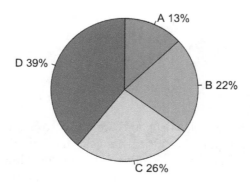

Figure A4.12.   Pie chart 5.

13.   Graphics-Plot

Please execute Program Plot1.R

If we want to have a scatterplot on **x** and **y**, we can simply enter the values of **x** and **y** as follows, and ask R to plot.

```
x<-c(1,2,3,4,5)
y<-c(2,4,6,8,20)
plot(x,y, xlab="label for x", ylab="label for y", main = "title")
```

Listing 13-1-Plot1.R

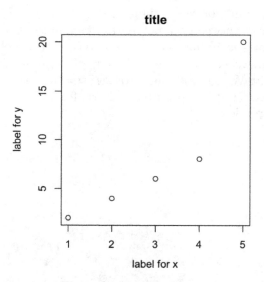

Figure A4.13.   Plot-1.

If we already have a data set and we want to use it, we can read it before we plot. Open the "Students.csv" file, where we can see that there are 10 students with StudentID, Gender, Height, and Weight. To read a csv file, we can use the **read.csv** function.

To plot the data of height versus weight, we can type:

```
plot(s$Height, s$Weight)
```

To set the label of the x-axis, the y-axis, and the title for the chart, we can use **xlab**, **ylab**, and **main**.

Please execute **Plot2.R**

```
s<-read.csv("Students.csv")
print(s)
plot(s$Height, s$Weight)
plot(s$Height, s$Weight, xlab="X-Height", ylab="Y-Weight",
main = "Height and Weight")
```

Listing 13-2-Plot2.R

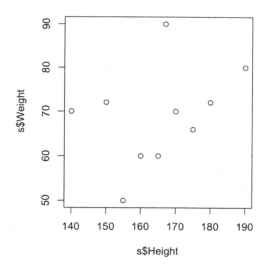

Figure A4.14.   Plot-2.

To get a histogram, we can use the **hist** function.

```
hist(s$Weight, xlab="Weight", ylab="Count", main = "Weight")
```

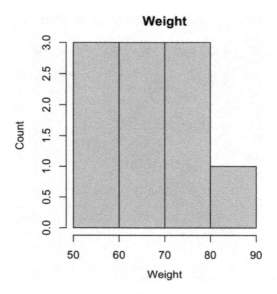

Figure A4.15.   Histogram.

14.   Graphics-Box Plot

First, let's have a simple data set for us to use and perform simple calculations by hand.

If we have 12 people in Hong Kong with heights (in cm) as follows, from low to high.

120, 130, 140, 150, 160, 170, 180, 190, 200, 210, 220, 230.

The median is the average of the 6th and 7th numbers when we have 12 numbers.

So, it is equal to $(170 + 180)/2 = 175$.

The first quantile separates 25% of the data from the remaining 75% of data.

So, it is in the $0.25(n + 1) = 0.25 \times 13 = 3.25$ ordered position.

Its value is then $= 140 + 0.25(150 - 140) = 142.5$.

The third quantile separates 75% of the data from the remaining 25% of data.

So, it is in the $0.75(n + 1) = 0.75 \times 13 = 9.75$ ordered position.

Its value is then $= 200 + 0.75(210 - 200) = 207.5$.

Please execute program **Box-Plot.R**

```
HK<-c(120, 130, 140, 150, 160, 170, 180, 190, 200, 210, 220, 230)
print(quantile(HK, type = 6))
   0%   25%   50%   75%  100%
120.0 142.5 175.0 207.5 230.0
```

Listing 14-1-Box-Plot.R

As there are different methods to calculate quantile, we have to specify that **type=6** for us to use the above method.

If we type **help("boxplot")**, we can know that it generates Box-and-Whisker Plot. It describes a data set with five key numbers: minimum, first quartile, median, third quartile, and the maximum.

Please execute **box-plot.R**

```
boxplot(HK, xlab='city', ylab='Height')
```

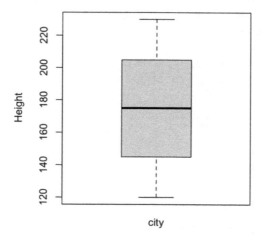

Figure A4.16.   Box plot 1 showing the heights of people in Hong Kong.

If we have data for other cities, we can plot them together.

```
SZ<-c(130,140,150,160)
SH<-c(150,160,170,180,190,200)
boxplot(HK, SZ, SH, xlab='city', ylab='Height')
```

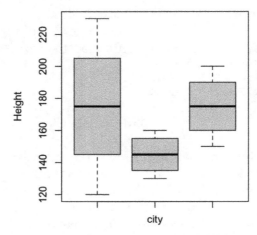

Figure A4.17.   Box plot 2 showing the heights of people in Hong Kong, Shenzhen, and Shanghai.

If we want to add a descriptor under each boxplot, we can add in **names=c(**"Hong Kong", "Shenzhen", "Shanghai"**)** into the following R line.

```
boxplot(HK, SZ, SH, xlab='Cities', ylab='Height',
names=c("Hong Kong", "Shenzhen", "Shanghai"))
```

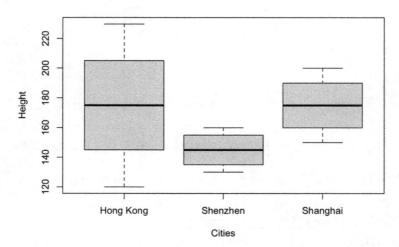

Figure A4.18.   Box plot 3 showing heights, with city names along the *x*-axis.

15. Graphics-ggplot

tidyverse is a collection of R packages.

Source: https://www.tidyverse.org/.

ggplot() can be used to declare the input data frame for a graphic and to specify the set of plot aesthetics.

Source: https://ggplot2.tidyverse.org/reference/ggplot.html.

Please install these packages if you have not done so before by typing the following two lines in R console.

```
install.packages("tidyverse")
install.packages("ggplot2")
```

For a data set of graphdata.csv as follows:

```
"","xdata","yval","time_series"
"1",1,2,"time_series1"
"2",2,4,"time_series1"
"3",3,6,"time_series1"
"4",4,8,"time_series1"
"5",5,10,"time_series1"
"6",1,11,"time_series2"
"7",2,12,"time_series2"
"8",3,13,"time_series2"
"9",4,14,"time_series2"
"10",5,15,"time_series2"
"11",1,13,"time_series3"
"12",2,15,"time_series3"
"13",3,17,"time_series3"
"14",4,19,"time_series3"
"15",5,20,"time_series3"
```

One common way to invoke **ggplot()** is to give a dataframe, and the aesthetics (**aes**) properties with a general form of **ggplot(df, aes(x, y, other aesthetics))**.

Please test graphdata.R

```
library(tidyverse)
library(ggplot2)
df<-read.csv("graphdata.csv")
print(ggplot(data = df, aes(x=xdata,
y=yval,group=time_series,color=time_series)) +
        geom_line() + geom_point() +
        ggtitle("Multiple lines with unique color"))
```

Listing 15-1-graphdata.R

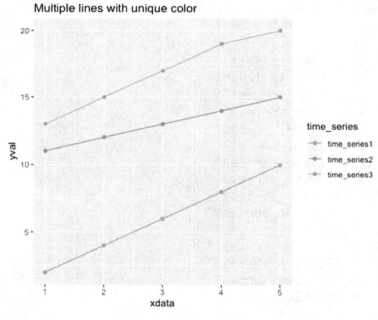

Figure A4.19.   ggplot 1.

If we only need to show a line without the point, we can put **geom_line()** only.

```
print(ggplot(data = df,
        aes(x=xdata,y=yval,
        group=time_series,color=time_series)) +
        geom_line() +
        ggtitle("Lines"))
```

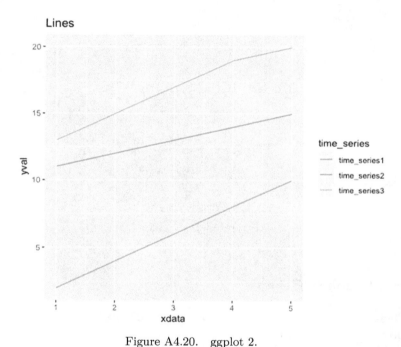

Figure A4.20.   ggplot 2.

If we only need to show points, we can put **geom_point()** only.

```
print(ggplot(data = df, aes(x=xdata,y=yval,
        group=time_series,color=time_series)) +
        geom_point() +
        ggtitle("Points"))
```

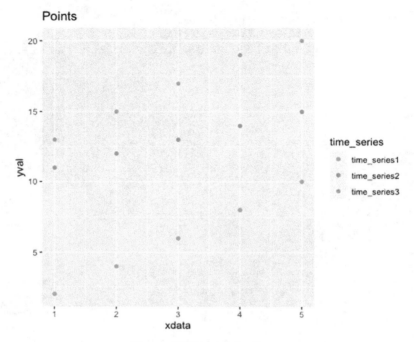

Figure A4.21.　ggplot 3.

16.　Graphics-Colors

There are 657 colors in R. We can type **colors()** in the console to look at their descriptions.

If we want to show colors 1 to 9, we can barplot 9 numbers (each of value 1 in the following example). We can also assign value other than 1. We can assign color names to a new variable **cc**. Then, we set **t** to be the bar height. Here, **rep** means replicates a number of times.

The **c** after **x<** - means combines for the following line:

```
x<-c(cc[1],cc[2],cc[3],cc[4],cc[5],cc[6],cc[7],cc[8],cc[9])
```

Please test Color.R

```
cc<-colors()
t<-rep(1,9)
x<-c(cc[1],cc[2],cc[3],cc[4],cc[5],cc[6],cc[7],cc[8],cc[9])
barplot(t, names.arg=x, col=x)
```

Listing 16-1-Color.R

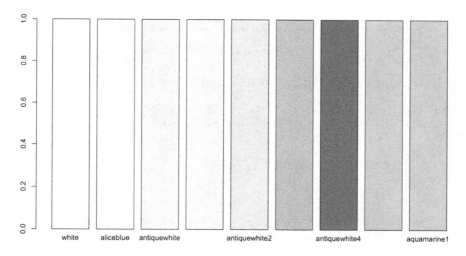

Figure A4.22.   Color 1.

If we also want to show the legend, we can add **legend.text** in the argument.

```
barplot(t, names.arg=x, legend.text=x, col=x)
```

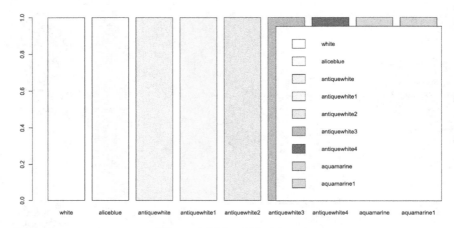

Figure A4.23.   Color 2.

If we want to show colors 10 to 18, we can type the following lines:

```
x<-c(cc[10],cc[11],cc[12],cc[13],cc[14],cc[15],cc[16],cc[17],cc[18])
barplot(t, names.arg=x, legend.text=x, col=x)
```

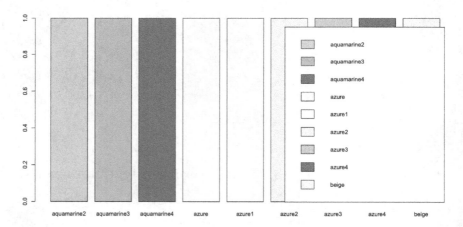

Figure A4.24.   Color 3.

17.   Word Cloud

Please install the **wordcloud** package if you have not done so before by typing the following line in R console.

```
install.packages("wordcloud")
```

If we have friends with English names, we can create a data set of their names and number of friends (frequency) with a particular English name. We can generate a word cloud by calling the `library(wordcloud)`.

The content of words.cvs is as follows:

```
Engname,Times
Peter,3
John,5
Mary,10
Howard,1
Jane,2
Sherry,5
Kitty,3
Connie,5
Stevie,3
Mark,4
```

Please test **WordCloud1.R**

```
library(wordcloud)
w<-read.csv("words.csv")
print(w)
wordcloud(words=w$Engname,
          freq=w$Times,
          max.words=5,
          min.freq=5,
          colors="red")
```

Listing 17-1-WordCloud1.R

We have specified in `words=w$Engname` that we want the words to come from the field `Engname` from data frame `w`.

`freq=w$Times` means that the frequency of the word comes from the field `Times` of data frame `w`.

If we only want to show a maximum of 5 words, we put `max.words=5`.

If we want the minimum frequency of a word to be 5 or more before we will show it, we put `min.freq=5`.

If we want to color the word cloud in red, we put `colors="red"`. The word cloud generated will be as follows:

Figure A4.25.   Word cloud 1.

If we want to specify the scale of showing the words, we can add in `scale=c(2,1)` to specify the scale of the highest frequency word to be 2 and the lowest frequency word to be 1.

Please test wordCloud2.R

```
library(wordcloud)
w<-read.csv("words.csv")
wordcloud(words=w$Engname,
          freq=w$Times,
          min.freq=1,
          colors="red", scale=c(2,1))
```

Listing 17-2-WordCloud2.R

The word cloud generated will be as follows:

Figure A4.26.   Word cloud 2.

If we want to use three different colors, we can specify
`colors=c("red","blue",green")`.
   Please test wordCloud3.R

```
library(wordcloud)
w<-read.csv("words.csv")
wordcloud(words=w$Engname,
          freq=w$Times,
          min.freq=1,
          colors=c("red","blue","green"), scale=c(2,1))
```

Listing 17-3-WordCloud3.R

The word cloud generated will be as follows:

Figure A4.27.   Word cloud 3.

If we want R to automatically generate a number of colors, we can use **colors=rainbow(nrow(w))**.

nrow(w) means the number of rows in **w**.

We can also specify **colors=rainbow(10)** if we enter a specific number of 10. Using **nrow(w)** is more general than using a specific number of 10.

Please test wordCloud4.R

```
library(wordcloud)
w<-read.csv("words.csv")
wordcloud(words=w$Engname,
          freq=w$Times,
          min.freq=1,
          colors=rainbow(nrow(w)), scale=c(2,1))
```

Listing 17-4-WordCloud4.R

Figure A4.28.   Word cloud 4.

18.   String

A string is a series of characters. It can include a to z, A–Z, 0–9, and other symbols. If we have a string, we can know how many characters it has by calling the function **nchar**, which means the number of characters.

```
s<-"abcde"
print(nchar(s))
[1] 5
```

To extract the characters within the string from a start position to a stop position, we can use **substr**, which means sub-string. If we want the character of a string from the first to the second position, we can type:

```
print(substr(s,1,2))
[1] "ab"
```

If we want the character in the third position, we can type:

```
print(substr(s,3,3))
[1] "c"
```

To print one character in one line, we can write the program as follows:

```
s<-"abcde"
for (i in 1:nchar(s)) print(substr(s,i,i)
[1] "a"
[1] "b"
[1] "c"
[1] "d"
[1] "e"
```

To reverse print one character at a time, we can write the program as follows:

```
s<-"abcde"
for (i in 1:nchar(s)) print(substr(s,i,i))
[1] "e"
[1] "d"
[1] "c"
[1] "b"
[1] "a"
```

To create a new string which is reversed, we can use for-loop and vary **i** from **nchar(s)** to 1. We set a string, **r**, to be empty before we execute the for-loop. So, we have **r< -""** (we type the double quotes symbol two times with nothing in between to indicate that the string is empty).

Please test **String1.R**

```
s<-"abcde"
for (i in 1:nchar(s)) print(substr(s,i,i))
[1] "e"
[1] "d"
[1] "c"
[1] "b"
[1] "a"
```

Listing 18-1-String1.R

We can modify the program slightly as follows:

```
s<-"abcde"
r<-""
for (i in nchar(s):1)
{
  r<-paste(r,substr(s,i,i),sep="")
  print(r)
}
print('end of loop')
print(r)
[1] "e"
[1] "ed"
[1] "edc"
[1] "edcb"
[1] "edcba"
[1] "end of loop"
[1] "edcba"
```

`r<-paste(r,substr(s,i,i,),sep="")` combines two strings **r** and `substr(s,i,i)`, and a separator, and saves the result into r. When we specify `sep=""`, it means that the separator is empty. If we want to have a comma between two strings, we put: `r<-paste(r,substr(s,i,i,),sep=",")`

If we want to convert an upper-case letter to a lower-case letter, we can use the function **tolower** as follows. If the character is already in lower case, **tolower** will keep it as lower case.

Please test **String2.R**

```
s<-"ABcde"
r<-""
for (i in nchar(s):1)
{
  c<-substr(s,i,i)
  lc<-tolower(c)
  r<-paste(r,lc,sep="")
  print(r)
}
[1] "e"
[1] "ed"
[1] "edc"
[1] "edcb"
[1] "edcba"
```

Listing 18-2-String2.R

If we want to keep a character which is a-z and 0-9, we can add in a condition to check the character, **lc**.

Please test **String3.R**

```
s<-"ABcde.,%!123"
r<-""
for (i in nchar(s):1)
{
  c<-substr(s,i,i)
  lc<-tolower(c)
  if (((lc>="a") & (lc<="z")) | ((lc>="0") & (lc<="9")))
    r<-paste(r,lc,sep="")
}
print(r)
[1] "321edcba"
```

Listing 18-3-String3.R

19.   Chi-Square Test

To run Chi-Square Test, we can execute the program Chi-Square.R

```
d<-read.csv("Chi-Square-Data.csv")
print(d)
dimnames(d)<-list(usage=c("Small","Medium","Large"),
gender=c("Female","Male"))
print(d)
result<-chisq.test(d)
print(result)
print(result$observed)
print(result$expected, digits=2)
    F  M
1 14  5
2  5  5
3  5 11
        Female Male
Small       14    5
Medium       5    5
Large        5   11

    Pearson's Chi-squared test

data:  d
X-squared = 6.3413, df = 2, p-value = 0.04198

        Female Male
Small       14    5
Medium       5    5
Large        5   11

        Female Male
Small     10.1  8.9
Medium     5.3  4.7
Large      8.5  7.5
Warning message:
In chisq.test(d) : Chi-squared approximation may be incorrect
```

Listing 19-1-Chi-Square.R

We read the data from the **Chi-Square-Data.csv** file and assign it to the data frame **d**, and get the following print result.

```
   F  M
1 14  5
2  5  5
3  5 11
```

We can use `dimnames(d)` to set the dimension names for the data frame **d**, and specify the names for the rows and the columns. We can get the following print result afterward.

```
       Female Male
Small      14    5
Medium      5    5
Large       5   11
```

To run Chi-Square test on the table of data frame **d**, we can use `result<-(chisq.test(d))` and print the result.

```
    Pearson's Chi-squared test

data:  d
X-squared = 6.3413, df = 2, p-value = 0.04198
```

We can print the observed frequency with `print(result$observed)`

```
       Female Male
Small      14    5
Medium      5    5
Large       5   11
```

To specify the minimum number of significant digits to be printed, we can use `print(result$expected, digits=2)`

```
       Female Male
Small    10.1  8.9
Medium    5.3  4.7
Large     8.5  7.5
```

When we run the program, we will get the following warning message:

```
Warning message:
In chisq.test(d) : Chi-squared approximation may be
incorrect
```

If we type **help("chisq.test")** in the R console, we can get the following messages about **simulate.p.value**:

```
It is "a logical indicating whether to compute p-values by
Monte Carlo simulation." The default is FALSE.
"If simulate.p.value is FALSE, the p-value is computed
from the asymptotic chi-squared distribution of
the test statistic."
```

R will issue a warning message of "Chi-squared approximation may be incorrect" under this situation. As we really want to compute the *p*-value from the asymptotic chi-squared distribution of the test statistic, we can ignore the warning.

20. Correlation

If we have collected data from customers of a restaurant for the first and the second visit, we can run a correlation as follows with the data file of **Restaurant.csv**.

Please execute **Correlation.R**

```
Restaurant<-read.csv("Restaurant.csv")
print(Restaurant)
print(cor.test(Restaurant$Pref1,Restaurant$Pref2))
   Respondent Gender Pref1 Pref2
1           1      M     5     4
2           2      M     6     5
3           3      M     7     6
4           4      M     4     3
5           5      M     5     4
```

6	6	M	6	5
7	7	M	4	2
8	8	M	5	5
9	9	M	6	6
10	10	M	7	6
11	11	F	3	3
12	12	F	4	5
13	13	F	5	4
14	14	F	4	5
15	15	F	4	4
16	16	F	3	4
17	17	F	4	4
18	18	F	5	6
19	19	F	3	4
20	20	F	5	6

```
    Pearson's product-moment correlation
data:   Restaurant$Pref1 and Restaurant$Pref2
t = 3.877, df = 18, p-value = 0.001105
alternative hypothesis: true correlation is not equal to 0
95 percent confidence interval:
 0.3308069 0.8602892
sample estimates:
      cor
0.6745771
```

Listing 20-1-Correlation.R

So, the correlation coefficient is equal to 0.6745881 in the last row. The null hypothesis is that the correlation coefficient is equal to zero. The alternative hypothesis is that the true correlation is not equal to 0. If the null hypothesis is true, the probability (p-value) is 0.001105. So, if we can tolerate an error of 5%, we will reject the null hypothesis and accept the alternative hypothesis that the correlation coefficient is not equal to zero.

We can also obtain correlation coefficients for male respondents and for female respondents respectively by using subset function.

Please execute Correlation-Gender.R

```
Restaurant<-read.csv("Restaurant.csv")
Male<-subset(Restaurant,Restaurant$Gender=="M")
print(cor.test(Male$Pref1,Male$Pref2))
Female<-subset(Restaurant,Restaurant$Gender=="F")
print(cor.test(Female$Pref1,Female$Pref2))



    Pearson's product-moment correlation

data:  Male$Pref1 and Male$Pref2
t = 6.3915, df = 8, p-value = 0.000211
alternative hypothesis: true correlation is not equal to 0
95 percent confidence interval:
 0.6714100 0.9798944
sample estimates:
      cor
0.9144599

    Pearson's product-moment correlation

data:  Female$Pref1 and Female$Pref2
t = 2.7735, df = 8, p-value = 0.02417
alternative hypothesis: true correlation is not equal to 0
95 percent confidence interval:
 0.1261035 0.9229191
sample estimates:
    cor
0.70014
```

Listing 20-2-Correlation-Gender.R

Thus, the correlation coefficient is 0.9144599 for male respondents, and 0.70014 for female respondents. The p-values are 0.000211 and 0.02417, respectively.

21. t-test

If we have collected data from customers of a restaurant for the first and the second visit, we can run t-test as follows:

Please execute t-test.**R**

```
Restaurant<-read.csv("Restaurant.csv")
print(t.test(Restaurant$Pref1-4))
```

One Sample t-test%

```
data:  Restaurant$Pref1 - 4
t = 2.7754, df = 19, p-value = 0.01205
alternative hypothesis: true mean is not equal to 0
95 percent confidence interval:
 0.1843941 1.3156059
sample estimates:
mean of x
      0.75
```

Listing 21-1-t-test.R

If we have the null hypothesis that preference for the first visit is equal to 4, we can put **Restaurant$Pref1~Gender** as an argument in **t.test** as shown above.

```
print(t.test(Restaurant$Pref1~Gender, data=Restaurant,
var.equal=TRUE))
```

Two Sample t-test

```
data:  Restaurant$Pref1 by Gender
t = -3.5032, df = 18, p-value = 0.002538
alternative hypothesis: true difference in means between group F
and group M is not equal to 0
95 percent confidence interval:
 -2.3995611 -0.6004389
sample estimates:
mean in group F mean in group M
            4.0             5.5
```

If we have the null hypothesis that preferences for the first visit for male customers and female customers are the same, we can put **Restaurant$Pref1~Gender** in **t.test** as shown above. **var.equal** is a logical variable indicating whether to treat the two variances as being equal for male customers and female customers.

```
print(t.test(Restaurant$Pref1, Restaurant$Pref2, paired=TRUE))
```

```
Paired t-test

data:  Restaurant$Pref1 and Restaurant$Pref2
t = 0.94006, df = 19, p-value = 0.359
alternative hypothesis: true mean difference is not equal to 0
95 percent confidence interval:
 -0.2452938  0.6452938
sample estimates:
mean difference
         0.2
```

If we have the null hypothesis that preferences for customers are the same for the first visit and the second visit, we can run paired *t*-test by putting **Restaurant\$Pref1** and **Restaurant\$Pref2** and **paired=TRUE** in the **t.test** as shown above.

```
Male<-subset(Restaurant,Restaurant$Gender=="M")
print(t.test(Male$Pref1, Male$Pref2, paired=TRUE))
```

```
Paired t-test

data:  Male$Pref1 and Male$Pref2
t = 5.0138, df = 9, p-value = 0.0007252
alternative hypothesis: true mean difference is not equal to 0
95 percent confidence interval:
 0.4939304 1.3060696
sample estimates:
mean difference
         0.9
```

If we have the null hypothesis that preferences for male customers are the same for the first visit and the second visit, we can run paired *t*-test by putting **Male\$Pref1** and **Male\$Pref2** and **paired=TRUE** in the **t.test** as shown above.

22. Analysis of Variance

If we have sales values of 10 stores when we have three different marketing promotion messages, we can run analysis of variance (ANOVA) as follows for the data file **ANOVA-Data.csv**.

Please execute **ANOVA-Data.R**

```
d<-read.csv("ANOVA-Data.csv")
print(d)
e<-aov(d$Sales~Message, data=d)
print(summary(e))
```

```
   Store Message Sales
1     1     One    10
2     2     One     9
3     3     One     8
4     4     One    10
5     5     One     7
6     6     One     6
7     7     One     7
8     8     One     9
9     9     One    10
10   10     One     8
11    1     Two     8
12    2     Two     7
13    3     Two     9
14    4     Two     8
15    5     Two     6
16    6     Two     4
17    7     Two    10
18    8     Two     7
19    9     Two     8
20   10     Two     6
21    1   Three    10
22    2   Three     8
23    3   Three     7
24    4   Three     5
25    5   Three     7
26    6   Three     4
27    7   Three     3
28    8   Three     5
29    9   Three     4
30   10   Three     6
            Df Sum Sq Mean Sq F value Pr(>F)
Message      2   31.4  15.700   4.964 0.0146 *
Residuals   27   85.4   3.163
---
Signif. codes:  0 '***' 0.001 '**' 0.01 '*' 0.05 '.' 0.1 ' ' 1
```

Listing 22-1-ANOVA-Data.R

The null hypothesis is that there is no difference among three different messages. If the null hypothesis is correct, the probability of getting the ANOVA result is only 0.0146. So, if we can accept an error of 5%, we will reject the null hypothesis and accept the alternative hypothesis that there is difference among the three groups.

23.   Regression-Bivariate

If we have a data set of weights and heights of 15 respondents, **DataReg.csv**, we can run a bivariate regression by executing **Regression-Bivariate.R**

```
d<-read.csv("DataReg.csv")
print(d)
result<-lm(Weight~Height, data=d)
print(summary(result))
```

	Respondent	Weight	Height
1	1	17	129
2	2	16	116
3	3	16	128
4	4	18	145
5	5	19	152
6	6	20	150
7	7	22	166
8	8	20	156
9	9	21	168
10	10	17	123
11	11	19	144
12	12	24	179
13	13	23	178
14	14	17	122
15	15	20	164

```
Call:
lm(formula = Weight ~ Height, data = d)

Residuals:
    Min      1Q  Median      3Q     Max
-1.1063 -0.6464  0.1932  0.5556  1.1690
```

```
Coefficients:
            Estimate Std. Error t value Pr(>|t|)
(Intercept) 2.250099   1.424624   1.579    0.138
Height      0.114977   0.009539  12.054 1.98e-08 ***
---
Signif. codes:  0 '***' 0.001 '**' 0.01 '*' 0.05 '.' 0.1 ' ' 1

Residual standard error: 0.7411 on 13 degrees of freedom
Multiple R-squared:  0.9179,    Adjusted R-squared:  0.9116
F-statistic: 145.3 on 1 and 13 DF,  p-value: 1.981e-08
```

Listing 23-1-Regression-Bivariate.R

After we have read the data.csv into the data frame **d**, we print it out as shown above. We can use **lm** to fit the linear regression model. We specify two variables, the **Weight** field of data frame **d** and the **Height** field of data frame **d**.

We save the model to result by

```
result<-lm(Weight~Height, data=d)
```

Then, we print the summary of the result by

```
print(summary(result))
```

t value is equal to estimate/standard error. So, we have $2.250099/1.424624 = 1.579$, and $0.114977/0.009539 = 12.054$.

The p-value is 1.98e-08 which is a scientific notation. We can use **options** as follows to print p-value as 0.0000000198.

```
options(scipen=999)
print(summary(result))

Call:
lm(formula = Weight ~ Height, data = d)

Residuals:
    Min      1Q  Median      3Q     Max
-1.1063 -0.6464  0.1932  0.5556  1.1690
```

```
Coefficients:
             Estimate Std. Error t value    Pr(>|t|)
(Intercept) 2.250099   1.424624   1.579        0.138
Height      0.114977   0.009539  12.054 0.0000000198 ***
---
Signif. codes:  0 '***' 0.001 '**' 0.01 '*' 0.05 '.' 0.1 ' ' 1

Residual standard error: 0.7411 on 13 degrees of freedom
Multiple R-squared:  0.9179,    Adjusted R-squared:  0.9116
F-statistic: 145.3 on 1 and 13 DF,   p-value: 0.00000001981
```

If we want to use scientific notation again, we can type:

```
options(scipen=0)
```

24. Regression-Multiple

If we have a data set of Sales, TV media spending, and digital media spending for 12 months, DataSales.csv, we can run multiple regression by executing Regression-Multiple.R

```
d<-read.csv("DataSales.csv")
print(d)
result<-lm(Sales~TVSpend+DigitalSpend, data=d)
print(summary(result))
```

	Month	Sales	TVSpend	DigitalSpend
1	1	820	183	148
2	2	805	113	185
3	3	987	196	189
4	4	718	166	119
5	5	772	160	143
6	6	863	171	173
7	7	895	194	165
8	8	923	156	194
9	9	914	148	199
10	10	683	117	142
11	11	645	140	120
12	12	671	116	146

```
Call:
lm(formula = Sales ~ TVSpend + DigitalSpend, data = d)

Residuals:
    Min      1Q  Median      3Q     Max
-16.796  -6.671   2.185   7.674  15.986

Coefficients:
              Estimate Std. Error t value Pr(>|t|)
(Intercept)    -1.6143    25.0922  -0.064     0.95
TVSpend         2.0122     0.1175  17.129 3.54e-08 ***
DigitalSpend    3.1059     0.1230  25.257 1.15e-09 ***
---
Signif. codes:  0 '***' 0.001 '**' 0.01 '*' 0.05 '.' 0.1 ' ' 1

Residual standard error: 11.27 on 9 degrees of freedom
Multiple R-squared:  0.9917,    Adjusted R-squared:  0.9898
F-statistic: 537.1 on 2 and 9 DF,  p-value: 4.345e-10
```

Listing 24-1-Regresssion-Multiple.R

After we have printed the data set, we can run linear model (**lm**) for multiple regression. We specify the dependent variable to be Sales and the independent variables to be TVSpend and DigitalSpend. Then, we print the summary of results.

25. Sentiment Analysis

If we have received a message from a person, how can we know what is the emotion and sentiment of this message?

Please install the following package.

```
install.packages("syuzhet")
```

"The name "Syuzhet" comes from Russian Formalists Victor Shklovsky and Vladimir Propp who divided narrative into two components, the "fabula" and the "syuzhet." Syuzhet refers to the "device" or technique of a narrative whereas fabula is the chronological order of events", (accessed on May 6, 2022), https://www.rdocumentation.org/packages/syuzhet/versions/1.0.6.

Introduction to the Syuzhet Package is available at: https://cran.r-project.org/web/packages/syuzhet/vignettes/syuzhet-vignette.html.

After we have installed the package, we can type:

```
library(syuzhet)
help("get_nrc_sentiment")
```

We can read from the bottom of the help content of the following web page and get more information. http://saifmohammad.com/WebPages/lexicons.html.

The "NRC" lexicon was developed by Mohammad, Saif M. and Turney, Peter D, accessed May 6, 2022, http://saifmohammad.com/WebPages/lexicons.html.

NRC is National Research Council Canada, accessed May 6, 2022, https://nrc.canada.ca/en/corporate/about-nrc.

"There are eight emotions (anger, fear, anticipation, trust, surprise, sadness, joy, and disgust) and two sentiments (negative and positive)", accessed May 6, 2022, http://saifmohammad.com/WebPages/lexicons.html.

Please execute **Sentiments-NRC.R**

```
print(get_nrc_sentiment('ugly'))
print(get_nrc_sentiment('upset'))
print(get_nrc_sentiment('ugly and upset'))
  anger anticipation disgust fear joy sadness surprise trust negative positive
1     0            0       1    0   0       0        0     0        1        0
  anger anticipation disgust fear joy sadness surprise trust negative positive
1     1            0       0    0   0       1        0     0        1        0
  anger anticipation disgust fear joy sadness surprise trust negative positive
1     1            0       1    0   0       1        0     0        2        0
```

Listing 25-1-Sentiments-NRC.R

Thus, 'ugly' has the emotion of **disgust** and is **negative**, 'upset' has the emotions of **anger** and **sadness** and is **negative**. Both words together then have the emotions of **anger**, **disgust**, and **sadness** and are counted as two negatives.

The number for 'ugly and upset' is the sum of that for 'ugly' and 'upset'.

Please continue executing the following lines in Sentiments-
NRC.R

```
d<-"Yesterday was Friday. I felt happy.
I had just finished preparing the teaching materials for my class in the
morning.
Then, I felt bored, and went for lunch.
A car driver was not following travel light and hit a dog.
I was angry that he did not pay attention to other people in the street."
e<-get_sentences(d)
print(e)
f<-get_tokens(d)
print(f)
```

```
[1] "Yesterday was Friday."
[2] "I felt happy."
[3] "I had just finished preparing the teaching materials for my class in the
morning."
[4] "Then, I felt bored, and went for lunch."
[5] "A car driver was not following travel light and hit a dog."
[6] "I was angry that he did not pay attention to other people in the street."
 [1] "yesterday" "was"        "friday"    "i"          "felt"       "happy"
 [7] "i"          "had"        "just"      "finished"   "preparing"  "the"
[13] "teaching"   "materials"  "for"       "my"         "class"      "in"
[19] "the"        "morning"    "then"      "i"          "felt"       "bored"
[25] "and"        "went"       "for"       "lunch"      "a"          "car"
[31] "driver"     "was"        "not"       "following"  "travel"     "light"
[37] "and"        "hit"        "a"         "dog"        "i"          "was"
[43] "angry"      "that"       "he"        "did"        "not"        "pay"
[49] "attention"  "to"         "other"     "people"     "in"         "the"
[55] "street"
```

We first assigned a paragraph to **d**. R can help us get each sentence
from the paragraph or get each word (**token**) from the paragraph as
shown in the results above.

Please continue executing the following lines in Sentiments-
NRC.R

```
snrc<-get_nrc_sentiment(e)
print(snrc)
```

	anger	anticipation	disgust	fear	joy	sadness	surprise	trust	negative	positive
1	0	0	0	0	0	0	0	0	0	0
2	0	1	0	0	1	0	0	1	0	1
3	0	0	0	0	0	0	0	0	0	0
4	0	0	0	0	0	0	0	0	0	0
5	1	0	0	0	0	0	0	0	1	0
6	1	1	1	0	1	0	0	1	1	2

So, each of the six sentences has the above emotions.

```
w<-colSums(snrc)
print(w)
         anger anticipation      disgust         fear      joy   sadness
             2            2            1            0        2         0
      surprise        trust     negative     positive
             0            2            2            3
```

We can add up the sum of each column by calling **colSums(snrc)** and saving it to **w**.

```
barplot(w, las=2, cex.names=0.5, col=rainbow(10),
main="example",xlab="Emotions/Sentiments",ylab="Scores")
```

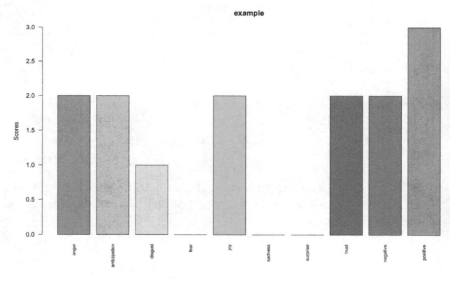

Figure A4.29.   Sentiment analysis 1.

We use **barplot** to show the results saved in **w**.

    las=2 asks R to put x labels vertically.

    cex.names=0.5 makes the size of the names on the label 50%.

We use **col=rainbow(10)** to indicate that we want R to automatically generate 10 colors for us.

If we have received messages from different people about Apple on Twitter, how do we know whether people are positive, neutral, or negative (sentiment) toward Apple?

We can read each message and give a sentiment score ourselves, or we can outsource to Amazon Mechanical Turk which is a global, on-demand, 24x7 workforce, accessed May 6, 2022, https://www.mturk.com/.

The data set of tweets.csv can be found online, accessed May 6, 2022, https://raw.githubusercontent.com/bdanalytics/Apple-Tweets/master/data/tweets.csv.

Please execute **Sentiments-NRC-Apple.R**

```
library(syuzhet)
d<-read.csv("Tweets.csv")
print.default(d, max=1)
s<-get_nrc_sentiment(d$Tweet)
barplot(colSums(s), las=2, cex.names=0.5, col=rainbow(10),
main="Apple Tweets",xlab="Emotions/Sentiments",ylab="Scores")

$Tweet
[1] "I have to say, Apple has by far the best customer care
service I have ever received! @Apple @AppStore"
 [ reached getOption("max.print") -- omitted 1180 entries ]

$Avg
[1] 2
 [ reached getOption("max.print") -- omitted 1180 entries ]

attr(,"class")
[1] "data.frame"
```

Listing 25-2-Sentiments-NRC-Apple.R

We can look at the first message by `print.default(d, max=1)` as shown above.

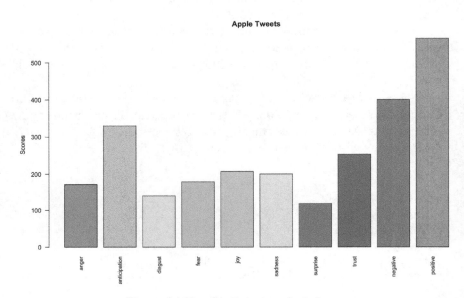

Figure A4.30.   Sentiment analysis 2.

26.   Web Scraping

To read the content of a web page to extract information into R, we can use the Package **rvest** which stands for "Easily Harvest (Scrape) Web Page."

More details about **rvest** are available at https://cran.r-project.org/web/packages/rvest/rvest.pdf.

I have created the following web page for us to scrape. https://sites.google.com/view/howardlam/publications/cases?authuser=0.

The screen capture is as follows:

Cases

- Howard Pong-yuen Lam, Hugh Thomas, Rosette Hang-yee Leung and Hanni Jie (2022), "OmniFoods: Plant-Based Pork from Hong Kong to the Rest of China," Ivey Publishing, 28 September 2022.

- Hang Yee Rosette Leung, Hugh Thomas, Hanni Jie, Pong Yuen Howard Lam (2022), "Green Monday: Flexitarianism, Innovation, and Endorsement," Ivey Publishing, 11 July 2022.

- Howard Pong-yuen Lam, Hugh Thomas, Keith C.H.Wong,(2020), "SenseTime Group Limited : Business Model and Expansion," Harvard Business Publishing, 19 July 2020.

- Hugh Thomas, Andrew C.F. Chan, Howard Pong-yuen Lam and Icy F.L. Ngai (2019), "Incubation and the Hong Kong Science and Technology Parks Corporation," Harvard Business Publishing, 16 August 2019.

- Andrew C.F. Chan, Howard Pong-yuen Lam and Icy F.L. Ngai (2019), "OpenSky.TV: Business Model From Content Creation, Curation, Consumption, Commercialization," Harvard Business Publishing, 3 May 2019.

- Kevin Y.F. Au, Howard Pong-yuen Lam, Lu, S.Y. and Ngai, F.L. Icy (2018), "Bamboos Health Care Holdings (Hong Kong) Ltd.: Business Model and Expansion," Harvard Business Publishing, 12 November 2018.

- Andrew C.F. Chan, Howard Pong-yuen Lam, Hugh Thomas, Andy K.C. Wong and Canice M.C. Kwan (2018), "AMOREPACIFIC Hong Kong: Marketing Korean Beauty Products," Harvard Business Publishing, 3 May 2018.

- Andrew C.F. Chan, Howard Pong-yuen Lam, Hugh Thomas and Elsie Tsui (2016), "Hung Fook Tong: From Hong Kong to China," Harvard Business Publishing, 30 May 2016.

- Kevin Y.F. Au, Andrew C.F. Chan, Howard Pong-yuen Lam and Cinty Li (2015), "TSL Jewellery: An Innovator Across Generations," Harvard Business Publishing, 24 Feb 2015.

Figure A4.31.   Web page cases.

Please execute **WebScraping-publications.R** after you have typed
install.packages("rvest") into the console of RStudio.

```
library(rvest)
webpage <- read_html("https://sites.google.com/view/howardlam/
publications/cases?authuser=0")
fields <- webpage %>%
  html_nodes(".XqQF9c") %>%
  html_text()
print(fields)
```

```
[1] "OmniFoods: Plant-Based Pork from Hong Kong to the Rest of China"
[2] "Green Monday: Flexitarianism, Innovation, and Endorsement"
[3] "SenseTime Group Limited : Business Model and Expansion"
[4] "Incubation and the Hong Kong Science and Technology Parks
Corporation"
[5] "OpenSky.TV: Business Model From Content Creation, Curation,
Consumption, Commercialization"
[6] "Bamboos Health Care Holdings (Hong Kong) Ltd.: Business Model
and Expansion"
[7] "AMOREPACIFIC Hong Kong: Marketing Korean Beauty Products"
[8] "Hung Fook Tong: From Hong Kong to China"
[9] "TSL Jewellery: An Innovator Across Generations"
```

Listing 26-1-WebScraping-publications.R

%>% means "pipe to."

So, web page is sent to **html_nodes** to detect areas of **".XqQF9c"** in the html file, which in turn is sent to **html_text()** to generate text.

".XqQF9c" is what you want to select. We can use Chrome browser to view a web page and find this string. The steps are as follows.

Choose "View" menu option from Chrome, then "Developer," "Inspect Elements." Then, put the mouse over the element that you want to inspect. You can find the string **".XqQF9c"**.

I had made a twenty-second video by using text-to-voice feature from CapCut video editing software, and posted it to YouTube (https://youtu.be/qYslT1lJFmw) and Tencent Video (https://v.qq.com/x/page/o35055t6ycc.html) on how to find the element.

The text retrieved are stored in fields. webpage and fields are variables set by the programmer. To examine it, you can type **print(fields)** and **str(fields)**. "https://sites.google.com/view/howardlam/publications/cases?authuser=0" is a string. It is the hyperlink for the web page that we want to scrape. I have created this web page.

I have created this web page for us to scrape. https://sites.google.com/view/howardlam/r-program/web-scraping?authuser=0.

The screen capture of it is as follows.

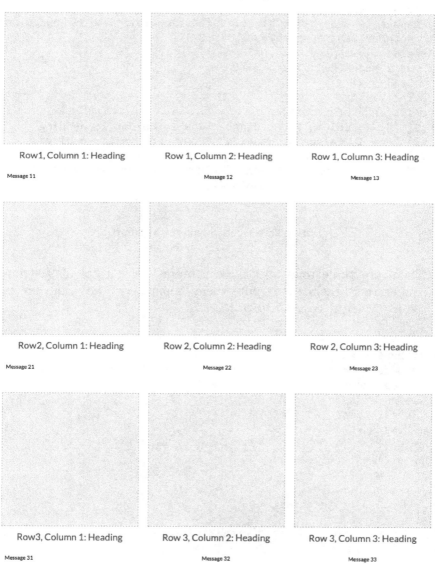

Figure A4.32. Web page row and column.

If we want to scrape this web page with rows and columns, we can execute **WebScraping-row-column1.R**

```
library(rvest)
webpage <- read_html("https://sites.google.com/view/howardlam/
r-program/web-scraping?authuser=0")
fields <- webpage %>%
  html_nodes(".CjVfdc") %>%
  html_text()
print(fields)
print(length(fields))
[1] "Row1, Column 1: Heading"  "Row 1, Column 2: Heading"
[3] "Row 1, Column 3: Heading" "Row2, Column 1: Heading"
[5] "Row 2, Column 2: Heading" "Row 2, Column 3: Heading"
[7] "Row3, Column 1: Heading"  "Row 3, Column 2: Heading"
[9] "Row 3, Column 3: Heading"
[1] 9
```

Listing 26-2-WebScraping-row-column1.R

There are three rows and three columns for a total of 9 strings. To extract them and put them separately, we can execute **WebScraping-row-column2.R**

```
library(rvest)
webpage <- read_html("https://sites.google.com/view/howardlam/
r-program/web-scraping?authuser=0")
fields <- webpage %>%
  html_nodes(".CjVfdc") %>%
  html_text()
print(fields)
print(length(fields))
# N = 9
N <-length(fields)
# M = 9/3 = 3 records
M <-N/3
# Set data to be a table with M (3) rows and 3 columns for
N (9) cells
```

```
data <- 1:N
dim(data)<-c(M,3)
# Initialize i and j to 1 to start
i<-1
j<-1
# Set done to be "N" to start a while loop
done="N"
while (done=="N")
{
  data[i,1]<-fields[j]
  data[i,2]<-fields[j+1]
  data[i,3]<-fields[j+2]
  j<-j+3
  i<-i+1
  if (j>N)
  {done="Y"}
}
write.csv(data, file = "outfile.csv")
[1] "Row1, Column 1: Heading"  "Row 1, Column 2: Heading"
[3] "Row 1, Column 3: Heading" "Row2, Column 1: Heading"
[5] "Row 2, Column 2: Heading" "Row 2, Column 3: Heading"
[7] "Row3, Column 1: Heading"  "Row 3, Column 2: Heading"
[9] "Row 3, Column 3: Heading"
[1] 9
```

Listing 26-3-WebScraping-row-column2.R

The content of the **outfile.csv** is as follows:

```
"","V1","V2","V3"
"1","Row1, Column 1: Heading","Row 1, Column 2: Heading","Row 1,
Column 3: Heading"
"2","Row2, Column 1: Heading","Row 2, Column 2: Heading","Row 2,
Column 3: Heading"
"3","Row3, Column 1: Heading","Row 3, Column 2: Heading","Row 3,
Column 3: Heading"
```

Appendix 5: Programming in Python

1. Installation

To download and install Python, please click on the Downloads button on the following web page, www.python.org, and follow the steps to install it.

After you have installed Python, you can start the Python console, and start using it to do simple operations (Chapter 2).

You can also install Anaconda so that you can more easily write, modify and execute Python programs in an environment (Chapter 3). To download it, please visit the following website. https://anaconda.com.

After you have learned how to write in one computer language, Python, you can also know the key computer programming concepts which are applicable to programming in other languages. For example, you can use Python to perform arithmetic operations, obtain values of functions, plot graphs, and get results from statistical tests.

2. Python Console

After you have downloaded Python, installed it, and run it on your computer, you will see the Python Console.

While you are at the Python Console, you will see the following sign which is a Python prompt. That is, Python is ready to take your command.

```
>>>
```

You can say hello to the world by typing

```
print('Hello World')
Hello World
```

We can treat Python console as a calculator, too. To calculate the sum of two numbers, you can type

```
8+2
10
```

When you see the Python prompt >>>, you can press the up arrow on your keyboard to get what you have typed previously.

You can also use print to tell Python that you want it to print the result for you to see.

```
print((8+2)*3)
30
```

To leave Python, you can type:

```
quit()
```

3. Anaconda/Spyder (Hello World, Comment, Input)

Although we can continue working on the Python console, it is better to use Anaconda and Spyder.

"Spyder is a free and open source scientific environment for Python", accessed April 16, 2022, https://www.spyder-ide.org/.

After you have started Anaconda and launched Spyder, you will see the following screen.

Figure A5.1. Screen of Spyder.

Afterward, it will be convenient to save Python programs (with file extension .py) and other data files together into a folder or the working directory.

We can say hello to the world by typing the following in the Console panel:

```
print("Hello World")
Hello World
```

You can also write a program in the left panel to do simple calculations. To run the program, just click on the green triangle, the fifth icon from the left top bar.

```
x=1
y=2
print(x+y)
3
```

This program assigns a value of 1 to x, a value of 2 to y, adds them up, and prints the sum.

While you are at Spyder, you can set the working directory to one that you have created by choosing "Python", "Preferences", "Current working directory" and then browse to the directory that you want to use.

If you want to remind yourself or let other programmers know the meaning of a line, you can add a comment line by putting a special symbol of # in a line. Python will ignore what you put after # because it knows that it is for humans to read, not for computers to read and execute.

```
L<-7 # Assigns the value of 7 to variable L
W<-2 # Assigns the value of 2 to variable W
print(L*W) # Print the result of L multiplied by W
 (area of a rectangle)
14
```

We can make a program more general by allowing users to enter the value for L and W.

Please execute **Area1.py** and click on the console panel before you enter 10 and 20.

```
print("Hello World")
L=input()
W=input()
Area=float(L)*float(W)
print(Area)
10
20
200.0
```

Listing 3-1-Area1.py

input() allows us to enter anything (including characters) and so we have to tell Python that we want to convert what we have entered (10) as numeric value. Then, Python will not treat it as the string '10'.

We can also use a prompt message to remind users as shown in the following program. Please execute **Area2.py** and click on the console panel before you enter 10 and 20.

```
print("Hello World")
L=input('Please enter the length ')
W=input('Please enter the width ')
Area=float(L)*float(W)
print(Area)
Please enter the length 10
Please enter the width 20
200.0
```

Listing 3-2-Area2.py

4.   Arithmetic Operations

We can use operators $(+ - * /)$ for adding, subtracting, multiplying, and dividing two numbers. We can use ** for raising to a power.

```
8-2
6

8*2
16

8/2
4

8**2
64

16**0.5
4.0

8+2*3
14
```

Because Python will calculate 2*3 to be 6 first, and then perform the calculation of 8+6.

```
(8+2)*3
30
```

Because Python will know that it has to calculate (8+2) to get 10 before 10 is multiplied by 3 to get 30.

5. Assignment Operations

We can assign a value to a variable by typing = as follows.

```
X=1
Y=2
Z=X+Y
print(Z)
3
```

= is what Python programming language has chosen to use as "an assignment operator" to tell the computer that we want it to calculate the value from the "right-hand side" and then assign to the variable in the "left-hand side."

Please note that we are not dealing with algebra here.

If we have initialized the value of **X** to be 1, **X+1** is then equal to 2. So, 2 will be assigned to the variable in the left hand side, **X**.

```
X=1
X=X+1
print(X)
2
```

In algebra, it is impossible that **X=X+1**.

Python treats capital letters and small letters differently. So, if you type **print(x)**, you will get an error, because Python does not have anything for **x**. Python only knows that there is a variable **X** (not **x**).

Similarly, you can type the following:

```
X=1
x=2
print(x)
2
```

X has a value of 1. **x** has a value of 2. **X** and **x** are two different variables.

If we want to manipulate multiple values, we can set up an array and name it as **X**.

```
X=[1,2,3,4,5]
print(X)
print(X[0])
print(X[1])
[1, 2, 3, 4, 5]
1
2
```

That is, there are five elements in the array **X**. We can refer to each element by putting the index **X[0]**, **X[1]**, **X[2]**, **X[3]**, **X[4]**.

6. Functions

First, let's have a simple data set for us to use and perform simple calculations manually.

Suppose we have 12 people with heights (in cm) as follows, from low to high.

120, 130, 140, 150, 160, 170, 180, 190, 200, 210, 220, 230.

The median is the average of the 6th and 7th numbers when we have 12 numbers. So, it is equal to $(170 + 180)/2 = 175$.

The first quantile separates 25% of the data from the remaining 75% of data. So, it is in the $0.25(n + 1) = 0.25 \times 13 = 3.25$ ordered position. Its value is then $= 140 + 0.25(150 - 140) = 142.5$.

The third quantile separates 75% of the data from the remaining 25% of data. So, it is in the $0.75(n+1) = 0.75 \times 13 = 9.75$ ordered position. Its value is then $= 200 + 0.75(210 - 200) = 207.5$.

Please execute heights.py

```
import statistics
data=[120, 130, 140, 150, 160, 170, 180, 190, 200, 210, 220, 230]
print("mean =",statistics.mean(data))
print("quantitles =",statistics.quantiles(data,n=4))
print("median =",statistics.median(data))
print("minimum =",min(data))
print("maximum =",max(data))
print("range =",max(data)-min(data))
print("number of items / length =",len(data))
print("sum = ",sum(data))
data.sort(reverse=True)
print(data)

mean = 175
quantitles = [142.5, 175.0, 207.5]
median = 175.0
minimum = 120
maximum = 230
range = 110
number of items / length = 12
sum =  2100
[230, 220, 210, 200, 190, 180, 170, 160, 150, 140, 130, 120]
```

Listing 6-1-heights.py

Python has a statistics module. For the list of functions, please refer to the following web page. https://docs.python.org/3/library/statistics.html.

We can also define our own function. https://docs.python.org/3/tutorial/controlflow.html#definingfunctions.

Please execute **function-program.py**

```
X=1
x=2
print(x)
def sum1toN(n):
    result = (1+n)*n/2
    return result

in_n = input('Please enter n ')
n = float(in_n)
print(sum1toN(n))
```

Please enter n 10
55.0

Listing 6-2-function-program.py

The sum of $1 + 2 + 3 + \cdots n$ is equal to $(1 + n) * n/2$.
We can also derive this result as follows:

$$s = 1 + 2 + 3 \cdots \cdots (n-2) + (n-1) + n$$

$$s = n + (n-1) + (n-2) \cdots + 3 + 2 + 1$$

If we add up the two equations, we will have

$$s + s = (1+n) + (2+n-1) + (3+n-2)$$
$$+ \cdots (n-2+3) + (n-1+2) + (n+1)$$

We can simplify and get

$$2s = (1+n) + (1+n) + \cdots + n) + \cdots (1+n) + (1+n) + (1+n)$$
$$2s = (1+n) * n$$
$$s = (1+n) * n/2$$

7. Library

Python has a number of useful packages. For the latest list of packages, please refer to https://pypi.org/.

For what has been installed in Spyder, type

```
pip list
```

For example, if we want to use wordcloud, we can install it by typing the following at the console of Spyder:

```
pip install wordcloud
```

The other useful packages are statsmodels, pandas, matplotlib, numpy.

```
pip install statsmodels
pip install pandas
pip install matplotlib
pip install numpy
```

In general, when we create our own Python program, it is better to avoid using the same name of a package to reduce any chance of confusion for Python and for other people to read our program.

8. Conditions

There are six relational operators for us to compare two variables.

< less than
> greater than
<= less than or equal to
>= greater than or equal to
== equal
!= Not equal

Please execute the program Relational-operator1.py

```
inx=input("Please enter a number ")
iny=input("Please enter a second number for comparison ")
x=float(inx)
y=float(iny)
if (x==y):print ("=")
if (x<=y):print("<=")
if (x>=y):print(">=")
if (x<y):print("<")
if (x>y):print(">")
if (x!=y):print("not equal")
print(x*y)
Please enter a number 2
Please enter a second number for comparison 3
<=
<
not equal
6.0
```

Listing 8-1-Relational-operator1.py

After we have typed a few keys and pressed enter for **inx**, Python will save the keys as a string, that is, a series of characters. If we enter **abc**, **inx** is "**abc**." If we enter **123**, **inx** is "**123**" which is a string.

We cannot multiply "**abc**" by 3. Similarly, we cannot multiply "**123**" by 3. We have to convert the string of "**123**" to a numeric value, either as integer by using **int(inx)** or as a floating point number by using **float(inx)** which is a number with a decimal point.

We can also combine two conditions with the symbol | or &.

| means or.

& means and.

condition 1 or condition2

condition1 | condition2 is TRUE when we have:
condition1 is TRUE, condition1 is TRUE.
Condition1 is TRUE, condition2 is FALSE.
Condition1 is FALSE, condition2 is TRUE.
Condition1 | condition2 is FALSE when we have:
condition1 is FALSE, condition2 is FALSE.

Condition 1 and condition2

condition1 & condition2 is TRUE when we have:
condition1 is TRUE, condition1 is TRUE.
Condition1 & condition2 is FALSE when we have:
condition1 is TRUE, condition2 is FALSE.
Condition1 is FALSE, condition2 is TRUE.
Condition1 is FALSE, condition2 is FALSE.

Please execute **Relational-operator2.py**

```
pip list
x=input("Please enter x ")
y=input("Please enter y ")
if ((x==1) | (x==2)):print ("x is equal to 1 or 2")
if ((x==1) & (y==1)):print ("x=1 and y=1")

Please enter x 1
Please enter y 2
X is equal to 1 or 2
```

Listing 8-2-Relational-operator2.py

For the program, **Multiple-choices.py**, we can execute different blocks of statements, depending on the choice of the user.

```
x=input("Please enter a choice A B C D ")
if (x=="A"):
    print("You have chosen A")
elif (x=="B"):
    print("You have chosen B")
elif (x=="C"):
    print("You have chosen C")
else:
    print("You have not chosen A, B, C")
```

Listing 8-3-Multiple-choices.py

We will have to indent (i.e., put some spaces at the front of the line) under a condition to make it easier for us to read lines under different conditions, and also for Python to know what to execute under each condition.

9. Loop

If we want to print numbers 1 to 5, we can type **print** 5 times.

```
print(0)
print(1)
print(2)
print(3)
print(4)
```

We can also perform the above step 5 times if we use a do loop.

Loop-do.py

```
for i in range(5):
    print(i)
0
1
2
3
4
```

Listing 9-1-Loop-do.py

```
for i in range(3,10):
    print(i)
3
4
5
6
7
8
9
```

"The given end point is never part of the generated sequence", accessed April 29, 2022, https://docs.python.org/3/tutorial/controlflow.html#for-statements.

```
sum=0
for i in range(1,4):
    sum=sum+i
print('sum =',sum)
sum = 6
```

We can use a for-loop to calculate the sum of 1 to 3.

When i is equal to 1, we calculate sum plus i as 0 plus 1 which is equal to 1. Then, we assign 1 to sum.

When i is equal to 2, we calculate sum plus i as 1 plus 2 which is equal to 3. Then, we assign 3 to sum.

When i is equal to 3, we calculate sum plus i as 3 plus 3 which is equal to 6. Then, we assign 6 to sum.

In this way, we can calculate the cumulative sum of 1+2+3.

In a for-loop, we need to specify a variable such as i.

If we use a while-loop, we can simply set a condition for the loop to be executed.

For example, we can set a variable such as **done** to be **"N"** (that is not done yet).

We can set variable i equal to 1 before we start running the while-loop.

While **done** is equal to **N**, we will execute a block of lines. We have to use indentation with spaces to indicate the lines that we want executed together as shown in the following program below.

Loop-while.py

```
done="N"
i=1
while (done=="N"):
    print(i)
    i=i+1
    if (i>5):done="Y"
1
2
3
4
5
```

Listing 9-2-Loop-while.py

So, we will print the value of **i**, increase the value of **i** by 1, and assign it back to **i**. In this case, we want to end the while-loop when **i** is greater than 5, because we only want to print 1 to 5.

To end the while-loop, we use if statement in the last line to check and change the value of variable **done** to another value which is not **N**. In the program, we have set **done** to **Y** which means Yes.

When **done** is equal to **Y**, the condition of **done** equal to **N** is **FALSE**. As a result, the while-loop will stop.

We can enhance the program to calculate the sum of 1 to 5.

```
done="N"
i=1
sum=0
while (done=="N"):
    sum=sum+i
    i=i+1
    if (i>5):done="Y"
print("sum = ",sum)
sum = 15
```

10.   Read and Write File

We can use Excel to create a file, and then save it as a comma-separated values (CSV) file.

For Python, if there is space before the field name, there will be problem for it to read in the data. So, if the first line has spaces, please eliminate all spaces.

That is, change StudentsID, Gender, Height, Weight to StudentID,Gender,Height,Weight.

We can use text editor to open the file and take out the spaces (if any).

For Apple, please right click the file, and choose **textedit** to open the file.

For Windows, please open the CSV file with Notepad or Wordpad.

If the content of Students.csv is as follows:

```
StudentID,Gender,Height,Weight
1,M,180,72
2,M,170,70
3,M,160,60
4,F,150,72
5,F,140,70
6,M,165,60
7,F,155,50
8,M,167,90
9,F,175,66
10,M,190,80
```

Please execute read-and-write-file1.py after installing pandas by typing the following in the console of Spyder:

```
pip install pandas
```

To read the above student file into s, type

```
pip install pandas
import pandas as pd
df = pd.read_csv('Students.csv')
print(df)
   StudentID Gender  Height  Weight
0         1      M     180      72
1         2      M     170      70
2         3      M     160      60
3         4      F     150      72
4         5      F     140      70
5         6      M     165      60
6         7      F     155      50
7         8      M     167      90
8         9      F     175      66
9        10      M     190      80
```

Listing 10-1-read-and-write-file1.py

"Pandas is a fast, powerful, flexible and easy to use source data analysis and manipulation tool, built on top of the Python programming language", accessed April 12, 2022, https://pandas.pydata.org/.

"In pandas, a data table is called a DataFrame", accessed April 30, 2022, https://pandas.pydata.org/docs/getting_started/index.html#getting-started.

A DataFrame has row and column. To display the dimension (the number of rows and the number of columns), type

```
pip install pandas
print(df.shape)
(10, 4)
```

To print the first 3 records, we can use head.

```
print(df.head(3))
   StudentID Gender  Height  Weight
0      1        M      180      72
1      2        M      170      70
2      3        M      160      60
```

To print the last 3 records, we can use tail.

```
print(df.tail(3))
   StudentID Gender  Height  Weight
7      8        M      167      90
8      9        F      175      66
9     10        M      190      80
```

Pandas treats ten records with index of 0–9. So, we have the above table with row 0, row 1, row 2, and so on.

"To access a group of rows and columns by label(s)", we can use loc as shown in the following, accessed April 12, 2022, https://matplotlib.org/stable/api/_as_gen/matplotlib. pyplot.boxplot.html.

```
e = df.loc[df['Gender']=='M']
print(e)
   StudentID Gender  Height  Weight
0      1        M      180      72
1      2        M      170      70
2      3        M      160      60
5      6        M      165      60
7      8        M      167      90
9     10        M      190      80
```

To know the column names in Pandas dataframe, we can use **list**.

```
print(list(df))
['StudentID', 'Gender', 'Height', 'Weight']
```

To write the content of a dataframe, e, to a CSV file, we can use:

```
e.to_csv('Students-male.csv', index=False)
```

The content of Students-male.csv is as follows:

```
StudentID,Gender,Height,Weight
1,M,180,72
2,M,170,70
3,M,160,60
6,M,165,60
8,M,167,90
10,M,190,80
```

If we do not specify **index=False**, we will get the following for Students-male.csv which may not be readable by other software.

```
,StudentID,Gender,Height,Weight
0,1,M,180,72
1,2,M,170,70
2,3,M,160,60
5,6,M,165,60
7,8,M,167,90
9,10,M,190,80
```

If we want to get content of a particular row and column, we can convert the whole dataframe to an array by executing **df.to_numpy()** in the program read-and-write-file2.py

```
print(list(df))
import pandas as pd
df = pd.read_csv('Students.csv')
data=df.to_numpy()
for i in range(0,6):
    print(data[i,1])
M
M
M
F
F
M
```

Listing 10-2-read-and-write-file2.py

It will print the content in row 0, 1, 2, 3, 4, 5, 6 for column 1.

Columns 0, 1, 2, 3 are for StudentID, Gender, Height, and Weight, respectively.

"Numpy is the fundamental package for scientific computing with Python", accessed May 12, 2022, https://numpy.org/.

If we want to create and write to another file, we can execute read-and-write-file3.py.

```python
import pandas as pd
df = pd.read_csv('Students.csv')
data=df.to_numpy()
article_revised=open('Students_revised.txt','w')
for i in range(0,6):
    article_revised.writelines(str(data[i,2])+'\n')
article_revised.close()
```

Listing 10-3-read-and-write-file3.py

So, we have opened the file Students_revised.txt for us to write (**w**) content to it.

If we want to print **data[i,2]** for height, we have to convert **data[i,1]** to a string with **str(data[i,2])** so that we can write it out with **writelines**. We have put '\n' in **writelines** because we want to print each line as a new line.

The content of Students_revised.txt is as follows:

180
170
160
150
140
165

If we want to read a text file, we can execute read-article.py

```
article=open('article.txt')
lines = article.readlines()
for i in range(len(lines)):
    print(lines[i].strip())
Marketing Department
Business School
The Chinese University of Hong Kong
```

Listing 10-4-read-article.py

The above three lines are the content for the file article.txt.

The program will read each line from the file into lines. Afterward, we can print out **lines[0]**, **lines[1]** and **lines[2]** by using a for loop with **i** varies from 0 to 2.

We have put in **.strip()** so that we can skip the return/new line at the end. If we do not have **.strip()**, the output of the program will have one empty line.

If we want to create a file for writing (**w**), we can execute read-and-write-article.py

```
article=open('article.txt')
lines = article.readlines()
for i in range(len(lines)):
    print(lines[i].strip())
article_revised=open('article_revised.txt','w')
article_revised.writelines(lines[0])
article_revised.close()
Marketing Department
Business School
The Chinese University of Hong Kong
```

Listing 10-5-read-and-write-article.py

For demonstration, we have created a new text file, **article_ revised.txt**, and written one line in it. The content of this text file is as follows:

```
Marketing Department
```

11. Graphics-Bar Chart

"Matplotlib is a comprehensive library for creating static, animated, and interactive visualization in Python", accessed April 12, 2022, https://matplotlib.org/.

Please install **pandas** and **matplotlib** by typing the following two lines in the console of Spyder.

```
pip install pandas
pip install matplotlib
```

For illustration, we have a CSV file with 4 students in Marketing, 6 in Accounting, 3 in Finance, 7 in Management.

Content of data-plot.csv is as follows:

```
subject,frequency
Marketing,4
Accounting,6
Finance,3
Managment,7
```

Please execute program Bar-chart-vertical.py

```
pip install pandas
pip install matplotlib
import pandas as pd
import matplotlib.pyplot as plt
df = pd.read_csv('data-plot.csv')
print(df)
x=df.subject
y=df.frequency
plt.bar(x,y, color=['black','red','green','blue'])

plt.title('Students by Major')
plt.ylabel('Count')
plt.xlabel('Major')
           subject        frequency
0          Marketing          4
1          Accounting         6
2          Finance            3
3          Management         7
```

Listing 11-1-Bar-chart-vertical.py

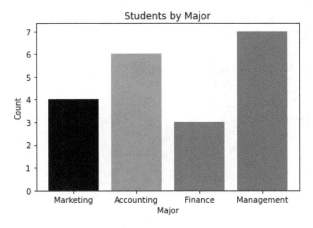

Figure A5.2.   Bar chart, vertical.

The first 2 lines **import pandas** and **matplotlib.pyplot** and refer them as **pd** and **plt** respectively, for us to refer to afterward.

After we have read in the data-plot.csv file, we can print it out to display its content.

We then set **x** to be the subject column of the data frame, and **y** to be the frequency column of the data frame.

Afterward, we can plot a bar chart with one color for each bar.

We can specify the title, the label for the y-axis, and the label for the x-axis with the following three lines:

```
plt.title('Students by Major')
plt.ylabel('Count')
plt.xlabel('Major')
```

To save the graph, you can right click on it, and save it to your computer.

To create a bar chart horizontally, we can simply use **barh** instead of **bar**.

Please execute program Bar-chart-horizontal.py

```
import pandas as pd
import matplotlib.pyplot as plt
df = pd.read_csv('data-plot.csv')
x=df.subject
y=df.frequency
plt.barh(x,y, color=['black','red','green','blue'])
plt.title('Students by Major')
plt.ylabel('Count')
plt.xlabel('Major')
```

Listing 11-2-Bar-chart-horizontal.py

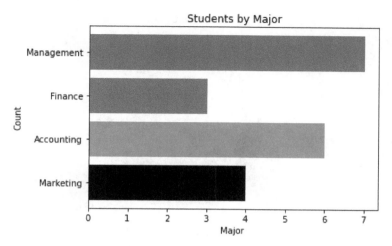

Figure A5.3. Bar chart, horizontal.

12. Graphics-Pie Chart

Please read the previous chapter about bar chart before you read this chapter.

Please execute program Pie-chart1.py

```
import pandas as pd
import matplotlib.pyplot as plt
df = pd.read_csv('data-plot.csv')
print(df)
plt.pie(df.frequency,labels=df.subject,autopct='%.2f%%')
plt.title('Students by Major')
```

Listing 12-1-Pie-chart1.py

We can generate a pie chart by specifying the data to be the frequency column of the data frame, **df.frequency**, and the labels to be the subject column of the data frame, **df.subject**.

```
plt.pie(df.frequency,labels=df.subject,autopct='%.2f%%')
```

autopct means that we want Python to generate percentage automatically with 2 decimal points and put % at the end for the

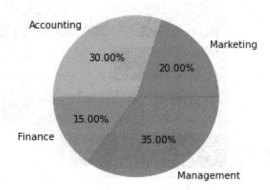

Figure A5.4.   Pie chart 1-1.

pie chart. `'%.2f%%'` is a string for format to inform Python how to plot the pie chart.

If we change the format string to `'%.0f%%'`, we will get a pie chart without decimal points.

```
plt.pie(df.frequency,labels=df.subject,autopct='%.0f%%')
```

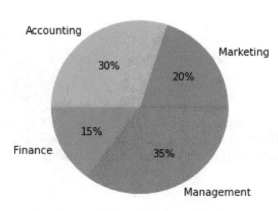

Figure A5.5.   Pie chart 1-2.

We can also set the start angle and whether we want to explode a certain part of the pie chart.

Please execute Pie-chart2.py

```
import pandas as pd
import matplotlib.pyplot as plt
df = pd.read_csv('data-plot.csv')
print(df)
my_colors=['blue','green','red','orange']
my_explode= (0, 0,0.1,0)
plt.pie(df.frequency,labels=df.subject,autopct='%.0f%%',
        startangle=90,explode=my_explode)
plt.title('Students by Major')
```

Listing 12-2-Pie-chart2.py

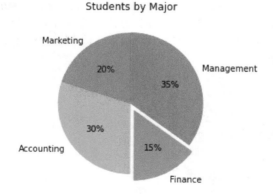

Figure A5.6.   Pie chart 2-1.

If we change my_explode= (0, 0,0.1,0) to my_explode= (0, 0,0.3,0), we can specify that the third label will be exploded further away from the center, that is, 0.3 instead of 0.1.

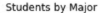

Figure A5.7.   Pie chart 2-2.

13.   Graphics-Plot

If we want to have a scatterplot on **x** and **y**, we can simply enter the values of **x** and **y** as follows, and ask Python to plot.

Please install **matplotlib** by typing the following line in the console of Spyder.

```
pip install matplotlib
```

Please execute Plot1.py

```
import matplotlib.pyplot as plt
x=[1,2,3,4,5]
y=[2,4,6,8,20]
plt.scatter(x,y,c="red")
```

Listing 13-1-Plot1.py

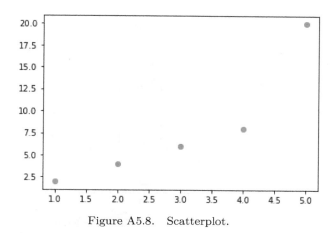

Figure A5.8. Scatterplot.

14. Graphics-Box Plot

Please install **matplotlib** by typing the following line in the console of Spyder.

```
pip install matplotlib
```

Please execute Box-Plot.py

```
import matplotlib.pyplot as plt
HK=[120, 130, 140, 150, 160, 170, 180, 190, 200, 210, 220, 230]
plt.boxplot(HK)
```

Listing 14-1-Box-Plot.py

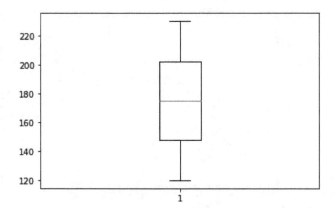

Figure A5.9.   Box Plot 1 for Hong Kong.

plt.boxplot tells Python that we want to draw a box and whisker plot.

"The box extends from the first quartile (Q1) to the third quartile (Q3) of the data, with a line at the median", accessed April 30, 2022, https://matplotlib.org/stable/api/_as_gen/matplotlib.pyplot.boxplot.html.

If we want to show data for another two cities, Shenzhen (SZ) and Shanghai (SH), we can add the following lines to the above program.

```
SZ=[130,140,150,160]
SH=[150,160,170,180,190,200]
cities=[HK, SZ, SH]
plt.boxplot(cities, labels=["Hong Kong","Shenzhen",
 "Shanghai"])
plt.title("Box plot title - cities")
```

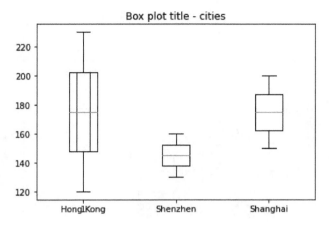

Figure A5.10.   Box Plot 2 for Hong Kong, Shenzhen, and Shanghai.

15.   Graphics-Colors

Python has a number of colors.
   Please execute **Color-program1.py**

```
import matplotlib.pyplot as plt
x=['A','B','C','D','E','F','G','H']
y=[2,4,3,1,5,6,1,7]
plt.bar(x,y, color=['black','red','green','blue',
 'white','yellow','magenta','cyan'],
      edgecolor='black')
plt.title('Title of chart')
plt.ylabel('y-label text')
plt.xlabel('x-label text')
```

Listing 15-1-Color-program1.py

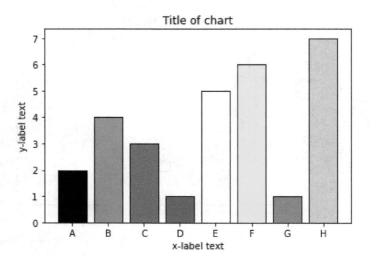

Figure A5.11.   Color chart 1.

edgecolor='black' in the above indicates to Python that we want to have a black border for each bar.

We can also use the first character of a color (except black) to get these 8 colors. For black color, we use **'k'** because blue color is **'b'**.

Please execute Color-program2.py to get the same chart as shown above.

```
import matplotlib.pyplot as plt
x=['A','B','C','D','E','F','G','H']
y=[2,4,3,1,5,6,1,7]
plt.bar(x,y, color=['k','r','g','b','w','y','m','c'],
        edgecolor='black')
plt.title('Title of chart')
plt.ylabel('y-label text')
plt.xlabel('x-label text')
```

Listing 15-2-Color-program2.py

matplotlib supports a list of named colors, accessed April 30, 2022, https://matplotlib.org/stable/gallery/color/named_colors.html.

Please execute Color-program3.py to look at some other colors.

```
import matplotlib.pyplot as plt
x=['A','B','C','D','E','F','G','H']
y=[2,4,3,1,5,6,1,7]
plt.bar(x,y, color=['gray','brown','tomato','skyblue',
  'lightgreen','navy','purple','pink'],
        edgecolor='black')
plt.title('Title of chart')
plt.ylabel('y-label text')
plt.xlabel('x-label text')
```

Listing 15-3-Color-program3.py

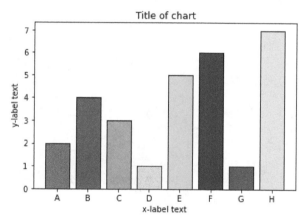

Figure A5.12.   Color chart 2.

16.   Word Cloud

If we have friends with the same English name, we can create a word cloud for these names saved in a CSV file.

word.csv

Peter,
Peter,

```
Peter
John,
John,
John,
Mary,
Howard,
Jane,
Jane,
Sherry,
Kitty,
Connie,
Catherine,
```

Please execute WordCloud1.py

```
import matplotlib.pyplot as plt
from wordcloud import WordCloud
text = open("words.csv").read()
print(text)
wordcloud=WordCloud().generate(text)
plt.imshow(wordcloud)
plt.axis("off")
```

Listing 16-1-WordCloud1.py

Figure A5.13.   Word Cloud 1.

We can change the width and height of the word cloud, and also its background color.

Please execute WordCloud2.py

```
import matplotlib.pyplot as plt
from wordcloud import WordCloud
text = open("words.csv").read()
print(text)
wordcloud=WordCloud(width=1000,height=500,
 background_color='white').generate(text)
plt.imshow(wordcloud)
plt.axis("off")
```

Listing 16-2-WordCloud2.py

Figure A5.14.   Word Cloud 2.

Other than white, we can also have blue, green, red, cyan, magenta, yellow, black.

17.   String

A string is a series of characters. It can include a to z, A-Z, 0 to 9, and other symbols.

We can express strings in Python in single quotes or double quotes with the same result, accessed April 29, 2022, https://docs.python. org/3/tutorial/introduction.html#strings.

```
print('abc')
abc
print("abc")
abc
print("I don't care")
I don't care
```

If we have a string, we can know how many characters it has by calling the function **len**, which means the length of the string in terms of number of characters.

Please execute **String1.py**

```
s="abcde"
print(len(s))
5

print(s[0])
print(s[1])
print(s[2])
a
b
c
```

Listing 17-1-String1.py

```
print(s[0:3])
abc
```

s[0:3] means that we want to get characters from position 0 (included) to 3 (excluded). Python Strings, accessed April 30, 2022, https://docs.python.org/3/tutorial/introduction.html#strings.

```
s="abcde"
for i in range(0,len(s)):
    print(s[i:i+1])
a
b
c
d
e
```

i is in the range of 0 to 4 (excluding 5). For print(s[i:i+1]), we will start with position **i** and exclude position **i+1**. So, we will have one character at position **i**.

```
s="abcde"
for i in range(len(s),-1,-1):
    print(i)
    print(s[i:i+1])
4
e
3
d
2
c
1
b
0
a
```

`for i in range(len(s),-1,-1)` means that we will start with `len(s)`, 5 in the example here, count down −1 each time, and end with position 0 (exclude position −1).

To create a new string which is reversed, we can set a string, `r`, to be empty before we execute the for loop. So, we have `r=""` (we type the double quotes symbol two times with nothing in between to indicate that the string is empty).

Please execute **String-reverse.py**

```
s="abcde"
r=""
for i in range(len(s),-1,-1):
    print(s[i:i+1])
    r=r+s[i:i+1]
print(r)
e
d
c
b
a
edcba
```

Listing 17-2-String-reverse.py

If we want to convert an upper-case letter to a lower-case letter, we can use `.lower()` as follows. If the character is already in lower case, `.lower()` will keep it as lower case.

    Please execute **String-lower.py**

```
s="ABcde"
r=""
for i in range(0,len(s)):
    c=s[i:i+1].lower()
    print(c)
    r=r+c
print(r)
a
b
c
d
e
abcde
```

Listing 17-3-String-lower.py

18. Chi-Square Test

To run Chi-Square Test, we can use the package of SciPy, "Fundamental algorithms for scientific computing in Python", accessed April 30, 2022, https://scipy.org/.

Please execute the program Chi-Square-test-program.py

```
from scipy import stats
data=[[3,10],[14,5],[5,2]]
results=stats.chi2_contingency(data,correction=True)
print(results)
(8.822081942824978, 0.012142531720281348, 2, array([ [
7.33333333,    5.66666667],
       [10.71794872, 8.28205128],
       [ 3.94871795,   3.05128205]]))
```

Listing 18-1-Chi-Square-test-program.py.

chi2_contigency is for "Chi-square test of independence of variables in a contingency table", accessed April 17, 2022, https://docs.scipy.org/doc/scipy/reference/generated/scipy.stats.chi2_contingency.html.

The data set is a table with three rows for usage (small, medium, large) and two columns for gender (female, male).

So, the Chi-square value is equal to 8.822. The p-value is equal to 0.0121.

The expected frequency is as shown in the array.

19. Correlation

If we have collected data from customers of a restaurant for the first and the second visit, we can save it in a CSV data file, Restaurant.csv

```
Respondent,Gender,Pref1,Pref2
1,M,5,4
2,M,6,5
3,M,7,6
4,M,4,3
5,M,5,4
6,M,6,5
7,M,4,2
8,M,5,5
9,M,6,6
10,M,7,6
11,F,3,3
```

```
12,F,4,5
13,F,5,4
14,F,4,5
15,F,4,4
16,F,3,4
17,F,4,4
18,F,5,6
19,F,3,4
20,F,5,6
```

We can run Correlation.py

```
import pandas as pd
from scipy import stats
data = pd.read_csv('Restaurant.csv')
x1 =data['Pref1']
x2 =data['Pref2']
results=stats.pearsonr(x1,x2)
print(results)
(0.674577091702233, 0.0011047079016250118)
```

Listing 19-1-Correlation.py

So, the value of the Pearson correlation coefficient is 0.6746 and the p-value is 0.0011.

"pandas is a fast, powerful, flexible, and easy to use open source data analysis and manipulation tool, built on top of the Python programming language", accessed April 17, 2022, https://pandas.pydata.org/.

"Pearson correlation coefficient and p-value for testing non-correlation", accessed April 17, 2022, https://docs.scipy.org/doc/scipy/reference/generated/scipy.stats.chi2_contingency.html.

20.   *t*-test

If we have collected data from customers of a restaurant for the first and the second visit, we can execute t-test-program1.py

```
from scipy import stats
import pandas as pd
d = pd.read_csv('Restaurant.csv')
visit1 = d['Pref1']
results=stats.ttest_1samp(a=visit1, popmean=4)
print(results)
Ttest_1sampResult(statistic=2.7753743355992,
 pvalue=0.012052476392025818)
```

Listing 20-1-*t*-test-program1.py

```
from scipy import stats
import pandas as pd
d = pd.read_csv('Restaurant.csv')
m = d.loc[d['Gender']=='M']
m1=m.Pref1
m2=m.Pref2
f = d.loc[d['Gender']=='F']
f1=f.Pref1
f2=f.Pref2
# Independent t-test
results=stats.ttest_ind(f1,m1)
print(results)
# t-test on two related samples
results=stats.ttest_rel(m1,m2)
print(results)
Ttest_indResult(statistic=-3.503245248726853,
 pvalue=0.0025383700074034749)
Ttest_relResult(statistic=5.0137741307804005,
 pvalue=0.0007252150276033929)
```

Listing 20-2-*t*-test-program2.py

So, the test statistic, t, is of value 2.7754, and the p-value is 0.0121, when we want to test whether the mean of visit1 is different from 4.

Please execute **t-test-program2.py**

So, for the independent t-test of female customers before visit and male customers before visit, the test statistic, t, is of value -3.5032, and the p-value is 0.0025.

For the t-test the paired samples of male customers before visit and after visit, the test statistic, t, is of value 5.0138, and the p-value is 0.0007.

21.   Analysis of Variance

As an example of the analysis of variance (ANOVA), we can use the data set of **ANOVA-Data.csv**, which has the Sales of 10 stores for three different messages.

```
Store,Message,Sales
1,One,10
2,One,9
3,One,8
4,One,10
5,One,7
6,One,6
7,One,7
8,One,9
9,One,10
10,One,8
1,Two,8
2,Two,7
3,Two,9
4,Two,8
5,Two,6
6,Two,4
7,Two,10
8,Two,7
9,Two,8
10,Two,6
1,Three,10
2,Three,8
3,Three,7
4,Three,5
5,Three,7
6,Three,4
7,Three,3
8,Three,5
9,Three,4
10,Three,6
```

Please execute **ANOVA-Program.py**
So, the test statistic is 4.9637 and the p-value is 0.0146.

```
from scipy import stats
import pandas as pd
d = pd.read_csv('ANOVA-Data.csv')
m1 = d.loc[d['Message']=='One']
m1Sales=m1.Sales
m2 = d.loc[d['Message']=='Two']
m2Sales=m2.Sales
m3 = d.loc[d['Message']=='Three']
m3Sales=m3.Sales
results=stats.f_oneway(m1Sales,m2Sales,m3Sales)
print(results)
F_onewayResult(statistic=4.963700234192038,
 pvalue=0.014594958916321215)
```

Listing 21-1-ANOVA-program.py

22. Regression-Bivariate

We can use **pandas** and **statsmodels** to run regression.

"pandas is a fast, powerful, flexible, and easy to use open source data analysis and manipulation tool, built on top of the Python programming language", accessed April 17, 2022, https://pandas.pydata.org/.

"statsmodels is a Python module that provides classes and functions for the estimation of many statistical models, as well as for conducting statistical tests", accessed April 17, 2022, https://www.statsmodels.org/stable/index.html.

For a data set of weight and height of 15 respondents, Reg-Data.csv

```
Respondent,Weight,Height
1,17,129
2,16,116
3,16,128
4,18,145
5,19,152
6,20,150
7,22,166
8,20,156
```

```
9,21,168
10,17,123
11,19,144
12,24,179
13,23,178
14,17,122
15,20,164
```

We can run a bivariate regression by executing **Regression-Bivariate.py**

```
import pandas as pd
import statsmodels.api as sm
data=pd.read_csv('RegData.csv')
x=data['Height']
y=data['Weight']
x=sm.add_constant(x)
results=sm.OLS(y,x).fit()
print(results.summary())
 OLS Regression Results
==============================================================================
Dep. Variable:                 Weight   R-squared:                       0.918
Model:                            OLS   Adj. R-squared:                  0.912
Method:                 Least Squares   F-statistic:                     145.3
Date:                Sun, 04 Dec 2022   Prob (F-statistic):           1.98e-08
Time:                        09:07:47   Log-Likelihood:                -15.716
No. Observations:                  15   AIC:                             35.43
Df Residuals:                      13   BIC:                             36.85
Df Model:                           1
Covariance Type:            nonrobust
==============================================================================
                 coef    std err          t      P>|t|      [0.025      0.975]
------------------------------------------------------------------------------
const          2.2501      1.425      1.579      0.138      -0.828       5.328
Height         0.1150      0.010     12.054      0.000       0.094       0.136
==============================================================================
Omnibus:                        2.064   Durbin-Watson:                   1.599
Prob(Omnibus):                  0.356   Jarque-Bera (JB):                1.012
Skew:                          -0.181   Prob(JB):                        0.603
Kurtosis:                       1.780   Cond. No.                     1.11e+03
==============================================================================
```

Listing 22-1-Regression-Bivariate.py

23. Regression-Multiple

For a data set of Sales, TV media spending, and digital media spending for 12 months, DataSales.csv

```
Month,Sales,TVSpend,DigitalSpend
1,820,183,148
2,805,113,185
3,987,196,189
4,718,166,119
5,772,160,143
6,863,171,173
7,895,194,165
8,923,156,194
9,914,148,199
10,683,117,142
11,645,140,120
12,671,116,146
```

We can run multiple regression with Regression-Multiple.py

```
import pandas as pd
import statsmodels.api as sm
data = pd.read_csv('DataSales.csv')
x=data[['TVSpend','DigitalSpend']]
y=data['Sales']
x=sm.add_constant(x)
results=sm.OLS(y,x).fit()
print(results.summary())
   OLS Regression Results
```

Dep. Variable:	Sales	R-squared:	0.992
Model:	OLS	Adj. R-squared:	0.990
Method:	Least Squares	F-statistic:	537.1
Date:	Sun, 04 Dec 2022	Prob (F-statistic):	4.35e-10
Time:	09:14:29	Log-Likelihood:	-44.369
No. Observations:	12	AIC:	94.74
Df Residuals:	9	BIC:	96.19
Df Model:	2		
Covariance Type:	nonrobust		

```
              coef    std err        t      P>|t|     [0.025     0.975]
---------------------------------------------------------------------------
const       -1.6143    25.092    -0.064     0.950    -58.377     55.148
TVSpend      2.0122     0.117    17.129     0.000      1.746      2.278
DigitalSpend 3.1059     0.123    25.257     0.000      2.828      3.384
===========================================================================
Omnibus:                0.918    Durbin-Watson:                   1.419
Prob(Omnibus):          0.632    Jarque-Bera (JB):                0.696
Skew:                  -0.227    Prob(JB):                        0.706
Kurtosis:               1.912    Cond. No.                     1.73e+03
===========================================================================
```

Listing 23-1-Regression-Multiple.py

24. Sentiment Analysis

If we have received a message from a person, how do we know what
is the sentiment of this message?

Please type the following line in the console of Spyder.

```
pip install vaderSentiment
```

"VADER (Valence Aware Dictionary and Sentiment Reasoner) is a
lexicon and rule-based sentiment analysis tool that is specifically
attuned to sentiments expressed in social media. It is fully open-
sourced [MIT License]", accessed May 11, 2022, https://github.com/
cjhutto/vaderSentiment.

"If you use either the data set or any of the VADER sentiment
analysis tools (VADER sentiment lexicon or Python code for rule-
based sentiment analysis engine) in your research, please cite the
above paper. For example:

Hutto, C.J. & Gilbert, E.E. (2014). VADER: A Parsimonious
Rule-based Model for Sentiment Analysis of Social Media Text.
Eighth International Conference on Weblogs and Social Media
(ICWSM-14). Ann Arbor, MI, June 2014," accessed May 11, 2022,
https://github.com/cjhutto/vaderSentiment#about-the-scoring.

Please execute vaderSentiment1.py for us to know the sentiment score of one sentence "I felt happy."

```python
from vaderSentiment.vaderSentiment import
 SentimentIntensityAnalyzer
sentence = "I felt happy."
print(sentence)
results = SentimentIntensityAnalyzer()
sentiment_dict = results.polarity_scores(sentence)
print(sentiment_dict['neg'])
print(sentiment_dict['neu'])
print(sentiment_dict['pos'])
print(sentiment_dict['compound'])
if sentiment_dict['compound'] >= 0.05:
    print("Positive")
elif sentiment_dict['compound'] <= - 0.05:
    print("Negative")
else:
    print("Neutral")
I felt happy.
0.0
0.351
0.649
0.5719
Positive
```

Listing 24-1-vaderSentiment1.py

"The compound score is computed by summing the valence scores of each word in the lexicon, adjusted according to the rules, and then normalized to be between -1 (most extreme negative) and $+1$ (most extreme positive). This is the most useful metric if you want a single unidimensional measure of sentiment for a given sentence. Calling it a 'normalized, weighted composite score' is accurate. It is also useful for researchers who would like to set standardized thresholds for classifying sentences as either positive, neutral, or negative. Typical threshold values (used in the literature cited on this page) are as follows:

positive sentiment: compound score $>= 0.05$

neutral sentiment: (compound score > -0.05) and (compound score < 0.05)

negative sentiment: compound score $<= -0.05$

NOTE: The compound score is the one most commonly used for sentiment analysis by most researchers, including the authors. The pos, neu, and neg scores are ratios for proportions of text that fall in each category (so these should all add up to be 1... or close to it with float operation)", accessed May 11, 2022, https://github.com/cjhutto/vaderSentiment#about-the-scoring.

Please execute vaderSentiment2.py for us to show the scores as percentages.

```python
from vaderSentiment.vaderSentiment import
 SentimentIntensityAnalyzer
sentence = "I felt happy."
print(sentence)
results = SentimentIntensityAnalyzer()
sentiment_dict = results.polarity_scores(sentence)
neg_value=sentiment_dict['neg']
neu_value=sentiment_dict['neu']
pos_value=sentiment_dict['pos']
print("sentence was rated as ", neg_value*100, "% Negative")
print("sentence was rated as ", neu_value*100, "% Neutral")
print("sentence was rated as ", pos_value*100, "% Positive")
print("Sentence was rated overall as", end = " ")
if sentiment_dict['compound'] >= 0.05:
    print("Positive")
elif sentiment_dict['compound'] <= - 0.05:
    print("Negative")
else:
    print("Neutral")
I felt happy.
sentence was rated as  0.0 % Negative
sentence was rated as  35.09999999999994 % Neutral
sentence was rated as  64.9 % Positive
Sentence was rated overall as Positive
```

Listing 24-2-vaderSentiment2.py

Please execute vaderSentiment3.py for us to show the scores as percentages and format them into two decimal points.

```
from vaderSentiment.vaderSentiment import
 SentimentIntensityAnalyzer
sentence = "I felt happy."
print(sentence)
results = SentimentIntensityAnalyzer()
sentiment_dict = results.polarity_scores(sentence)
neg_value=sentiment_dict['neg']*100
neu_value=sentiment_dict['neu']*100
pos_value=sentiment_dict['pos']*100
neg_formated=":.2f".format(neg_value)
neu_formated=":.2f".format(neu_value)
pos_formated=":.2f".format(pos_value)
print("sentence was rated as ", neg_formated, "% Negative")
print("sentence was rated as ", neu_formated, "% Neutral")
print("sentence was rated as ", pos_formated, "% Positive")
print("Sentence was rated overall as", end = " ")
if sentiment_dict['compound'] >= 0.05:
    print("Positive")
elif sentiment_dict['compound'] <= - 0.05:
    print("Negative")
else:
    print("Neutral")
I felt happy.
sentence was rated as  0.00 % Negative
sentence was rated as  35.10 % Neutral
sentence was rated as  64.90 % Positive
Sentence was rated overall as Positive
```

Listing 24-3-vaderSentiment3.py

Please execute vaderSentiment4.py for us to define (**def**) a function **sentiment_scores** with argument sentence, and for the main program to call the function thrice for 3 sentences.

```
from vaderSentiment.vaderSentiment import
 SentimentIntensityAnalyzer
def sentiment_scores(sentence):
    print(sentence)
    results = SentimentIntensityAnalyzer()
    sentiment_dict = results.polarity_scores(sentence)
    neg_value=sentiment_dict['neg']*100
    neu_value=sentiment_dict['neu']*100
    pos_value=sentiment_dict['pos']*100
    neg_formated=":.2f".format(neg_value)
    neu_formated=":.2f".format(neu_value)
    pos_formated=":.2f".format(pos_value)
    print("sentence was rated as ", neg_formated, "% Negative")
    print("sentence was rated as ", neu_formated, "% Neutral")
    print("sentence was rated as ", pos_formated, "% Positive")
    print("Sentence was rated overall as", end = " ")
    if sentiment_dict['compound'] >= 0.05:
        print("Positive")
    elif sentiment_dict['compound'] <= - 0.05:
        print("Negative")
    else:
        print("Neutral")
sentence1 = "Yesterday was Friday."
sentiment_scores(sentence1)
sentence2 = "I felt happy."
sentiment_scores(sentence2)
sentence3 = """I had just finished
 preparing the teaching materials for my class in the morning."""
sentiment_scores(sentence3)
Yesterday was Friday.
sentence was rated as  0.00 % Negative
sentence was rated as  100.00 % Neutral
sentence was rated as  0.00 % Positive
Sentence was rated overall as Neutral
I felt happy.
sentence was rated as  0.00 % Negative
sentence was rated as  35.10 % Neutral
sentence was rated as  64.90 % Positive
Sentence was rated overall as Positive
I had just finished
 preparing the teaching materials for my class in the morning.
sentence was rated as  0.00 % Negative
sentence was rated as  100.00 % Neutral
sentence was rated as  0.00 % Positive
Sentence was rated overall as Neutral
```

Listing 24-4-vaderSentiment4.py

The file Sentences.txt has the following five sentences.

```
Yesterday was Friday. I felt happy.
I had just finished preparing the teaching materials
 for my class in the morning.
Then, I felt bored, and went for lunch.
A car driver was not following traffic light and
 hit a dog.
I was angry that he did not pay attention to other
 people in the street.
```

We can read each sentence into the program vaderSentiment5.py and send each sentence to **sentiment_scores** function.

```python
from vaderSentiment.vaderSentiment import
 SentimentIntensityAnalyzer
def sentiment_scores(sentence):
    print(sentence)
    results = SentimentIntensityAnalyzer()
    sentiment_dict = results.polarity_scores(sentence)
    neg_value=sentiment_dict['neg']*100
    neu_value=sentiment_dict['neu']*100
    pos_value=sentiment_dict['pos']*100
    neg_formated=":.2f".format(neg_value)
    neu_formated=":.2f".format(neu_value)
    pos_formated=":.2f".format(pos_value)
    print("sentence was rated as ", neg_formated, "% Negative")
    print("sentence was rated as ", neu_formated, "% Neutral")
    print("sentence was rated as ", pos_formated, "% Positive")
    print("Sentence was rated overall as", end = " ")
    if sentiment_dict['compound'] >= 0.05:
        print("Positive")
    elif sentiment_dict['compound'] <= - 0.05:
        print("Negative")
    else:
        print("Neutral")

article=open('Sentences.txt')
lines = article.readlines()
for i in range(len(lines)):
    sentiment_scores(lines[i].strip())
    print("")
```

Listing 24-5-vaderSentiment5.py

```
Yesterday was Friday. I felt happy.
sentence was rated as   0.00 % Negative
sentence was rated as  57.50 % Neutral
sentence was rated as  42.50 % Positive
Sentence was rated overall as Positive

I had just finished preparing the teaching materials
 for my class in the morning.
sentence was rated as   0.00 % Negative
sentence was rated as  100.00 % Neutral
sentence was rated as   0.00 % Positive
Sentence was rated overall as Neutral

Then, I felt bored, and went for lunch.
sentence was rated as  23.10 % Negative
sentence was rated as  76.90 % Neutral
sentence was rated as   0.00 % Positive
Sentence was rated overall as Negative

A car driver was not following traffic light and
 hit a dog.
sentence was rated as   0.00 % Negative
sentence was rated as  100.00 % Neutral
sentence was rated as   0.00 % Positive
Sentence was rated overall as Neutral

I was angry that he did not pay attention to
 other people in the street.
sentence was rated as  18.80 % Negative
sentence was rated as  73.90 % Neutral
sentence was rated as   7.40 % Positive
Sentence was rated overall as Negative
```

So, "article" stores the whole content of Sentences.txt. Afterward, we assign all lines from article.readlines() to lines.

If there are five lines, len(lines) is equal to 5. Len means length. We can get these five lines with **lines**[0], lines[1], lines[2], lines[3], and lines[4]. So, we can use a for loop to change **i** from 0 to 4 to get these five lines.

We use `.strip()` to strip out the newline character of each line read from the txt file. We have `print("")` as the last line within the for loop of **i**, because we want to print an empty string `""` (two double quotes) to generate an empty line.

If we want to count the total number of positive, negative, and neutral sentences, we can execute vaderSentiment6.py

```
from vaderSentiment.vaderSentiment import
 SentimentIntensityAnalyzer
def sentiment_scores(sentence):
    global tpositive, tnegative, tneutral
    print(sentence)
    results = SentimentIntensityAnalyzer()
    sentiment_dict = results.polarity_scores(sentence)
    neg_value=sentiment_dict['neg']*100
    neu_value=sentiment_dict['neu']*100
    pos_value=sentiment_dict['pos']*100
    neg_formated=":.2f".format(neg_value)
    neu_formated=":.2f".format(neu_value)
    pos_formated=":.2f".format(pos_value)
    print("sentence was rated as ", neg_formated, "% Negative")
    print("sentence was rated as ", neu_formated, "% Neutral")
    print("sentence was rated as ", pos_formated, "% Positive")
    print("Sentence was rated overall as", end = " ")
    if sentiment_dict['compound'] >= 0.05:
        tpositive=tpositive+1
        print("Positive")
    elif sentiment_dict['compound'] <= - 0.05:
        tnegative=tnegative+1
        print("Negative")
    else:
        tneutral=tneutral+1
        print("Neutral")
tpositive=0
tnegative=0
tneutral=0
article=open('Sentences.txt')
lines = article.readlines()
for i in range(len(lines)):
    sentiment_scores(lines[i].strip())
    print("")
print("Total positive", tpositive)
print("Total negative", tnegative)
print("Total neutral", tneutral)
```

Listing 24-6-vaderSentiment6.py

```
Yesterday was Friday. I felt happy.
sentence was rated as   0.00 % Negative
sentence was rated as  57.50 % Neutral
sentence was rated as  42.50 % Positive
Sentence was rated overall as Positive

I had just finished preparing the teaching
 materials for my class in the morning.
sentence was rated as   0.00 % Negative
sentence was rated as  100.00 % Neutral
sentence was rated as   0.00 % Positive
Sentence was rated overall as Neutral

Then, I felt bored, and went for lunch.
sentence was rated as  23.10 % Negative
sentence was rated as  76.90 % Neutral
sentence was rated as   0.00 % Positive
Sentence was rated overall as Negative

A car driver was not following traffic light
 and hit a dog.
sentence was rated as   0.00 % Negative
sentence was rated as  100.00 % Neutral
sentence was rated as   0.00 % Positive
Sentence was rated overall as Neutral

I was angry that he did not pay attention to
 other people in the street.
sentence was rated as  18.80 % Negative
sentence was rated as  73.90 % Neutral
sentence was rated as   7.40 % Positive
Sentence was rated overall as Negative

Total positive 1
Total negative 2
Total neutral 2
```

The line **global tpositive, tnegative, tneutral** defines these three variables as global variables. That is, their values can be set and changed in the main program, and also within a single function.

If we want to analyse the sentiment of each word instead of a sentence, we can first extract each word from a paragraph. We will use **nltk**. "It provides a suite of text processing libraries for classification, tokenization, ..." accessed May 12, 2022, https://www.nltk.org/.

Please execute text1.py

```
import nltk text ="""" I worked for a long time, and felt tired
yesterday. I felt sad when I had dinner alone at 9pm. """
words=nltk.word_tokenize(text) n=len(words) for i in range(n):
    print(words[i])
fd = nltk.FreqDist(words)
print(fd.most_common(3))
print(fd.tabulate(3))
I
worked
for
a
long
time
,
and
felt
tired
yesterday
.
I
felt
sad
when
I
had
dinner
alone
at
9pm
.
[('I', 3), ('felt', 2), ('.', 2)]
   I felt   .
   3    2    2
None
```

Listing 24-7-text1.py

We use three double quotes `"""` to indicate the beginning and ending of a paragraph in different lines of the Python program. Hence, we can have the three lines in the program for the variable text as follows:

```
text =""" I worked for a long time, and felt tired yesterday.
I felt sad when I had dinner alone at 9pm.
"""
```

We tokenize the whole text to generate a number of words. We find out the total number of words first with `n=len(words)` so that we can then specify `n` in the for loop. `n` is equal to 23 in our example.

The following three lines let us know the frequency distribution of words.

```
fd = nltk.FreqDist(words)
print(fd.most_common(3))
print(fd.tabulate(3))
```

We see that 'I' appears 3 times, 'felt' appears two times, and full stop '.' appears 2 times.

Please execute text2.py

```
import nltk text =""" I worked for a long time, and felt tired
yesterday. I felt sad when I had dinner alone at 9pm. """
words=nltk.word_tokenize(text) n=len(words) for i in range(n):
    words[i]=words[i].lower()
print("change all letters to lower case")
print(words)
stopwords = nltk.corpus.stopwords.words("english")
filtered_words=[]
for i in range(n):
    if words[i] not in stopwords:
        filterwords=filtered_words.append(words[i])
print("filtered words")
print(filtered_words)
```

We use `words[i]=words[i].lower()` to convert all letters to lower case. We set `filtered_words=[]` to be empty before we start checking each of the `words[i]` to see whether it is in the list of `stopwords` or not. If it is not, we will append `words[i]` to `filtered_words`.

If we want to know the list of `stopwords`, we can `print(stopwords)` to generate the following list of `stopwords`.

```
change all letters to lower case
['i', 'worked', 'for', 'a', 'long', 'time', ',', 'and', 'felt',
 'tired', 'yesterday', '.', 'i', 'felt', 'sad', 'when', 'i',
 'had', 'dinner', 'alone', 'at', '9pm', '.']
filtered words
['worked', 'long', 'time', ',', 'felt', 'tired', 'yesterday',
 '.', 'felt', 'sad', 'dinner', 'alone', '9pm', '.']
```

Listing 24-8-text2.py

```
['i', 'me', 'my', 'myself', 'we', 'our', 'ours',
'ourselves', 'you', "you're", "you've", "you'll",
"you'd", 'your', 'yours', 'yourself', 'yourselves',
'he', 'him', 'his', 'himself', 'she', "she's", 'her',
'hers', 'herself', 'it', "it's", 'its', 'itself',
'they', 'them', 'their', 'theirs', 'themselves',
'what', 'which', 'who', 'whom', 'this', 'that',
"that'll", 'these', 'those', 'am', 'is', 'are', 'was',
'were', 'be', 'been', 'being', 'have', 'has', 'had',
'having', 'do', 'does', 'did', 'doing', 'a', 'an',
'the', 'and', 'but', 'if', 'or', 'because', 'as',
'until', 'while', 'of', 'at', 'by', 'for', 'with',
'about', 'against', 'between', 'into', 'through',
'during', 'before', 'after', 'above', 'below', 'to',
'from', 'up', 'down', 'in', 'out', 'on', 'off',
'over', 'under', 'again', 'further', 'then', 'once',
'here', 'there', 'when', 'where', 'why', 'how', 'all',
'any', 'both', 'each', 'few', 'more', 'most', 'other',
'some', 'such', 'no', 'nor', 'not', 'only', 'own',
'same', 'so', 'than', 'too', 'very', 's', 't', 'can',
'will', 'just', 'don', "don't", 'should', "should've",
'now', 'd', 'll', 'm', 'o', 're', 've', 'y', 'ain',
'aren', "aren't", 'couldn', "couldn't", 'didn',
"didn't", 'doesn', "doesn't", 'hadn', "hadn't", 'hasn',
"hasn't", 'haven', "haven't", 'isn', "isn't", 'ma',
'mightn', "mightn't", 'mustn', "mustn't", 'needn',
"needn't", 'shan', "shan't", 'shouldn', "shouldn't",
'wasn', "wasn't", 'weren', "weren't", 'won', "won't",
'wouldn', "wouldn't"]
```

We can combine **vaderSentiment** and **nltk** to count the number of words which are positive, negative, and neutral. Please execute text3.py

```python
from vaderSentiment.vaderSentiment import
 SentimentIntensityAnalyzer
def sentiment_scores(sentence):
    global tpositive, tnegative, tneutral
    results = SentimentIntensityAnalyzer()
    sentiment_dict = results.polarity_scores(sentence)
    if sentiment_dict['compound'] >= 0.05:
        print("positive",sentence)
        tpositive=tpositive+1
    elif sentiment_dict['compound'] <= - 0.05:
        print("negative",sentence)
        tnegative=tnegative+1
    else:
        tneutral=tneutral+1
tpositive=0
tnegative=0
tneutral=0

import nltk
text =""" I worked for a long time, and felt tired yesterday.
I felt sad when I had dinner alone at 9pm.
"""
words=nltk.word_tokenize(text)
n=len(words)
for i in range(n):
    words[i]=words[i].lower()
stopwords = nltk.corpus.stopwords.words("english")
filtered_words=[]
for i in range(n):
    if words[i] not in stopwords:
        filterwords=filtered_words.append(words[i])
print(filtered_words)
n=len(filtered_words)
for i in range(n):
    sentiment_scores(filtered_words[i])
print("Total positive", tpositive)
print("Total negative", tnegative)
print("Total neutral", tneutral)
```

```
['worked', 'long', 'time', ',', 'felt', 'tired', 'yesterday',
'.', 'felt', 'sad', 'dinner', 'alone', '9pm', '.']
negative tired
negative sad
negative alone
Total positive 0
Total negative 3
Total neutral 11
```

Listing 24-9-text3.py

25. Web Scraping

To read the content of a web page and extract information from it, we can use the packages called **requests** and **Beautiful Soup**.

"Requests is an elegant and simple HTTP library for Python, built for human beings.", accessed May 10, 2022, https://docs.python-requests.org/en/latest/.

"Beautiful Soup is a library that makes it easy to scrape information from web pages.", accessed May 10, 2022, https://pypi.org/project/beautifulsoup4/.

Please type the following lines in the console of Spyder.

```
pip install requests
pip install bs4
```

Then, execute Webscraping-publications.py

```
import requests webpage =
requests.get("https://sites.google.com/view/howardlam/
 publications/cases?authuser=0")
# print(webpage.text)

from bs4 import BeautifulSoup
page = BeautifulSoup(webpage.text, 'html.parser')
print(page.title)

publications=page.select('.XqQF9c')
for title in publications:
    print(title.text)


<title>Howard LAM - Cases</title>
OmniFoods: Plant-Based Pork from Hong Kong to the Rest of China
Green Monday: Flexitarianism, Innovation, and Endorsement
SenseTime Group Limited : Business Model and Expansion
Incubation and the Hong Kong Science and Technology Parks
 Corporation
OpenSky.TV: Business Model From Content Creation, Curation,
 Consumption, Commercialization
Bamboos Health Care Holdings (Hong Kong) Ltd.: Business Model
 and Expansion
AMOREPACIFIC Hong Kong: Marketing Korean Beauty Products
Hung Fook Tong: From Hong Kong to China
TSL Jewellery: An Innovator Across Generations?
```

Listing 25-1-Webscraping-publications.py

I have created the following web page for us to scrape.

https://sites.google.com/view/howardlam/publications/cases?authuser=0.

The screen capture is as follows:

Cases

- Howard Pong-yuen Lam, Hugh Thomas, Rosette Hang-yee Leung and Hanni Jie (2022), "OmniFoods: Plant-Based Pork from Hong Kong to the Rest of China," Ivey Publishing, 28 September 2022.

- Hang Yee Rosette Leung, Hugh Thomas, Hanni Jie, Pong Yuen Howard Lam (2022), "Green Monday: Flexitarianism, Innovation, and Endorsement," Ivey Publishing, 11 July 2022.

- Howard Pong-yuen Lam, Hugh Thomas, Keith C.H.Wong,(2020), "SenseTime Group Limited : Business Model and Expansion," Harvard Business Publishing, 19 July 2020.

- Hugh Thomas, Andrew C.F. Chan, Howard Pong-yuen Lam and Icy F.L. Ngai (2019), "Incubation and the Hong Kong Science and Technology Parks Corporation," Harvard Business Publishing, 16 August 2019.

- Andrew C.F. Chan, Howard Pong-yuen Lam and Icy F.L. Ngai (2019), "OpenSky.TV: Business Model From Content Creation, Curation, Consumption, Commercialization," Harvard Business Publishing, 3 May 2019.

- Kevin Y.F. Au, Howard Pong-yuen Lam, Lu, S.Y. and Ngai, F.L. Icy (2018), "Bamboos Health Care Holdings (Hong Kong) Ltd.: Business Model and Expansion," Harvard Business Publishing, 12 November 2018.

- Andrew C.F. Chan, Howard Pong-yuen Lam, Hugh Thomas, Andy K.C. Wong and Canice M.C. Kwan (2018), "AMOREPACIFIC Hong Kong: Marketing Korean Beauty Products," Harvard Business Publishing, 3 May 2018.

- Andrew C.F. Chan, Howard Pong-yuen Lam, Hugh Thomas and Elsie Tsui (2016), "Hung Fook Tong: From Hong Kong to China," Harvard Business Publishing, 30 May 2016.

- Kevin Y.F. Au, Andrew C.F. Chan, Howard Pong-yuen Lam and Cinty Li (2015), "TSL Jewellery: An Innovator Across Generations," Harvard Business Publishing, 24 Feb 2015.

Figure A5.15.   Webpage-cases.

We get the HTML text file of this web page. HTML stands for Hyper-Text Mark-up Language. So, if we have a file **w.html**, we can use a browser to open the file, and the browser will display a web page based on the text messages in **w.html**. Similarly, if we have a Microsoft Word file **w.docx**, we can use Word to open it.

print(webpage.text) will print the HTML file that we have just got.

Afterward, we send **webpage.text** to **Beautiful Soup** and ask it to analyze/parse it so that we can choose what we want to get after parsing. For example, we can print the title of the web page.

".XqQF9c" is what you want to select. We can use Chrome browser to view a web page and find this string. The steps are as follows.

Choose "View" menu option from Chrome, then "Developer," "Inspect Elements." Then, put the mouse over the element that you want to inspect. You can find the string ".XqQF9c".

I had made a 20 s video by using text-to-voice feature from CapCut video editing software, and posted it to YouTube (https://youtu.be/qYslTllJFmw) and Tencent Video (https://v.qq.com/x/page/o35055t6ycc.html) on how to find the element.

If we want to scrape a web page with rows and columns, we can execute **Webscraping-row-column1.py**

```
import requests
webpage = requests.get("https://sites.google.com/view/
  howardlam/r-program/web-scraping?authuser=0")
from bs4 import BeautifulSoup
page = BeautifulSoup(webpage.text, 'html.parser')
messages=page.select('.CjVfdc')
for m  in messages:
    print(m.text)
Row1, Column 1: Heading
Row 1, Column 2: Heading
Row 1, Column 3: Heading
Row2, Column 1: Heading
Row 2, Column 2: Heading
Row 2, Column 3: Heading
Row3, Column 1: Heading
Row 3, Column 2: Heading
Row 3, Column 3: Heading
```

Listing 25-2-Webscraping-row-column1.py

I have created this web page for us to scrape.

https://sites.google.com/view/howardlam/r-program/web-scraping?authuser=0.

The screen capture of it is as follows:

Web Scraping

Row1, Column 1: Heading	Row 1, Column 2: Heading	Row 1, Column 3: Heading
Message 11	Message 12	Message 13
Row2, Column 1: Heading	Row 2, Column 2: Heading	Row 2, Column 3: Heading
Message 21	Message 22	Message 23
Row3, Column 1: Heading	Row 3, Column 2: Heading	Row 3, Column 3: Heading
Message 31	Message 32	Message 33

Figure A5.16.   Webpage-row-column.

We can also save the text to an array data structure for us to manipulate in the program later. Please execute **Webscraping-row-column2.py**

```
import requests
webpage = requests.get("https://sites.google.com/view/
 howardlam/r-program/web-scraping?authuser=0")
from bs4 import BeautifulSoup
page = BeautifulSoup(webpage.text, 'html.parser')
Lines = []
messages=page.select('.CjVfdc')
for m  in messages:
    Lines.append(m.text)
print("array")
for L in Lines:
    print(L)
array
Row1, Column 1: Heading
Row 1, Column 2: Heading
Row 1, Column 3: Heading
Row2, Column 1: Heading
Row 2, Column 2: Heading
Row 2, Column 3: Heading
Row3, Column 1: Heading
Row 3, Column 2: Heading
Row 3, Column 3: Heading
```

Listing 25-3-Webscraping-row-column2.py

We first set **Lines** to be empty with **[]** (that is, the left bracket and the right bracket).

We use **Lines.append(m.text)** to append each line of text from **m.text** to the array.

We print out each element of the array at the end of the program.

We can also save the content to a text file so that we can use it in the future. Please execute **Webscraping-row-column3.py**

```
import requests
webpage = requests.get("https://sites.google.com/view/
 howardlam/r-program/web-scraping?authuser=0")
from bs4 import BeautifulSoup
page = BeautifulSoup(webpage.text, 'html.parser')
f = open("outfile.txt","w")
messages=page.select('.CjVfdc')
for m  in messages:
    f.write(m.text)
    f.write("\n")
f.close()
```

Listing 25-4-Webscraping-row-column3.py

The content of output.txt is as follows:

```
Row1, Column 1: Heading
Row 1, Column 2: Heading
Row 1, Column 3: Heading
Row2, Column 1: Heading
Row 2, Column 2: Heading
Row 2, Column 3: Heading
Row3, Column 1: Heading
Row 3, Column 2: Heading
Row 3, Column 3: Heading
```

We first open a file **"outfile.txt"** for us to write over it and so we specify **"w"**.

We write the content of **m.text** to the file with **f.write (m.text)**. We then write a return character with **f.write("\n")** so that we can end the current line and go to a new line. We close the file at the end of the program.

Index

9 789811 278693